ALL ABOUT KALA-SHILP

BUDHDEO PRASAD

ALL ABOUT KALA-SHILP

(NIFT, NID, B. ARCHITECTURE, NATA, & B.F.A.)
CEPT, PEARL, APEEJAY, SYMBIOSIS, SRISHTI, IIT-CEED & POLYTECHNIQUE. ETC.

ENTRANCE EXAMINATION

BY
BUDHDEO PRASAD

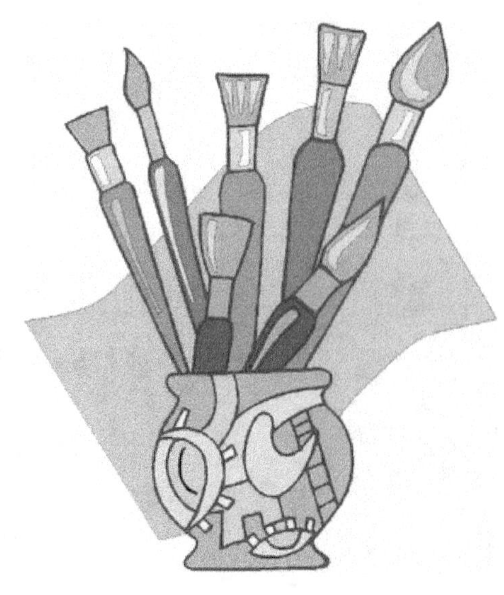

Name of the Book	:	**ALL ABOUT KALA-SHILP**
Author	:	B U D H D E O P R A S A D (An Art Teacher & Artist)
		B.A.(Hons.), M.Fine
1st Edition	:	February 2020
Publisher	:	**Kala- Shilp Prakashan**
		Kankarbagh, Patna - 20
Email	:	**kalashilpprakashan@gmail.com**
WhatsApp no.	:	**+91- 9546817753.**
Website	:	www.kalashilpprakashan.com

Decleration: **Publication has used some scattered materials from the internet to study for the students, sometime it may be copyright. For which publication reveals gratitude.**

Distributor :
GYAN GANGA Ltd
Patna, BIHAR
Gyan Ganga Trade Centre
Chamanchak, New Bypass Road,
Opp. Patrakar Nagar Thana,
 Patna - 27.
Mob. 9304826650, 9304826651, 9771492804.
Gyan Ganga,
Boring Road
3rd Floor, M-2/38, S. K. Puri, Patna - 01.
Mob:- 9304826652,53,53.
Gyan Ganga
Om Vihar Complex, Kadam Kuwan,
Patna- 03.
Mob:- 9304826655, 9771492969
Gyan Ganga
Gopal Market, Naya Tola, Patna.
Mob:- 9304826656, 9386589048.

Gyan Ganga
Vishal Bhawan, Near Saguna More,
Patna-03,
Mob:- 06115-222455.
Gyan Ganga Bhagalpur
Sharad Chandra Path, Masakchak-01,
Mob:- 7091492222, 0641-2408619.
Gyan Ganga Ranchi
Circular Road, Opp. Ranchi Women's
College, Ranchi, **Jharkhand**- 834001
Mob:- 9304826657, 0651-2563570.
Gyan Ganga Deoghar
Caster Town, Near Vijya Bank,
Deoghar, **Jharkhand**
Tel:- 9934013006, 9801694787
Gyan Ganga Jamsedpur
Line no.-14, Kashi-B, Near Bharat
Transport, Sakshi,
Jamsedpur-01, **Jharkhand**
Mob:- 7070096299, 9934013006.

Dedicated to my father

Late Dijan Prasad

PREFACE

This book covers every types and variation of questions from sketching/Drawing part in NID, NIFT, B.ARCH., NATA, B.F.A. etc. entrance exams. The book is profusely illustrated. Conceptual approaches are given in very simple form. Ideas have been taken from available syllabus and sample questions of the above courses. The candidate can perform in a very short time and time is precious for everyone. Hope you will benefit more from this book.

Budhdeo Prasad

ART AS A CAREER
(NID, NIFT, B. ARCH, NATA, B.F.A, CEPT, PEARL, APEEJAY, SYMBIOSIS, SRISHTI, & IIT-CEED)

Simple though it may seem the term Art has very broad connotations. Loosely defined the term denotes anything and everything that is aesthetically appealing, visually delightful, and requiring certain skills. Accordingly art includes a number of things: painting, sculpture, sketching, cartooning, dance, music, singing, poetry, ceramics and pottery, photography, flower arrangement, interior designing and yes. even cooking!!!

In modern times, however, Art has been broadly categorized into two-three groups e.g. performing arts, visual arts and fine arts etc. The latter encompasses sculpture, painting, sketching, drawing and graphics.

India has a rich tradition and heritage of art. There are many individuals who have attained the acme of fame. Yet there remain innumerable nameless, inconspicuous but highly talented artists, who make significant contributions to art. From painters of Kalighat pat (Kolkata) Pattachitra (orissa), Kalamkari (Hyderabad) Madhubani (Bihar) to those of Pichwari (Rajasthan) Chamba (HimachalPradesh) there are indeed hordes and hordes of them, who eventually pass into oblivion, unwept and unsung.

The minimum qualification for taking up the course is Class 12, For the degree courses, there is an entrance test in which the aptitude of a person is checked. You may have to make a still life sketch as well as a free-hand drawing on any medium from given topics. There is also a general awareness section in which general knowledge question are asked. The next step in the admission process is the interview. A person should have substantial portfolio to display during the interview.

It is important to practice drawing at home. For help and guidance, one can approach students of the arts colleges or even the faculty members. In certain cities, those who have just graduated organize crash courses too. Free-hand drawing must be practiced too and the best of the work should be selected for the portfolio.

NATIONAL INSTITUTE OF DESIGN (NID)

UG Undergraduate 4 years Academic Programs

Product design	Furniture & interior Design
Transportation Design	Ceramic & Glass Design
Toy Design	Textile Design
Apparel Design & Merchandising	Lifestyle Accessory Design
Graphic Design	Animation Film Design
Film & Video Communication	Strategic Design Managements
New Media Design	Software & User Interface Design
Information & Digital Design	Design for Retail Experiences
Design for Digital Experience	

NATIONAL INSTITUTE OF FASHION TECHNOLOGY (NIFT)

UG Undergraduate 4 years Academic Programs

Fashion & Apparel	Fashion & Textile
Fashion & Life style Accessories	Fashion & Communication
Fashion Technology	Knitwear Design
Leather Design (Footwear)	Garments Manufacturing technology
Personal Product & Interior Accessories	

COMMON ENTRANCE EXAMINATION FOR DESIGN (CEED-IIT)

Post graduate programs in Design

Industrial Design

Animation Design

Product Design and Engineering

Visual Communication Design

Interaction Design

BACHELOR OF ARCHITECTURE & NATA

Undergraduate 5 years

Drawing Engineer

Architecture

Film & Television Institute of India (FTII)

Film direction

Ideography

Cinematography

Film Editing

BACHELOR OF FINE ART (B.F.A.)

Painting

Graphics &

Sculpture

Applied art/Commercial art

PLACEMENTS

Art Teacher	Quality Controller	Merchandising
Lecturer	Sampling Coordinator	Boutique or Gallery Owner
Professor	Production Manager	Accessory designer
Curator	Graphic Designer	Film direction
Graphic Artist	Makeup artist	Cinematography
Stage & Set Designer	Photographer	Ideography
Freelance Artist	Textile designs for apparel or	Film Editing
Sculptor	home furnishing industry.	Product Design
Cartoonist	Designer for furnishing or floor	Furniture & interior Design
Commercial Artist	coverings	Transportation DesignCeramic
Interior Decorator	Home Stylists	& Glass Design
Designer	Design Coordinators	Toy Design & Development
Visualizer Illustrator	Fashion Designers in the Apparel	Textile Design
Advertising Agencies	industry and related life style	Apparel Design &
Publishing Houses	sectors	Merchandising
Event Management Firms	Fashion coordinators stylists	Lifestyle Accessory Design
Multimedia & Web Design Firms	Brand Designers	Graphic Design
Television Product Houses	Visual Merchandisers in retail	Animation Film Design
Textile	stores	Film & Video Communication
Merchandiser	Product developers in Design	New Media Design
		Information & Digital Design

ALL ABOUT KALA-SHILP

CONTENTS

***TOTAL PAGE - 248**
COLOUR PLATES - 8

FUNDAMENTALS OF PAINTING

INTRODUCTION

Painting can be defined as portraying an object through the medium of colours or in black and white. A painter work with pigments usually applied to a flat surface by means of a spatula, palette, knife or brush. Today computers can also be used to paint pictures on the screen and later printed, either in colour or in black and white, and as required.

Before you formally learn the techniques of drawing and painting, you must be familiar with things which you will require as an artist. You must have the following essential materials which you can buy from the local store.

Papers

Paper is available in smooth, rough, extra rough, board or mount board, in white or coloured. You can buy the paper as per your requirement. _Use smooth cartridge paper or tinted paper(hot pressed) for fine detailed work and shading work, rough handmade paper(cold pressed) may be used for water colour. You can buy sketch- books containing nearly all of these papers.

Pencil

Lead pencil are the most common and cheapest drawing tools. They can make the delicate marks, fuzzy gray marks, rich velvety marks etc. They are graded from H-8H (the hardest) to B-8B (the softest) but the marks they make very greatly according to the paper used. Generally use HB for drawing & 2B-6Bare very popular for shading work.

Chalks and Crayons

Working with charcoal sticks(willow and vine twings), crayons and chalks offers you the opportunity to build up areas of tone as well as vary the line thickness qualities. The major advantage of these tools is the wide variety of tones and marks available, some created by blurring with your finger, or highlighting with an eraser.

Erases/Rubber

These are needed from time to time, to erase charcoal or pencil completely or to produce highlights. The best type of eraser is one made of putty. After rubbing a line, the rubber should be cleaned properly with a clean and rough cloth. Modern plastic erasers are to use. Try to makes very little use of the eraser.

Pens

The most basic form of pen is a sharp stick dipped in ink, which gives a reasonably good line of informal quality. Pens can be cut from large feathers and used as quills, or a reed can be cut an used as in the traditional reed pen. In both cases, cut the end at a steep angle and slit the point. Ordinary steel-nibbed pens obtainable from stationers or art shop, are most commonly used (wash them in soap before using them). In commercial drawing various sizes of speed ball pen, sketch pen, boll-point pen felt -tipped pen and technical pen are used.

Ink

These can be either waterproof or water-soluble. Waterproof inks are usually used for line and wash work, so that the drawing is not disturbed by the addition of subsequent washes. Black ink is most commonly used, and some artists and black fountain pen ink, or black or sepia manuscript ink, very useful as these do not clog the nib.

Chinese stick ink gives beautiful greys and a soft black; dissolve the solid ink stick by rubbing it into a saucer.

When you wish to dilute inks, use distilled water or rain-water. Tap water can cause many inks to curdle and many watercolor inks to fade rapidly.

Colors

The colours make a drawing beautiful and attractive. Color is used according to the nature of creation and paper. In painting, usually three kinds of color are used- dry colors, water colors(Transprant) and oil color(opaque). Dry colors are pastels, pastel crayons, color pencils and colors sketch pens. In water color, there are tubes, tablets, photo colors and poster colors. oil colors are usually available in tubes and these are used by mixing turpentine or linseed oil in it.

Brushes

The brushes is also an essential instruments for an artist. They can be of various types-thick, thin, round or flat. The hair of brush can be both soft and hard. The brushes are used according to the needs of painting. Brushes meant for water colour should be long and soft .Sable hair brushes give good result.Hard hair brushes are used in oils. Usually, brushes of 1,2,3,4,5,and 6 numbers are used in painting and wide flat brush are used for applying washes and texture.

Other things

An artist requires some other essential items such as instrument box, 'T' and set square, ceramic or plastic palette for mixing color , glass or mug for water, boards pins for attaching paper to the drawing board, rubber solution, fevicol for sticking paper ,sharpener and clean white clothe etc.

MEDIA AND MEDIUM OF COMPOSITION

INTRODUCTION

Drawing and Painting is one of the oldest of the visual arts, and one of the most important. Each section features a different painting medium and its characteristics, as well as the numerous types of substrates (papers and surfaces), the tools of the trade, and other art materials and equipment that complement that particular medium. You'll learn how to create many exciting effects with each medium, and a wealth of full-color photos will give you a better understanding of how to achieve such results.

SURFACES/SUPPORT/GROUNDS

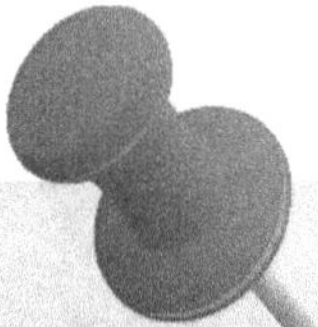

Drawing

Drawing can be finished worse of art or preparatory studies for paintings and other visual arts. They can be made using a wide variety of drawing instruments such as pencils, graphite sticks, chalks, charcoal, pens and inks. The most common drawing instrument is the graphite pencil. A graphite pencil consists of a thin rod of graphite mixed with clay, encased in wood. Charcoal is one of the oldest drawing instruments. It is produced by firing twigs of willow, vine, or other woods at high temperatures in airtight containers. Erasers can be used to rub out marks made by drawing materials such as graphite pencils or charcoal, or to achieved a particular effect-such as smudging. Fixative is often applied-using a mouth diffuser or aerosol spray fixative-to prevents smudging once a drawing is finished

Painting Dry-Medium Tools: (Fig-1)
1. Pencil
2. Wax Crayons
3. Charcoal
4. Graphite Stick(Sanguine)
5. Chalk
6. Pastel pencil
7. Pastel Stick with protective paper cover

Wet-Medium Tools: (Fig-2)
1. Brush
2. Writing Pen
3. Technical pen
4. Ball-point pen
5. Felt-tipped pen
6. Broad-tipped felt pen

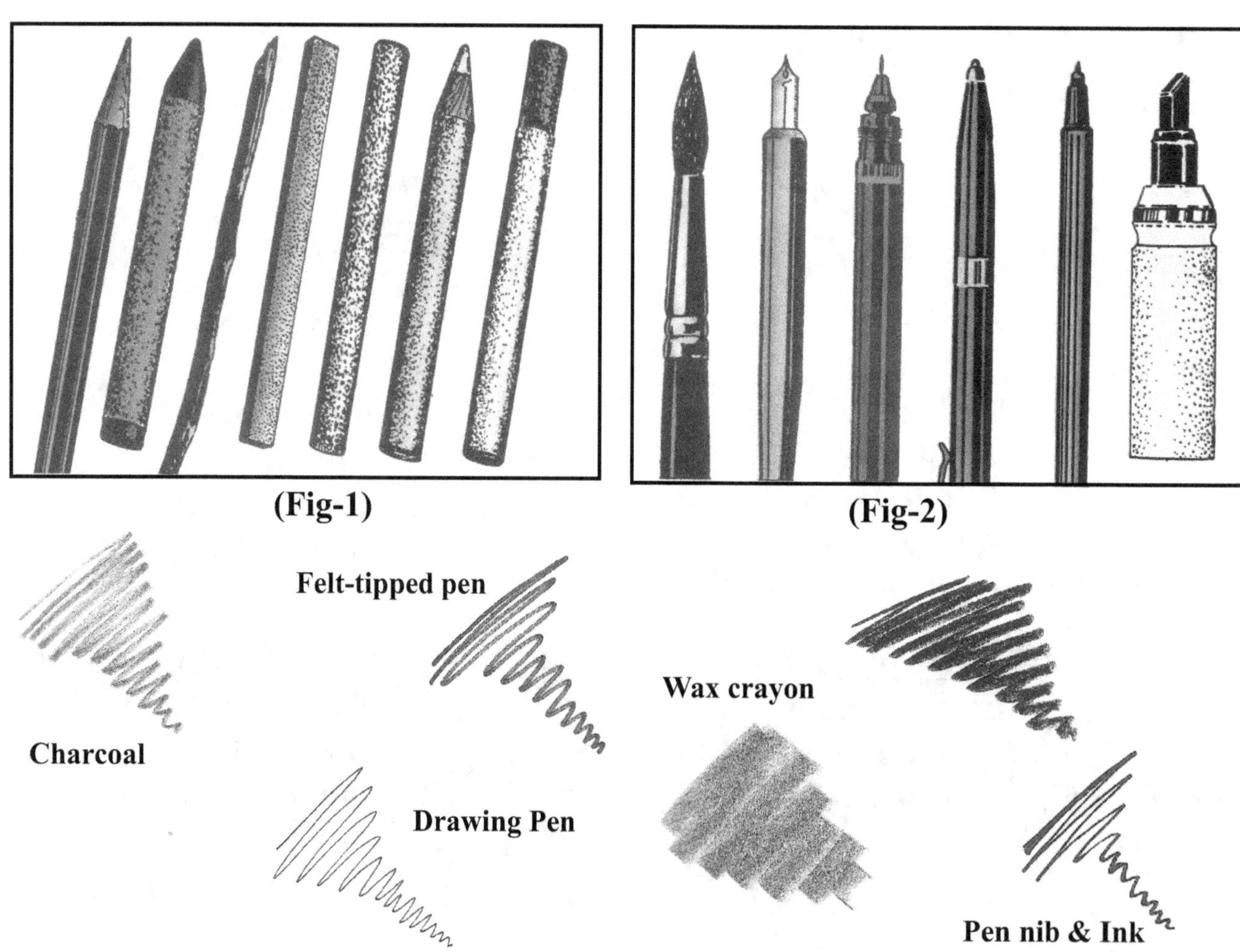

Colour Pencils

Colored pencils consist of a wooden shaft that is filled with colored pigment. This pigment is held together by a binder, that when spread over a surface, transfers color. Colored pencils, as a medium, are a popular choice for many artists. This is partly because they are so widely available, portable, and relatively inexpensive. When used correctly, colored pencil drawings can be rich with color and resemble a painting The center of the pencil is a pigmented core that is held together by a binder. The binder of the pencil affects how it performs on a surface. Most pencils feature a wax-based binder, while others are oil-based, or gum-based (watercolor pencils).

Colour pencils are available under various brands. The hardness and softness of the pencils may vary in different brands.The pencils are produced with primary colours, mixed colours and their light and dark shades, thus there are 12-120 shades of colours that are available in the market now. A box of 36 or 48 shades is convenient for handling. The color can be fluidly applied on a surface because of wax in its lead. Different tones can be obtained by controlling pressure on the pencil. There is ample scope for selection of colours due to availability of individual shades of appropriate colours. The sharpness of the pencil tip makes it possible to work with fine details. Due to wax in the pigment, work once done with pencil cannot be erased. The Doodling, Hatching (diagonal lines),Cross-hatching and Tonal gradation made by progressively reducing the pressure are intrusting techniques of colour pencil

Colour pencil can be used on papers of various textures including glossy surfaces , so selection of appropriate paper according to the subject is possible. Tinted paper, mount board, box board, etc. can also be used at a times. Apart from these, other accessories needed are cutter, pencil holder, butter paper, etc.

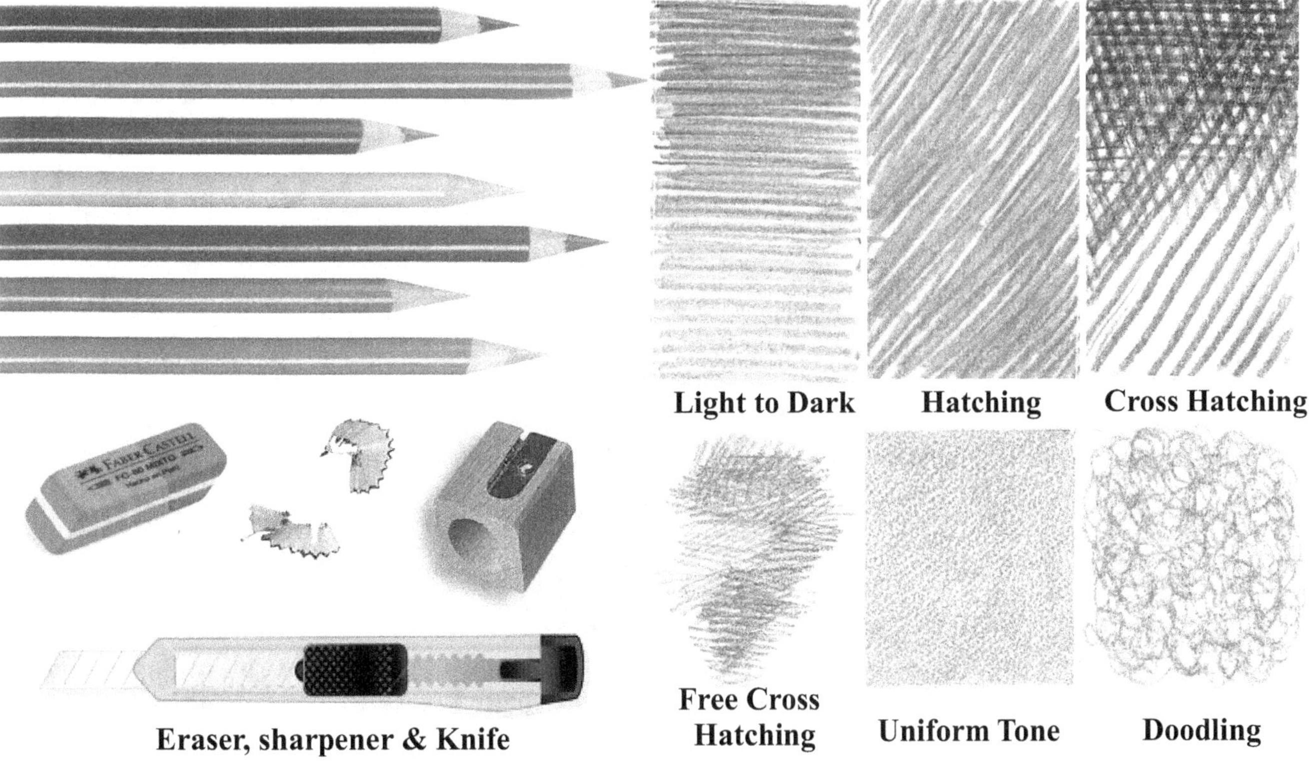

Eraser, sharpener & Knife

Pastels

Pastels are sticks of pigment made by mixing ground pigment with chalk and a binding medium, such as gum arabic. They vary in hardness depending on the proportion of the binding medium to the chalk. Soft pastel- the most common form of pastel-contains just enough binding medium to hold the pigment in stick form. Pastels can be applied directly to any support (surface) with sufficient tooth (texture). When a pastel is drawn over a textured surface, the pigment crumbles and lodges in the fibers of the support.

Pastel marks have a particular soft, matt quality and are suitable for techniques such as blending, scumbling, and feathering. Blending is a technique of rubbing and fusing two or more colours on the support using fingers or various tools such as tortillons (paper stumps), soft hair brushes, putty erasers, and soft bread. Scumbling is a technique of building up layers of pastel colours. The side or blunted tip of a soft pastel is lightly drawn over an under painted area so that patches of the colour beneath show through. Feathering is a technique of applying parallel strokes of colour with the point of a pastel, usually over an existing layer of pastel colour. A thin spray of fixative can be applied using a mouth diffuser or aerosol spray fixative to a finished pastel painting, or in between layers of colour to prevent smudging.

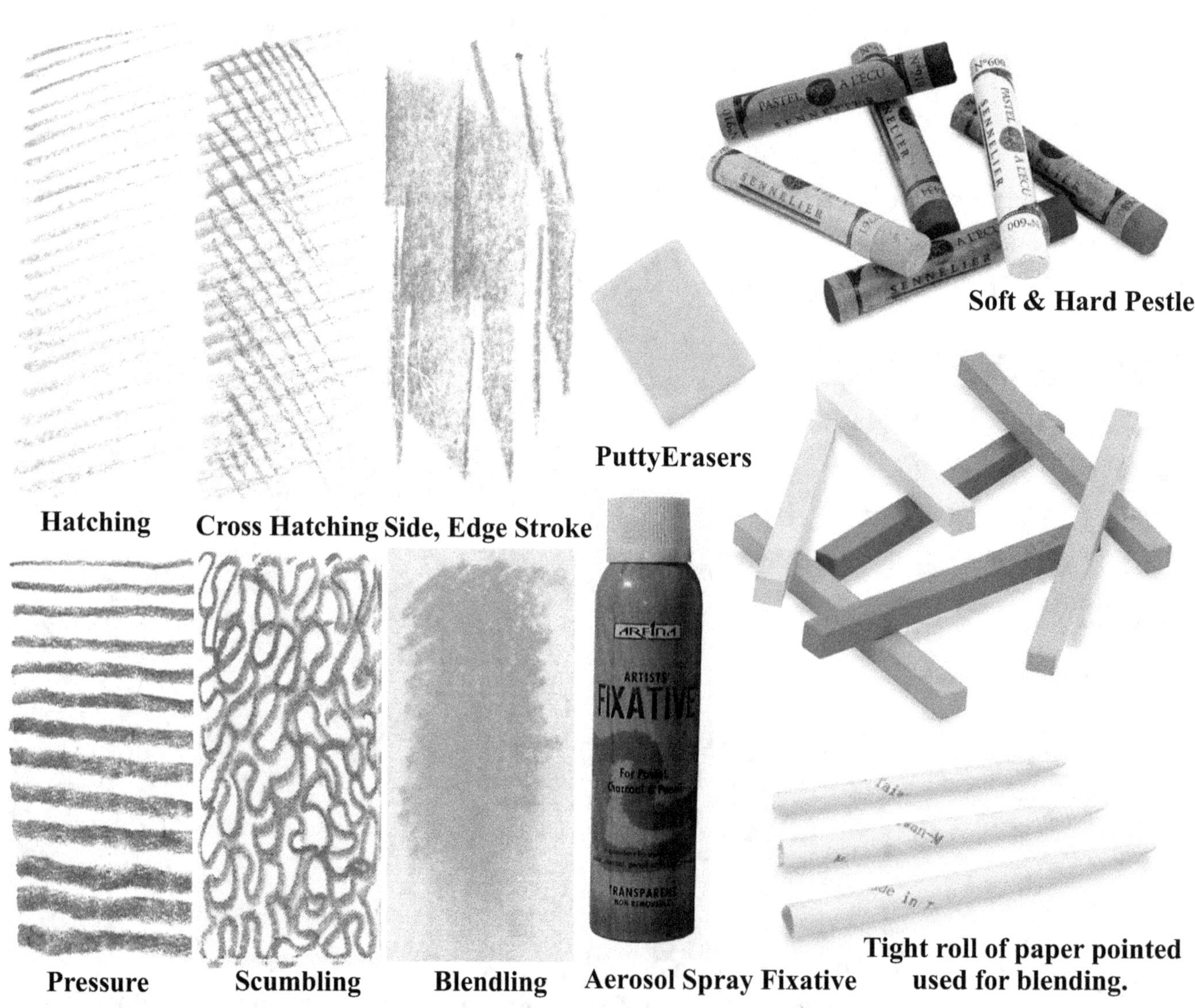

Watercolour

Water colour paint is made of ground pigment mixed with a water-soluble binding medium, usually gum arabic. It is usually applied to paper using soft hair brushes such as sable, goat hair, squirrel, and synthetic brushes. Watercolours are often diluted and applied as overlaying washes (thin, transparent layers) to build up depth of colour. Washes can be laid in a variety of ways to create a range of different effects. For example, a wet-in-wet wash can be achieved by laying a wash can be achieved by laying a wash on top of another wet wash. The two washes blend together to give a fused effect. Sponges are used to modify washes by soaking up paint so that areas of pigment are lightened or removed from the paper. Watercolours can also be applied undiluted-a technique known as dry brush-to create a broken colour effect. Watercolours are generally transparent and allow light to reflect from the surface of the paper through the layers of paint to give a luminous effect. They can be thickened and made opaque by adding body colour (Chinese white).

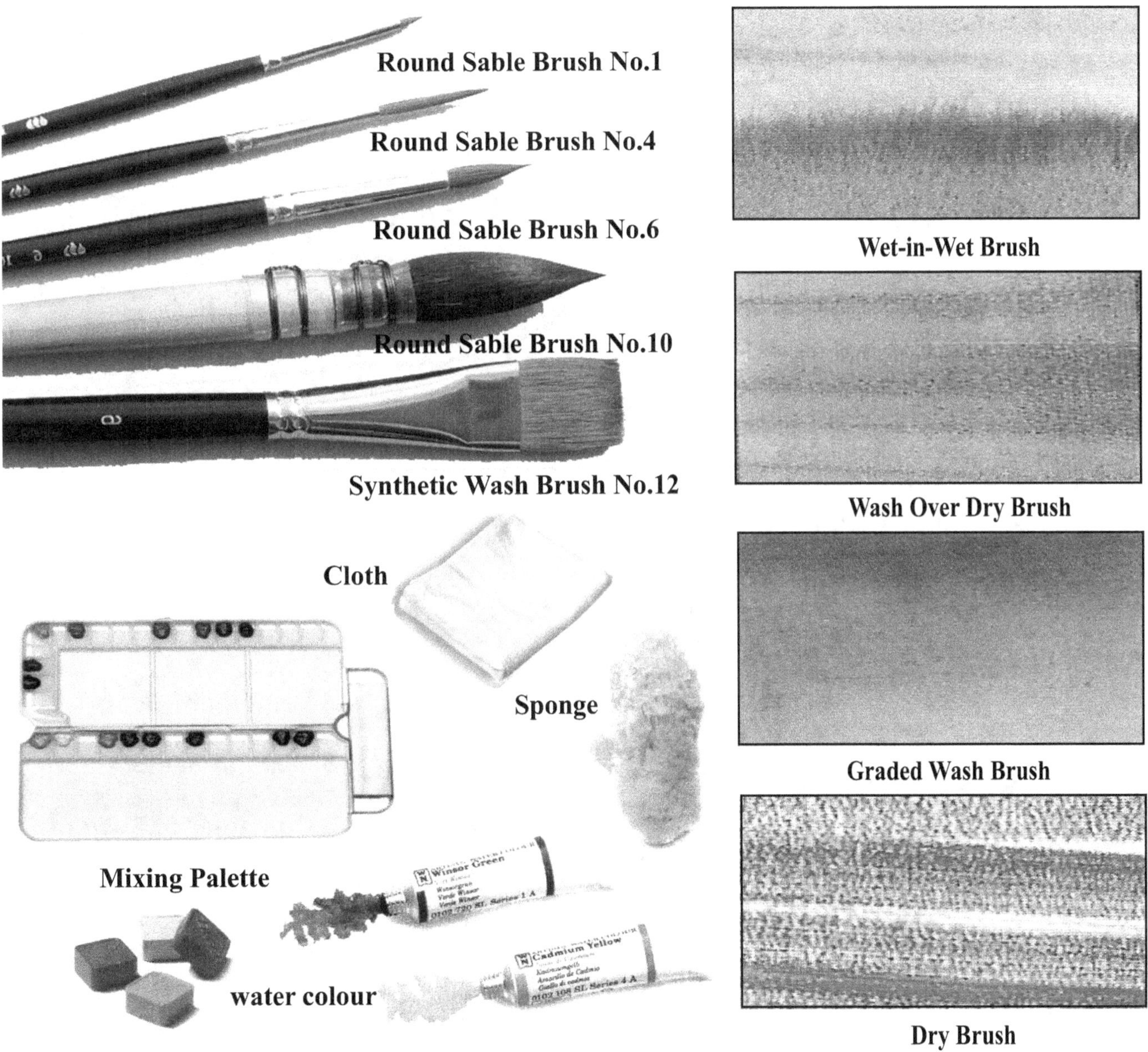

Oils

Oils paints are made by mixing and grinding pigment with a drying vegetable oil such as linseed oil. The paint can be applied to many different surfaces and textures-the most common being canvas. Before painting, the canvas is stretched on a wooden frame and its surface is prepared with layers of size (glue) and primer. The two main types of brushes used in oil painting are stiff hog hair bristle brushes generally used for covering large areas; and soft hair brushes made from sable or synthetic material-generally used for fine detail. Other tools, including painting knives, can also be used to achieve different effects. Oil paint can be applied thickly (a technique known as impasto), or can be thinned down using a solvent - such as turpentine or white sprit. Varnishes are sometimes applied to finished paintings to protect their surface and to give them a matt or gloss finish.

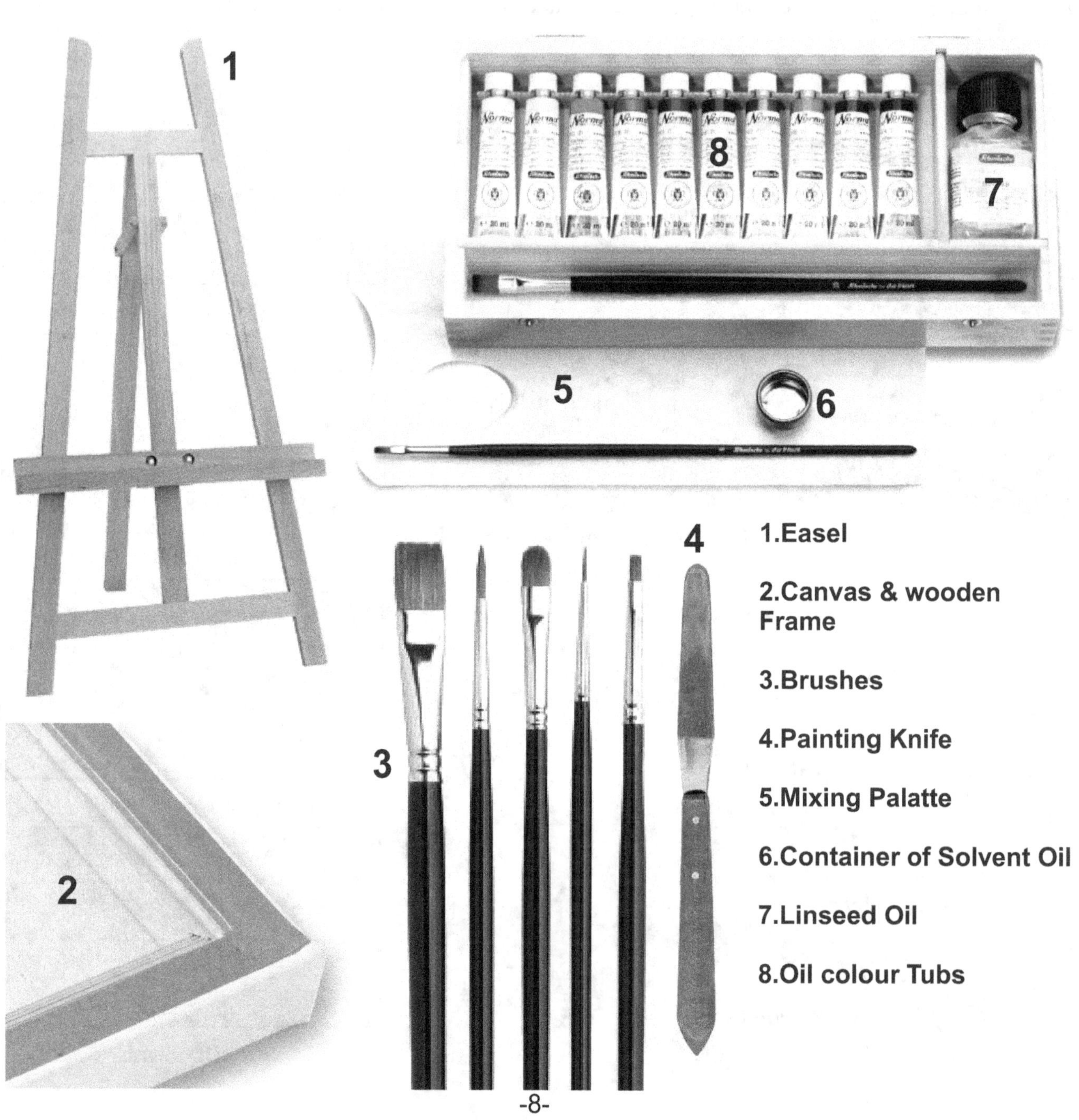

1.Easel

2.Canvas & wooden Frame

3.Brushes

4.Painting Knife

5.Mixing Palatte

6.Container of Solvent Oil

7.Linseed Oil

8.Oil colour Tubs

Acrylics

Acrylic paints is made by mixing pigment with a synthetic resin. It can be thinned with water but dries to become water insoluble. Acrylics are applied to many surfaces, such as paper and acrylic-primed board and canvass. A variety of brushes, painting knives, rollers, air-brushes, plastic the versatility of acrylics makes them suitable for a wide range of techniques. They can be used opaquely or -by adding water- in a transparent, watercolour style. Acrylic mediums can be added to the paint to adjust its consistency for special effects such as glazing and impasto (ridges of paint applied in thick strokes) or to make it more matt or glossy. Acrylics are quick-drying, which allows layers of paint to be applied on top of each other almost immediately.

Wet-in-Wet Brush

Opaque Over Transparent

Broken Colour

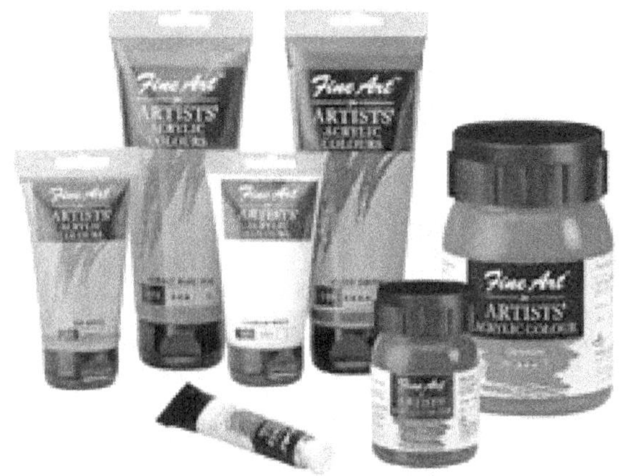

Colours

**Brushes &
Flexile Blades**

An Introduction of print making

Printmaking is a sometimes misunderstood aspect of visual art. Printmaking involves the creation of a master plate from which multiple images are made. Simply put, the artist chooses a surface to be the plate. This could be linoleum, styrofoam, metal, cardboard, stone or any one of a number of materials. Then the artist prepares the printing plate by cutting, etching or drawing an image onto the plate. Ink or colour is applied (in a variety of ways) and paper is pressed onto the plate either by hand or by way of a hand-run printing press. The finished print is pulled from the plate. A certain number of prints are pulled, the plate is destroyed so that more prints won't be printed later, thus ensuring the value of the edition. Often the first three or four prints of are different than the rest of the edition. These first prints are called artist's proofs. The number of prints pulled from one plate is called an edition.

Intaglio

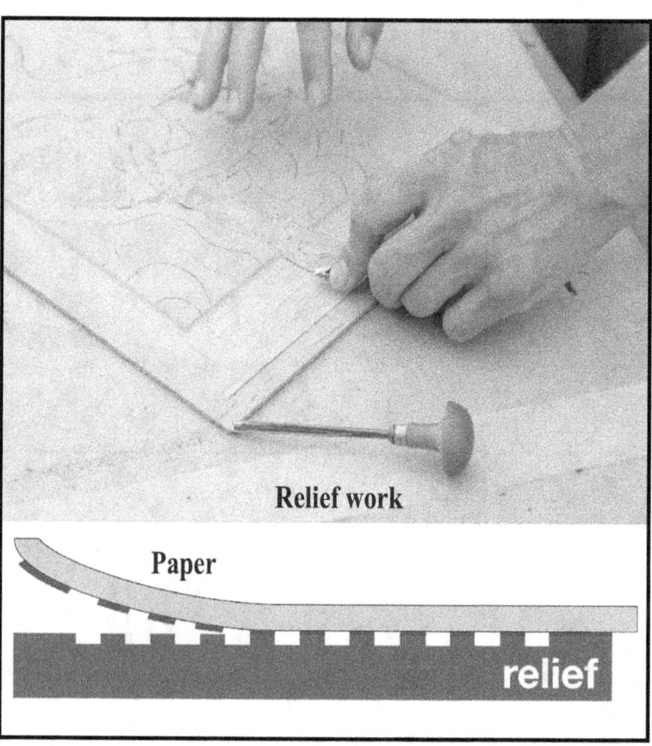

Relief

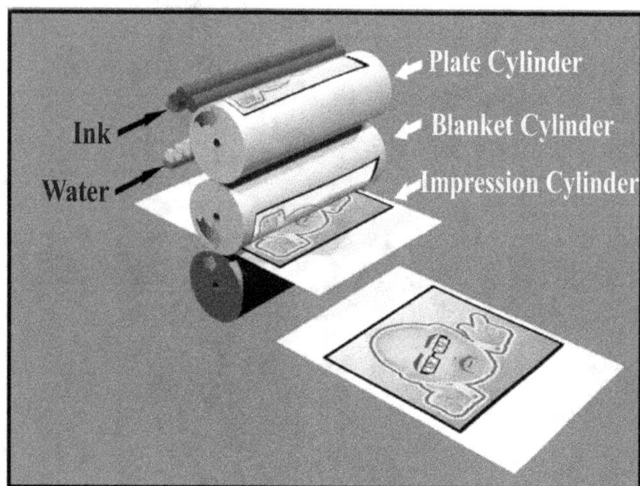

Off-Set Lithography

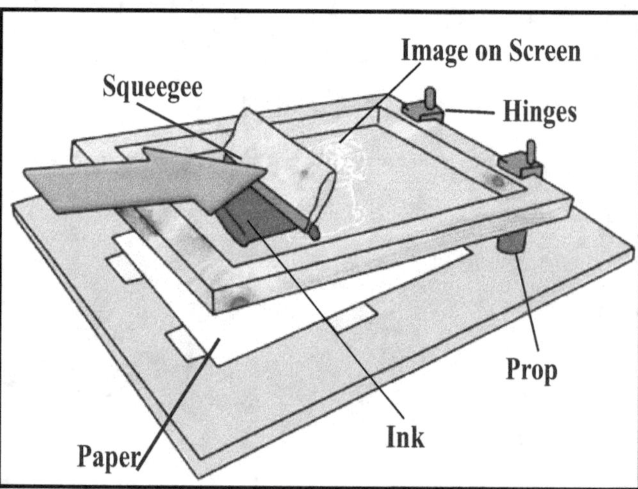

Screen Printing

Print Making (Graphics)

Prints are made by five basic printing processes **intaglio, lithographic, relief, screen and offset**.

In **<u>intaglio printing,</u>** lines are engraved or etched into the surface of a metal plate. Lines are engraved by hand using sharp metal tools. They are etched by corroding the metal plate with acid, using acid-resistant ground to protect the areas not to be etched. The plate is then inked and wiped, leaving the grooves filled with ink and the surface clean. Dampened paper is laid over the plate, and both paper and plate are passed through the rollers of an etching press. The pressure of the rollers forces the paper into the grooves, so that it takes up the ink, leaving an impression on the paper.

In **<u>relief printing,</u>** the non-printing areas of a wood or linoleum block are cut away using gouges, knives, and other tools. The printing areas are left raised in relief and are rolled with ink. Paper is laid on the inked block and pressure is applied by means of a press or by burnishing (rubbing) the back of the paper. The most common forms of relief printing are woodcut, wood engraving and linocut.

<u>Lithographic printing</u> is based on the antipathy between grease and water. An image is drawn on a surface-usually a stone or metal plate-with a greasy medium, (lithographic ink). The greasy drawing is fixed on to the plate by applying an acidic solution, such as gum arabic. The surface is then dampened and rolled with ink. The ink adheres only to the greasy areas and is repelled by the water. Paper is laid on the plate and pressure is applied by means of a press.

The **<u>Offset Printing</u>** is as against direct printing, offset has the advantage of printing the same image that is worked on a plate, rather than giving a mirror image. This process overtook lithography and could be operated manually or through the machine, in the printing process. A large rubber-covered blanket cylider on an offset press first picks up the impression from the inked plate and transfers the imprint onto a sheet of paper, which has been damped and placed to receive the print. The plate has to be re-inked by hand.

<u>Screen Printing/Silk Screen Printing</u> is known as hand printing, with various methods being used. The basic screen printing kit consists of a wooden frame with a silk mesh stretched tout on one side, a flat baseboard, the hingeber joining them and a flexible rubber or synthetic squeegee (rubber edged tool) to force the colour through the fine mesh to print on the paper registered on the base-board. Frames can come in several sizes and are made from wood plywood, tubular steel or aluminum. The mesh was originally of silk, though now nylon Terylene, polyester, copper and stainless steel are used. The fineness of the mesh governs the amount of ink that is deposited on the paper below. A film stencil is attached to the mesh. A liquid filler such as PVA(polyvinyl acetate emulsion paint), acquer, cellulose or ink is then applied with brush, scraper or finger for textural variation. Candles and wax crayons can also be used as fillers. The liquid filler is poured along one end of the frame while the paper is clamped to the baseboard. The squeegee then drags the liquid filler across the entire face of the mesh, forcing it through to print an image. In resent time photo-stencils have also been used in screen printing.

Computer Graphics

Computer graphics are very useful. It involves creativity, art, technology and the communication of ideas. It encourages students to reach beyond the boundaries of traditional graphic design and explore the huge potential of the digital environment.

Computer-generated imagery is used for movie making, video game and computer program development, scientific modeling, and design for catalogs and other commercial art. Some people even make computer graphics as art.

During mid 1980s, the arrival of desktop publishing and the introduction of graphic art software applications introduced a generation of designers to computer image manipulation and 3D image creation that had previously been laborious. Computer graphic design enabled designers to instantly see the effects of layout or typographic changes without using any ink in the process, and to simulate the effects of traditional media without requiring a lot of space.

Just see the flexibility of the medium. For a designer on the move, it is an office on the go, a compact work studio full of innumerous tools. This helps you working without mixing colours with water or oil on a pallet and away from clogging air brush, cleaning brush after every use and also a wrong colour stroke. It has an undo command that comes to your rescue, if you have done something unwanted and want to go back to your previous work.

The computer is loaded with varied software and tools. This huge array of tools follow your command. The precision of a computer remains unmatched. A line can be drawn in curve, straight, angular, thin, thick, etc. of a choice with the help of a line tool. The attributes are defined in the dialogue box. You can cut it, copy it, and paste it any number of times, at any desired place in the design. It can be undone if anything goes wrong and can repeat any command without any problem. Most software provides a whole range of calligraphy tools with varied styles.

All computers use an operating system and some software to follow commands. Software is basically of two types, vectors and rasters. Let us see what these vector and raster based software are?

1.Vector Based Software :(such as those created in Adobe Illustrator)This software is linear in nature, all kind of line based work is done through this kind of software, and inside shapes you can add colour fills. Because everything is generated based around this, vectors can be resized to any size without any loss of quality.

2.Raster Based Software:(sometimes referred to as bitmap images)are made up of thousands of pixels which determine the colour and form of the image.

Photos are raster images. Photoshop is the most common raster editor, enabling you to manipulate the colour and other properties of the pixels. This kind of software produces images that are softer at the edges. They are ideal for editing photo and image activities. When enlarged beyond its actual size they become hazy.

Traditional tools such as pencils or markers are often used to develop graphic design ideas, even when computers are used for finalization. Computers are generally considered to be an indispensable tool used in the graphic design industry. Computers and software applications are more effective production tools when combined with traditional methods.

The thumbnail sketches or rough drafts on paper can be used rapidly to refine and produce the idea on the computer in a hybrid process. This hybrid process is especially useful in logo design.

The thumbnail sketches or rough drafts on paper can be used rapidly to refine and produce the idea on the computer in a hybrid process. This hybrid process is especially useful in logo design.

Rapid production from the computer allows designers to explore multiple ideas quickly and with more detail than could be achieved by traditional hand-rendering or paste-up on paper. Software enables the designer to venture through the creative process more quickly experimenting with tools and methods, be they traditional or digital. Ideas explored using pencil and paper are executed using fonts, clipart, stock photos, or rendering filters on the computer. One of the key features of graphic design is that it involves selecting the appropriate image making tools out of its ability to generate meaning rather than preference.

COMPUTER IMAGE EFFECT

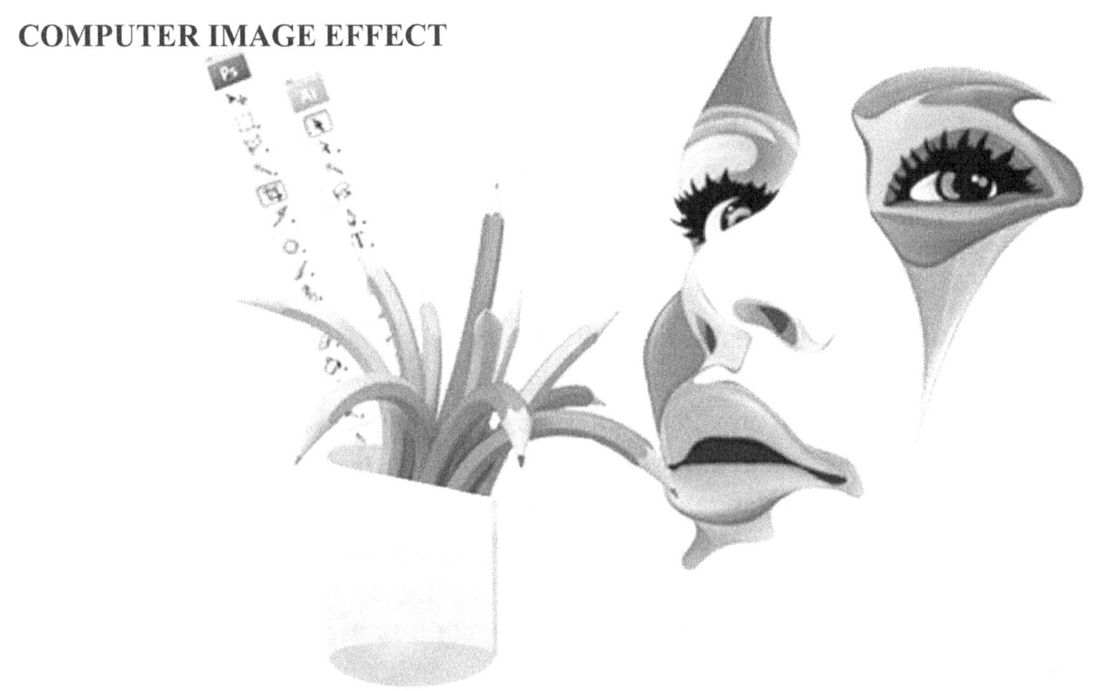

3D Computer graphics Image

Vector Graphics

Raster Graphics

Sculpture

The two traditional methods of making sculpture are **<u>carving and modelling.</u>**

A **<u>carved</u>** sculpture is made by cutting was the surplus from a block of **hard material** such as stone, marble, or wood. The tools used for carving very according to the material being carved. Heavy steel points, claws, and chisels that are struck with a lump hammer are generally used for stone and marble. Sharp gouges and chisels that are struck with a wooden mallet are used for wood. Sculptures formed from hard materials are generally finished by filing with rasps, rifflers, and other abrasive implements.

<u>Modelling</u> is process by which shapes are built up, using malleable materials such as clay, plaster and wax. The material is cut with wire ended tools and modelled with the fingers or a variety of hardwood and metal implements. For wood, is used to provide internal support. Sculptures formed in soft materials may harden naturally or can be made more durable by firing in a kiln. Modelled sculptures are often first designed in was or another material to be cast later in a metal such a bronze. The development of many new materials in the 20th century has enabled sculptures to experiment with new techniques such as construction (joining preformed pieces of material such as machine components, mirrors, and furniture) and kinetic (mobile) sculpture. sculptures formed in soft materials may harden naturally or can be made more durable by firing in a kiln. Modelled sculptures are often first designed in was or another material to be cast later in a metal such a bronze. The development of many new materials in the 20th century has enabled sculptures to experiment with new techniques such as construction (joining preformed pieces of material such as machine components, mirrors, and furniture) and kinetic (mobile) sculpture.

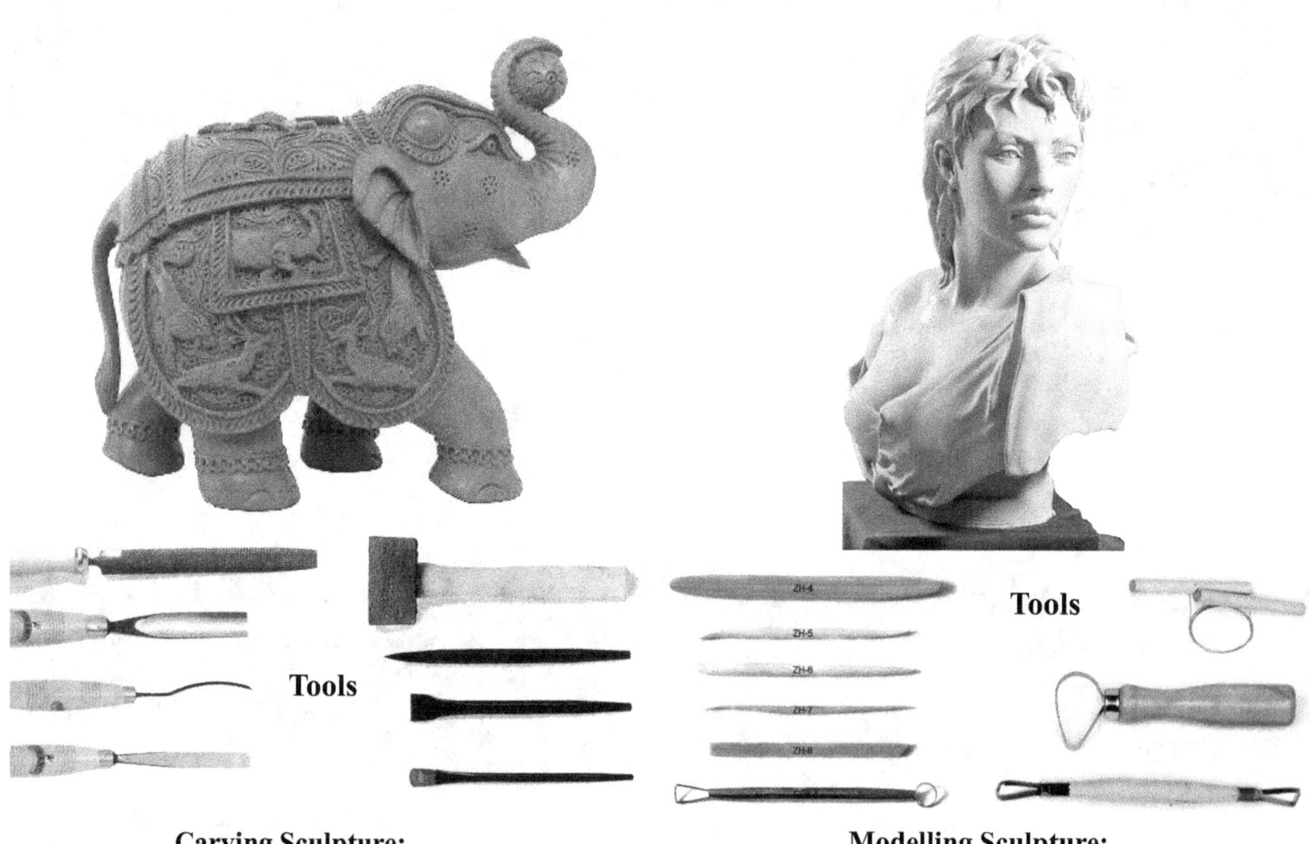

| Carving Sculpture: | Modelling Sculpture: |
| Hard Material(Stone, Marble, Wood) | Soft Material(Clay, Plaster, Wax) |

ELEMENTS AND PRINCIPLES OF ART

INTRODUCTION

It is very clear that all facts of nature cannot be put on paper, still, with the right combination of lines, tones, space perspective and composition, we can recollect and communicate our experience and make the viewer a participant in out multi sensed response to nature.

LINE: The path of a moving point at the edge of a flat shape, or outline of a solid object. It is longer than it is wider. Lines do have some width as well as length, this is called measure. Types of line refers to straight, curvy, horizontal, vertical, diagonal, zigzag, implied, and angular.   Direction pertains to the movement that a line may have or seem to indicate. Location refers to the placement of a line.

Horizontal lines run parallel such as ===

Vertical lines run up and down such as |||||

Diagonal lines are slanting lines such as \\\\\

Angled lines are a combination of diagonal lines such as /\/\/\ ><<>

Curved lines are curly and express movement such as ~~~~~

SHAPE: Shape is a two-dimensional area made by connecting lines that establish the contour of an object. Shapes may be positive or negative.   Shapes may stand out also by a difference of value, color, or texture.

FORM: The three dimensional projection of shape, it has volume, dimension, appears to have mass. This element is frequently used in sculpture. It may also refer to the overall organization of the work of art, as a second meaning

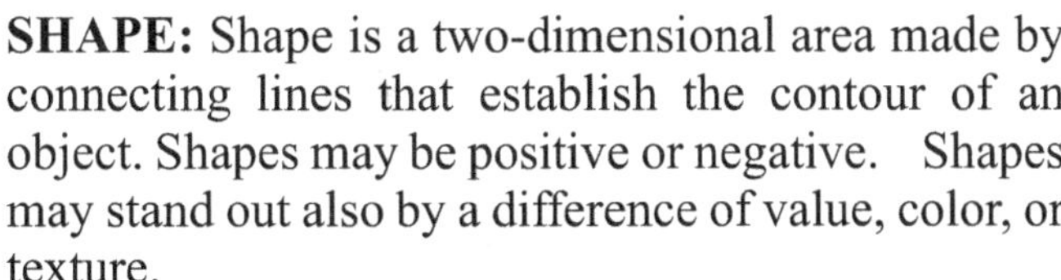

TEXTURE: Texture refers to the surface quality of "feel" or an object, such as roughness, smoothness, or softness. Actual texture can be felt while simulated texture are implied by the way the artist renders areas of the picture.

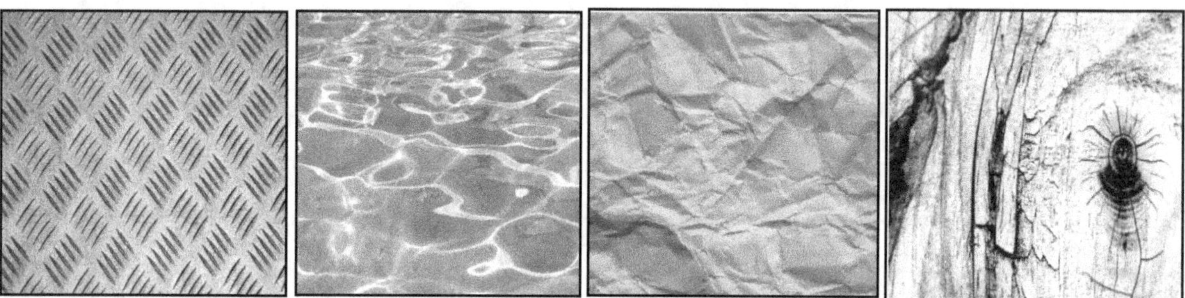

SPACE: Space refers to the distance or area between round above, or withing things. It can be a description for both two and three dimensional portrayals.

Space in other sense refers to the area, which is used in painting. How we use that areas while making picture, depends upon our mental caliber. This defined area can be used in different ways with different thoughts. If we give a defined area for drawing to ten different students, each of them will use the area in different way. In other words all those pictures will differ from each other.

EMPHASIS: In a picture, a particular part is given more importance than others. This effect is called emphasis. Actually, in every drawing there is a focal point which highlights the main theme of the drawing. And, for a picture to be lively, the emphasis of the focal point is necessary. This can be created through contrast in forms and colours.

Emphasis in a composition refers to developing points of interest to pull the viewer's eye to important part of the body of the work.

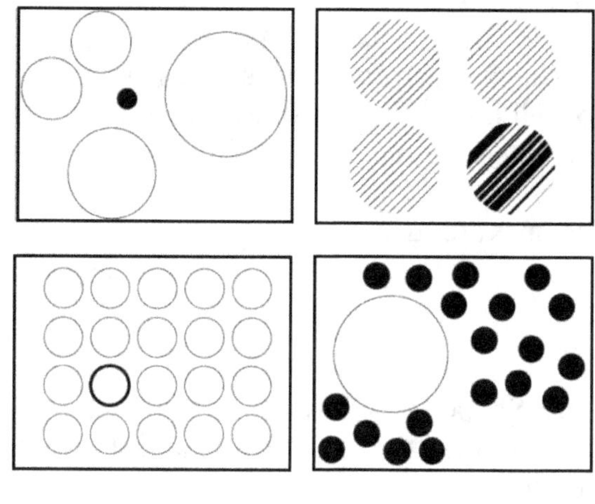

PROPORTION: Proportion or scale refers to the relationships of the size of objects in body of work. Proportions gives a sense of size seen as a relationship of objects. such as smallness or largeness.

BALANCE: Balance is another important aspect of art. Sometimes a Drawing or a Painting looks heavy on one side owing to a too big or too dark element. Sometimes it gives a thing sensation as if it is going to fall down on the heavy side. A balance of heaviness has to be achieved while painting. Our eye should be able to move with ease all over the object. Balance can be achieved by the help of lines, shapes, light and shade, colour and texture.

Balance can divided in two manners: Formal Balance and Informal Balance.

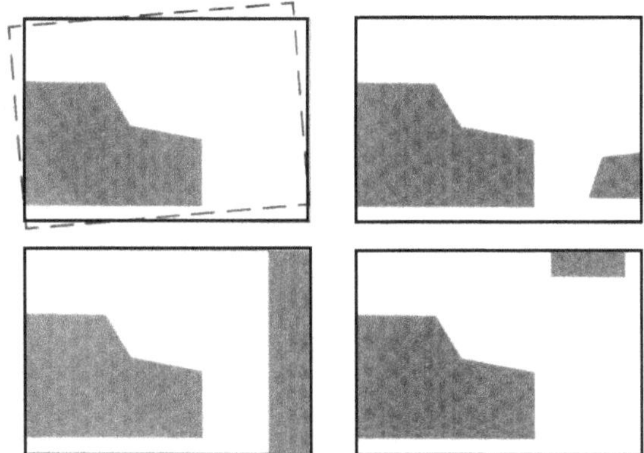

(i) FORMAL BALANCE: When the components are equally distributed on both the sides of a object, it is said to be formal balance.

(ii) INFORMAL BALANCE: When the components are not equally distributed on both the sides of a object and the balance is achieved by adjusting the shape, size, colour or tone etc., then it is called informal balance.

HARMONY : Harmony is achieved in a body of work by using similar elements throughout the work, or you can say they are the same family. for example, square, rectangle, parallelogram similarly we have colours of the same family like red, orange and yellow.

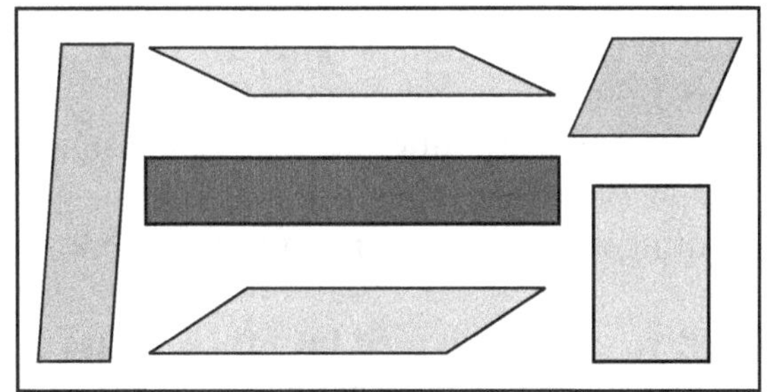

RHYTHM: Forms repeated within the picture give rise to an effect called rythm. Rythm in a picture suggests movement and life, the feeling of energy and force. It is of special importance in decorative design.

Movement of a line or shape in regular succession of intervals creates rhythm. Rhythm in music pleases the ear. After grasping all these facts one can draw things from memory and imagination.

Rythm is a type of moment in drawing and painting. It is seen in repetition of shapes and colour.

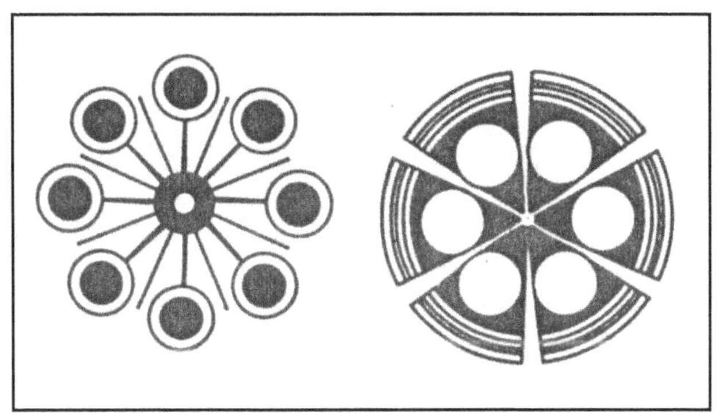

PERSPECTIVE

INTRODUCTION

Perspective is used in drawing and painting to help and create a sense of depth and space. Perspective is the art representing said objects on a flat surface as they are seen to be by the eye in other words, it is the way to make perceived objects look right.'

Now there is a wide difference between what you know about a thing and how your eyes see that thing. For example, suppose you are contemplating the view of a street which has a row of identical houses on either side. The houses at the far end appear to the eye smaller than those near to you. How small they appear to be in the picture depends on the length of the streets, the longer the street, the smaller the far houses. A man walking away from you would seem to be smaller and smaller as farther and farther he goes.

Perspective is also useful in showing the third dimension of an object.

In vast fields while seeing far away, we find the sky meeting the ground. This place is called the horizon. If a line is drawn on the same plane as the eyes and is parallel to the ground, it is called horizon line. The horizon line gets higher or lower according to the plane of sight. In the sketch of the railway line and trees on both sides, the place of horizon and point of vision are shown.

Methods of construction perspectives exist, including:
*Freehand sketching (common in art)
*Graphically constructing (once common in architecture)
*Using a perspective grid
*Computing a perspective transform (common in 3D computer applications)

Perspective can be divided into three types :
    a)   Linear perspective
    b)   Circular perspective
    c)   Colour perspective

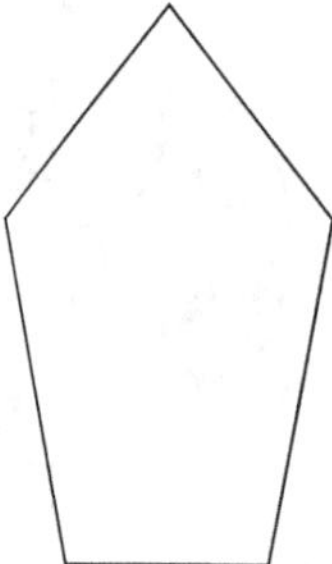
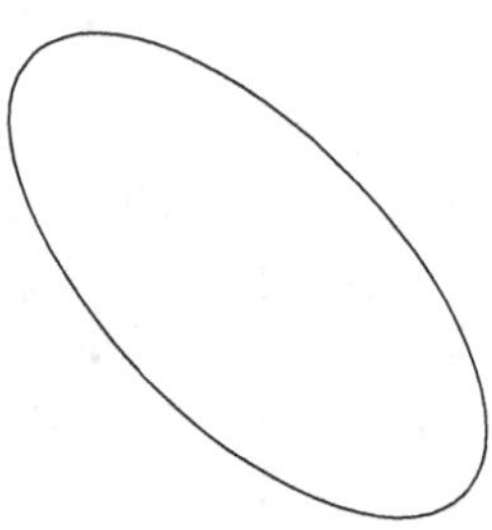
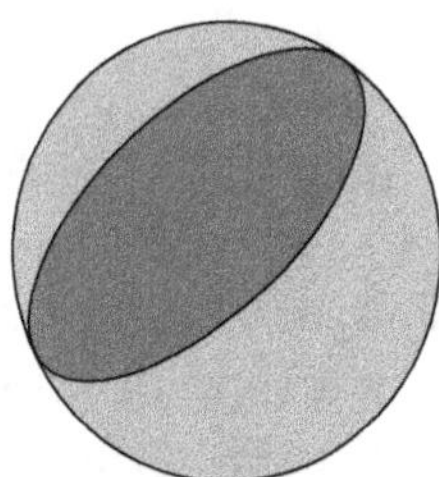

Linear perspective

Any object as it goes farther in distance becomes smaller in height and width. For example, see the picture given below. The height of the tree trunk that is nearest to you, is seen the biggest, while the second that is farther is seen smaller and the third one that is still farther seen more smaller. All the lines when increased in distance seem to meet at the horizon.

Circular Perspective

In this perspective, all the circular lines tend to become more circular when raised above the eyesight. Similar effect occurs again when the circular lines are seen below the eyesight. On both sides of the eyesight level, if the object is placed at an equal distance the ovals on both the sides look similar. And these ovales while moving away from eyesight become smaller.

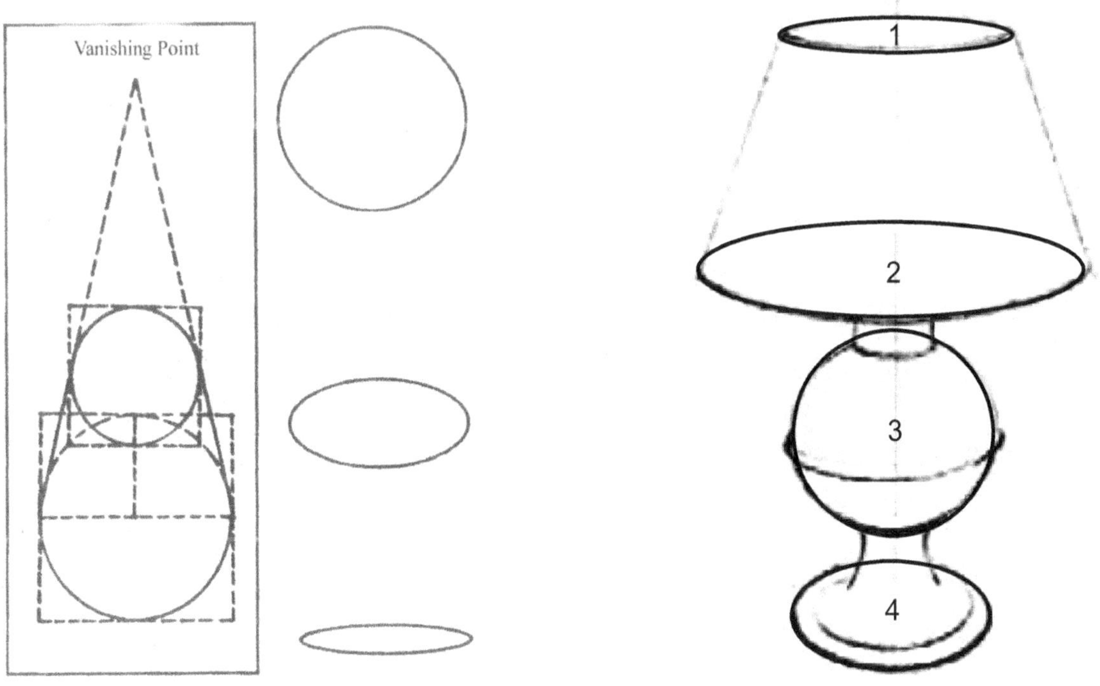

Colour Perspective

It is very important to create an illusion of solidity of the object in an object drawing. Either a round object or a square cube should be three dimensional in appearance. All objects rest on space. The depth of this space could be achieved by the use of bright and warm colours in the foreground and softer blurring colour in the background. Define the shaded part of the object and mark the lighted part carefully. Use bright colours (yellow, white, red etc.) for the lighted portion and darker shade (Brown, gray, blue etc.) for the shadows.

A still life does not appear beautiful and realistic till the colours are filled in it. Colours show the completeness and solidity of the objects. The effects of light and shadow have to be created carefully while putting the colours.

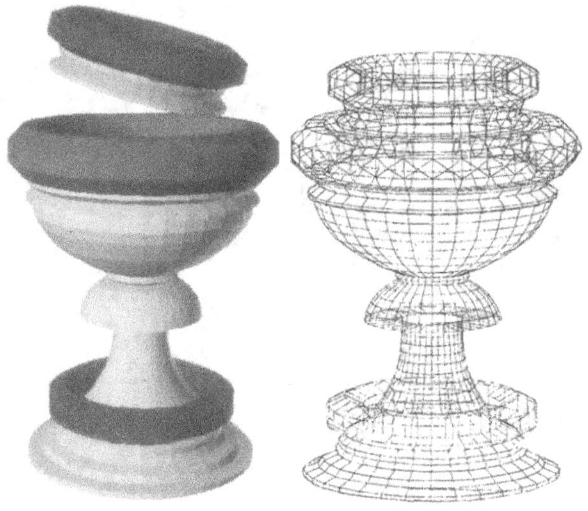

POINT OF VIEW

The most common categorizations of artificial perspective are one-, two- and three-point. The names of these categories refer to the number of vanishing points in the perspective drawing.

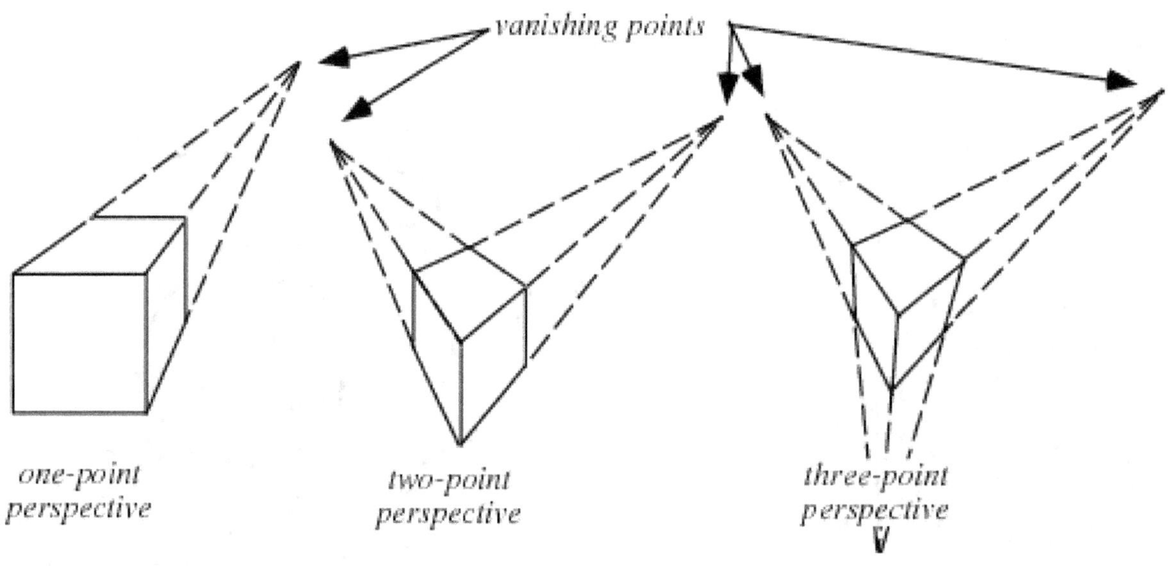

One-point perspective:

One-point perspective drawing means that the drawing has a single vanishing point, usually (though not necessarily) directly opposite the viewer's eye and usually (though not necessarily) on the horizon line. All lines parallel with the viewer's line of sight recede to the horizon towards this vanishing point. One point perspective has also been called central perspective and single-point perspective. This type of perspective is typically used for images of roads, railway tracks, hallways, or buildings viewed so that the front is directly facing the viewer.

Two-point perspective:

A two-point drawing would have lines parallel to two different angles. Any number of vanishing points are possible in a drawing, one for each set of parallel lines that are at an angle relative to the plane of the drawing. There are no longer any planes parallel to the picture plane. However the vertical lines are still drawn parallel to one another and at right angles to the ground plane. It is at this stage that perspective drawing starts to become more awkward because the second vanishing point is often situated well outside the frame of the picture. If both vanishing points are situated within the picture frame, the angles of objects appear to be extremely foreshortened.

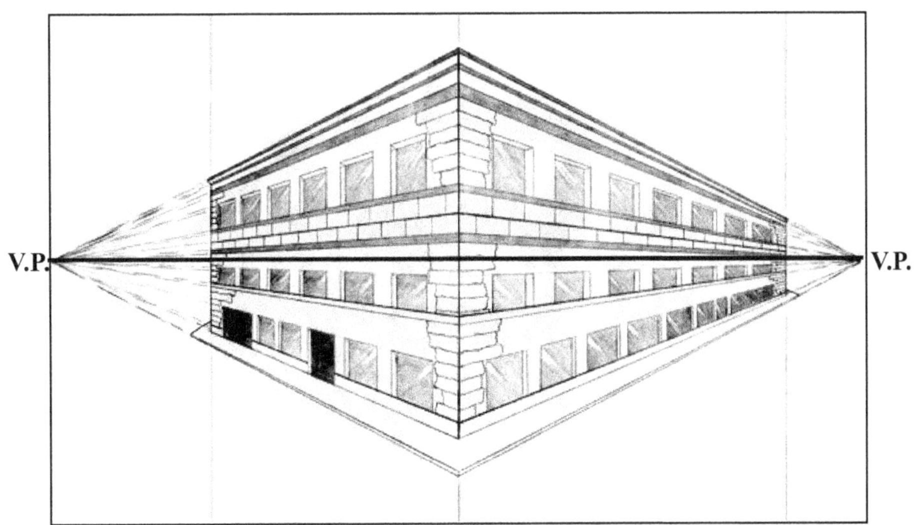

Three-point perspective:

Three Point Perspective is the most complex form of perspective drawing. Three point perspective uses three sets three vanishing points to draw each object. This technique is most commonly used when drawing buildings viewed from a low **(BIRDS VIEW POINT)** or high **(WORM or ANTS VIEW POINT)** eye-level. The low eye level in our illustration above creates the illusion that its box shape is towering above us. It naturally gives it the scale of a tall building.

In one and two point perspective, the picture plane is fixed at right angles to the ground plane. In three point perspective, the picture plane seems to be set at an angle as the viewer tends to tilt their head back or forward to look up or down from the eye level. You will not use the horizontal or the vertical line. Three point perspective is also used in action **(ANIMATION)** drawing.

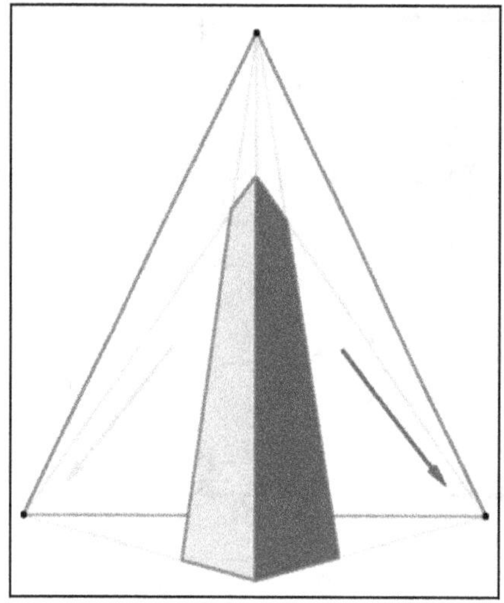

(WORM or ANTS EYE VIEW)

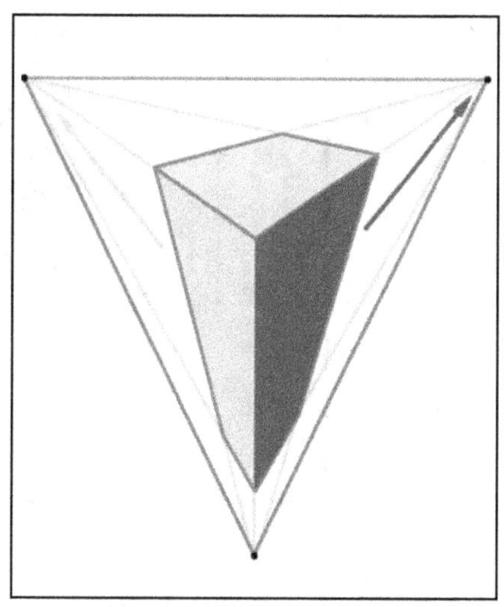

(BIRDS EYE VIEW)

Perspective of Reflection & Shadow

The perspective of reflection often causes difficulty; the trick here is to imagine the flat plane of the water surface continuing right to the foot of the object reflected, and the construction in fig.1 indicates how much of the reflection you will see. Finally, the construction in fig. 2 tells you how to determine the size and position of cast shadows.

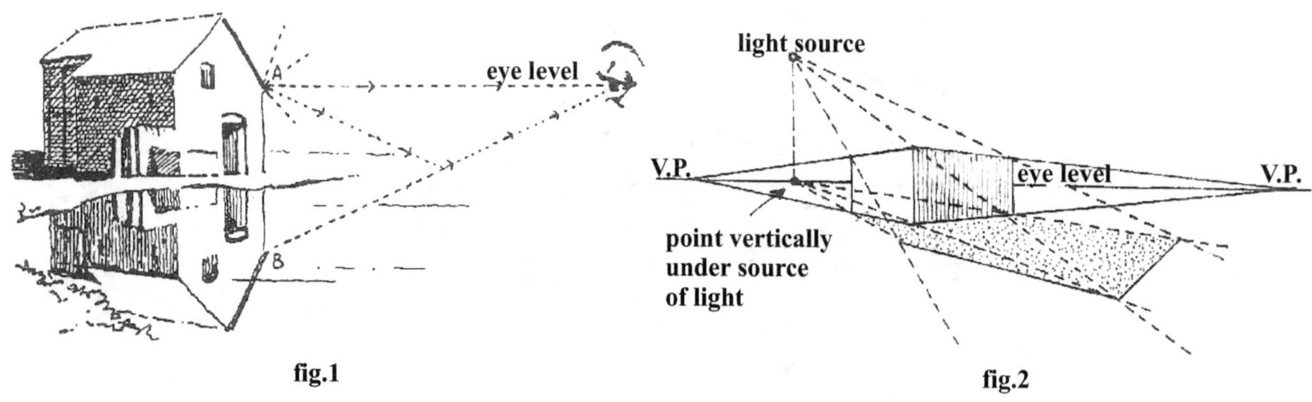

COLOUR AND COLOUR SCHEME

INTRODUCTION

Colour is the most exciting element of a painting. Colours make a sketch viable and affect the emotions directly. They make a picture attractive and lovely. They affect thoughts, mood, action and even health. The world cannot be imagined without colours various emotions and feeling can be expressed by colours. Nature presents from morning till night an array of spectacular colours. We jump with joy when we see a coloured dancing butterfly or colourful peacock. Let's also study the relationship of such colours to each other and their effect on mind.

Types of Colours:-Colours are of three types:-

1) Primary Colours   **2) Secondary Colours**   **3) Intermediate Colours**

Primary Colour : Red, Yellow and Blue are primary colours because they cannot be prepared by mixing other colours.

Secondary Colour : Orange, Green and Violet are secondary colours. By mixing any two primary colours a new colour i.e. secondary colour con be obtained.

Red + Blue = Violet/ Yellow + Blue = Green/ Red + Yellow = Orange

Intermediate Colour : All the colours which lie between primary and secondary colours are called intermediate colors, e.g., yellow- green, blue-green, blue-violet , red-violet, red orange and yellow-orange.

Opposite or Contras Colours: When two contrasting or complementary colours are put together, they create distracting or vibrating effect.

Yellow x Violet, Blue x Orange, Red x Green

Neutral Colours : Neutral colours are black and white. These colours make the other colours light or dark.

Tint :   White plus any one colour makes tint.: Tint is the lightest part of colour, for example, pink is the tint of red, we can say that by mixing the white   colour with any primary colour, the light effect of colour obtained will be called the tint of the primary colours.

Shaded Tint : Black Colour+ Primary colour. If we mix black colour with any primary colour we get the tint shade of that primary colour.

Warm Colours: Warm colours do not mean they have heat, but their effect on mind is warm. These colours give us the feelings of warmth or heat. The red colour of the rising sun is warm colour. The colour scheme of warm colours has red in common. Colours like red, purple, violet and orange when used together in a picture, create warm feeling.

Cool Colours : The blue colour of sky and ocean gives us the feelings of coolness. It is, therefore, a cool colour. A colour scheme where blue colour is prominent, is called cool colour scheme.

Monochromatic colours scheme: This scheme uses one colour in all tints and shade.

Polychromatic colour scheme: This colour scheme uses two or more colour combinations Black and whita can also be used. Every colour scheme gives a different feel.

EFFECT OF COLOURS :

Red: Red symbolises passion, strength, aggression, desire, energy, fire, sex, love, romance, excitement, heat, arrogance, ambition, leadership, courage, masculinity, power, danger, blood, war, anger, revolution, and radicalism.

Yellow: Yellow typically symbolises sunlight, joy, happiness, optimism, intelligence, idealism, spirituality, wealth (gold), summer, hope, liberalism, wonder, gladness, sociability, and
friendship.

Blue: Blue creates a feeling of overwhelmingness. It is seen as trustworthy, dependable and a symbol of commitment. It is the colour of sky and the sea, and it invokes the feeling of rest, serenity. It is calming, cooling and helps the intuition.

Orange: Orange typically symbolises sacrifice (especially costumes of a saints are orange), happiness, energy (rising sun), balance, heat, fire, enthusiasm, flamboyance, playfulness, and desire.

Green: Green symbolises intelligence, nature (green forest), spring, fertility, youth, environment, wealth, money, prosperity, good luck, vigour, generosity, grass, coldness, life, eternity earth, sincerity, renewal, natural abundance, growth, health, balance, harmony, stability, calming, and creative intelligence.

Violet: Violet is a combination of red and blue. It symbolises royalty, nobility, envy, sensuality, spirituality, creativity, wealth, cosmos, ceremony, mystery, wisdom, enlightenment, pride, and romanticism.

Brown: Brown symbolises calm, boldness, depth, natural organisms, nature, richness, rusticity, stability, tradition, anachronism, fascism, boredom, dullness, filth, heaviness, poverty, roughness, earth, wholesomeness, steadfastness, simplicity, friendliness, and dependability.

White: White is considered as the symbol of light (moonlight as well as sunlight), reverence, purity, truth, peace, innocence, cleanliness, simplicity, security, humility, life.

Black: Black symbolises absence, mystery, evil, death, fear, emptiness, darkness, seriousness, conventionality, rebellion, anarchism, sorrow.

Grey: Grey is a combination of white and black. It stands for, humility, respect, reverence, stability, subtlety, old age or Colour grey hair, pessimism, boredom, decay, dullness, pollution, urbanity, neutrality, mourning, and formality.

COLOUR THEORY:

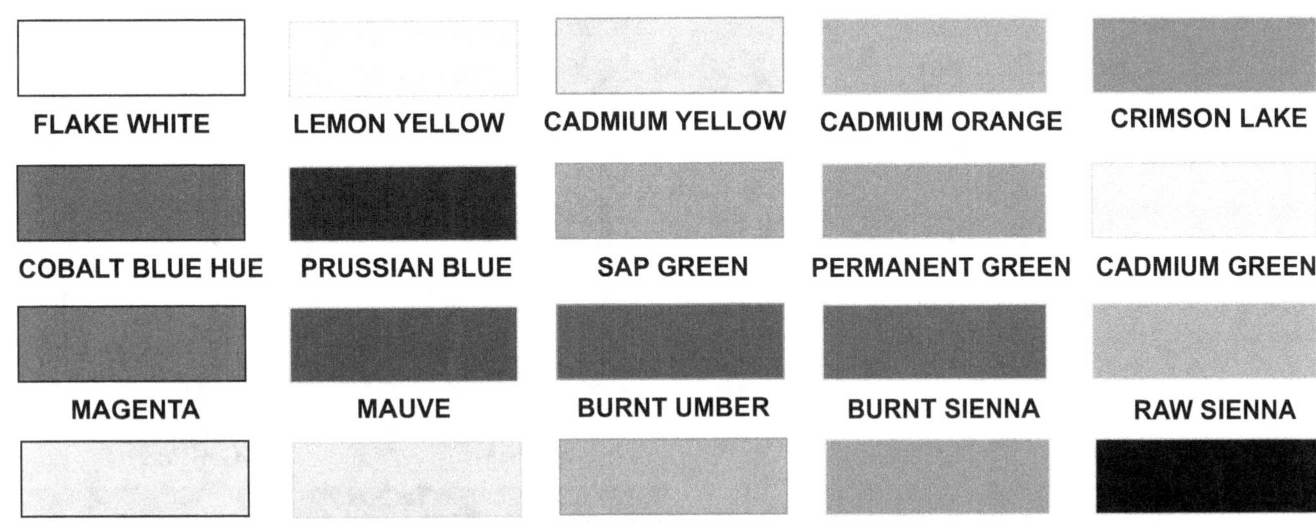

COLOUR WHEEL

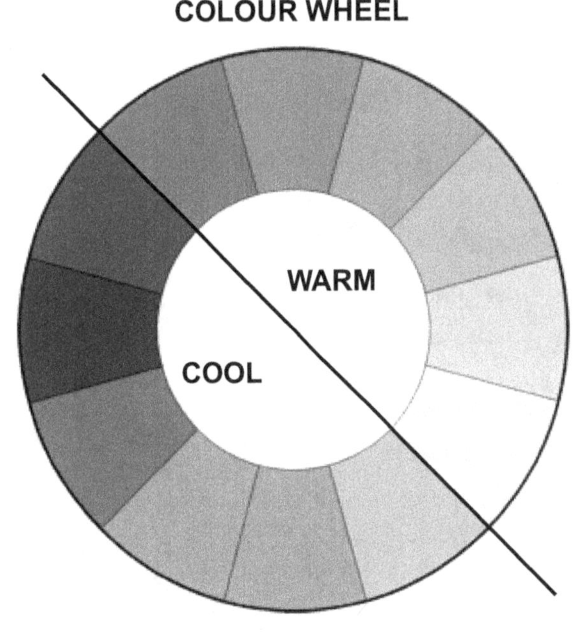

PRIMARY COLOUR   SECONDARY COLOUR

COLOUR MIXING

BROWNS & GRAYS

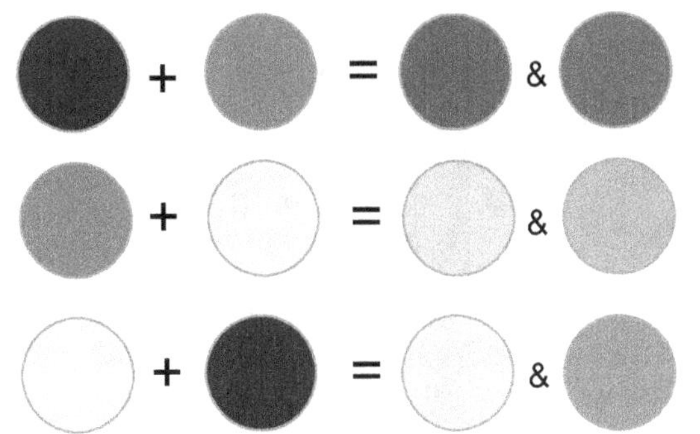

A

ANALOGOUS COLOURS

OPPOSITE or CONTRAST COLOUR
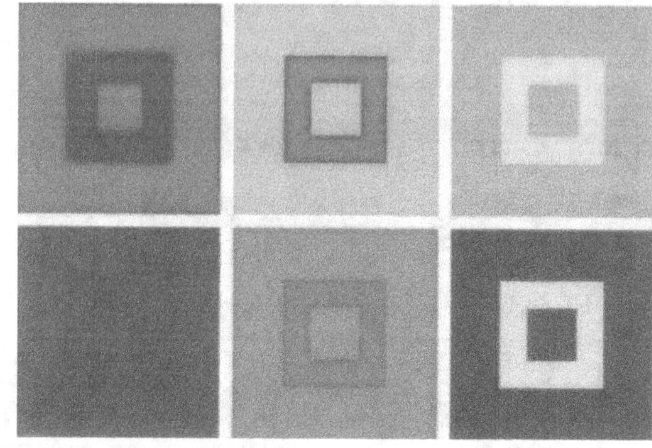

SHADE **COLOUR VALUE** TINT

MONOCHROMATIC SCHEME

POLYCHROMATIC SCHEME

DESIGN:

GEOMETRICAL
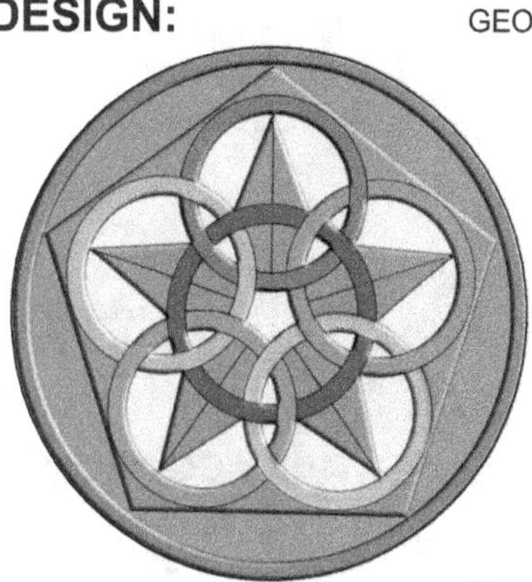

NEUTRAL
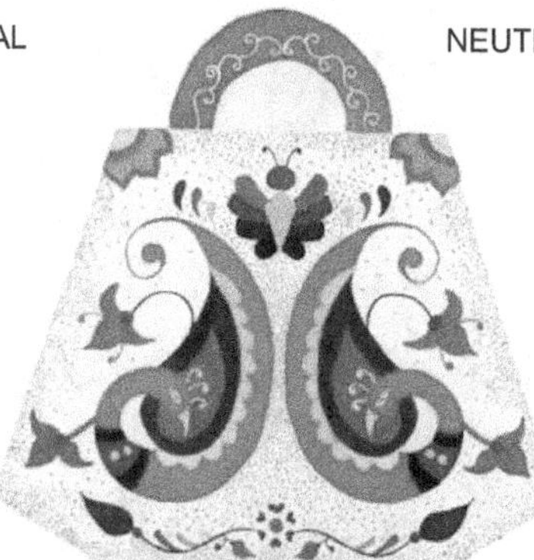

COOL COLOURS

DECORATIVE

ABSTRACT

WARM COLOURS
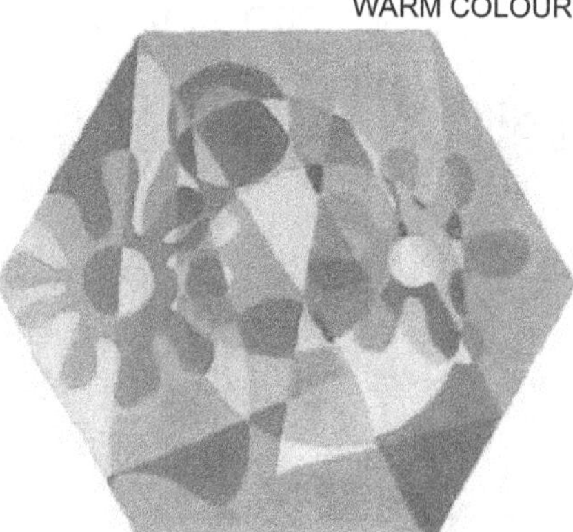

B

COMPOSITION
(HOW TO MAKE A PAINTING)

INTRODUCTION

Composition in painting means selection and arrangement of animate or inanimate objects within the given space to express the artist's ideas or imagination properly and effectively. At the very beginning, we may go for non-figarative composition.

EXERCISE

GEOMETRICAL FORM OF COMPOSITION:

Take one black sheet of paper. Cut it in different shapes circle, triangle, square or rectangle. Instead of one black colour, you may go for different colour paper also Lay these cut pieces on a light colour sheet or white sheet of paper in different ways to cover the empty space of the paper. It helps to develop the basic compositional idea, which will also help to develop the idea of proper balancing of the covered area. The covered area is known as positive space and uncovered area is negative space.

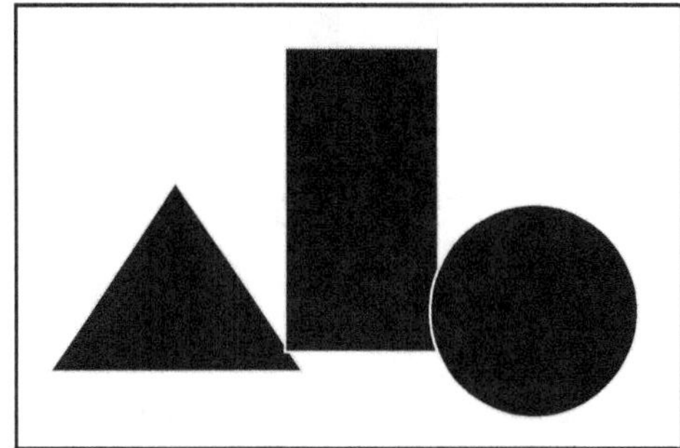

Positive and Negative space: Space and shape, two of the elements, work together to form a finished work of art. There are two kinds of space: Positive and Negative. Positive spaces are those occupied by the main subjects of the work. The negative spaces are the areas around and behind the positive spaces .Negative space can also be referred as the background. It is a very effective way of creating relationships between objects in a drawing.

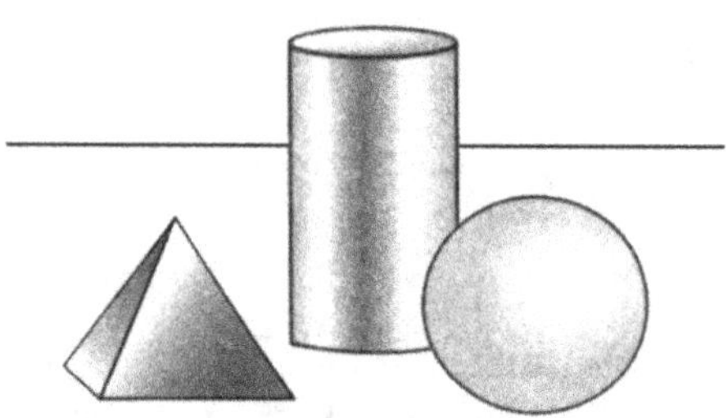

Framing and Horizon: A strange composition may be created by knowledge of compositional design formats or shapes. There are some examples.

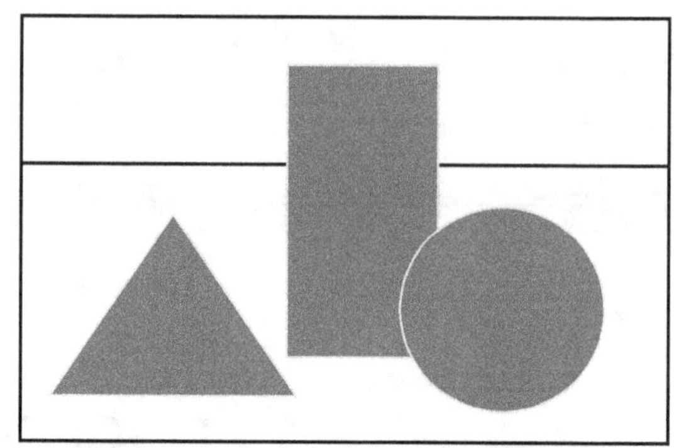

High Horizon

Central Horizon in Vertical

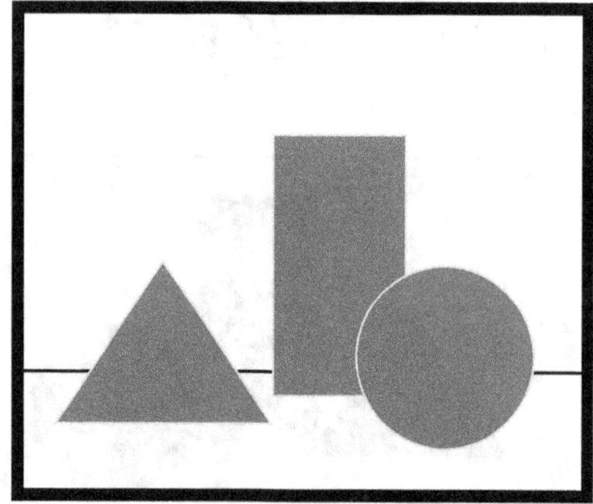

Low Horizon

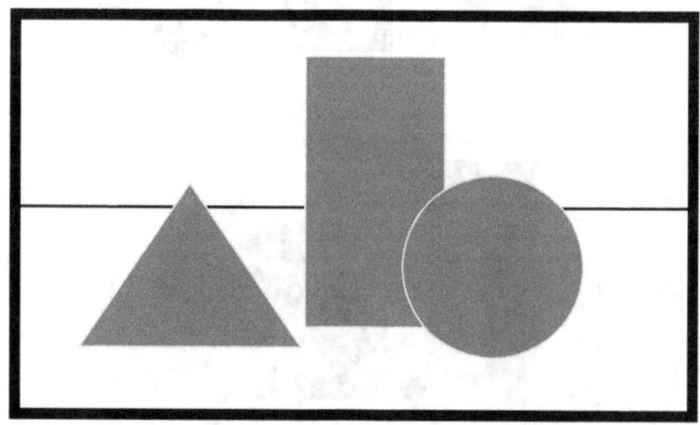

Central Horizon in Horizental

AVOID THE FOLLOWING MISTAKES IN COMPOSITION

Subject should not be drawn on a single line.

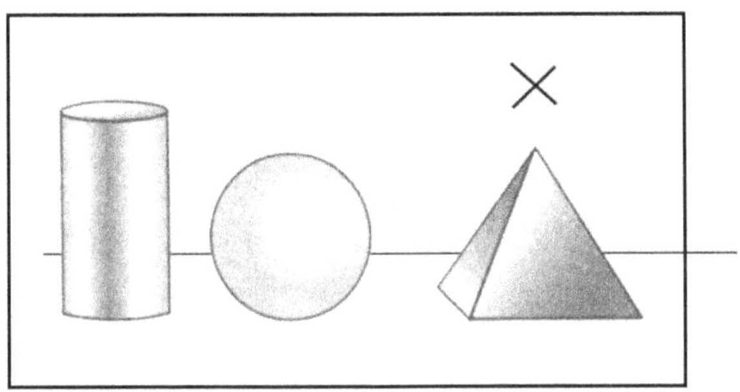
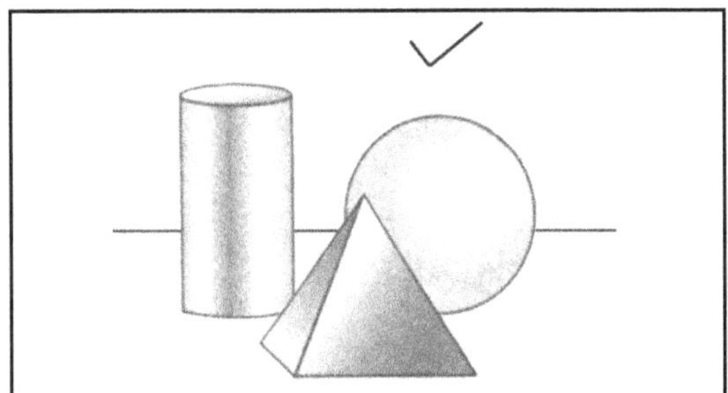

Subject in the drawing should not be too small.

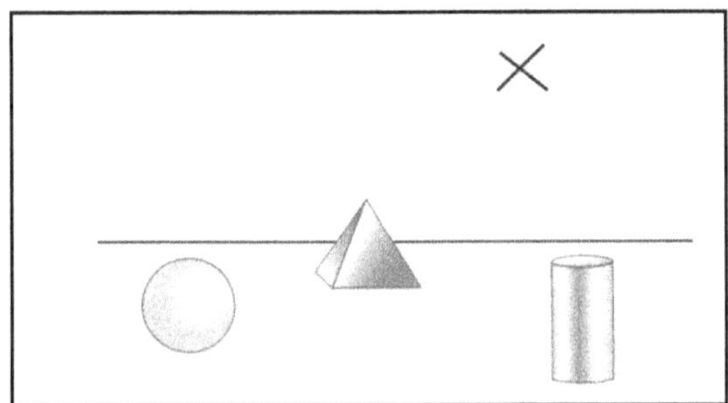
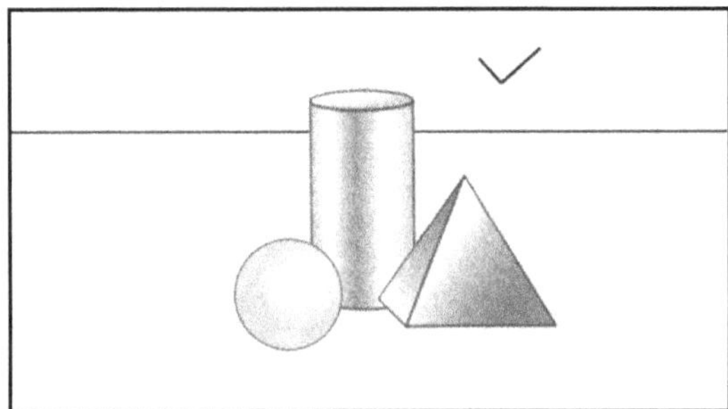

Subjects in the drawing should not be shown doing identical action and the forms should not appear to independent and unrelated.

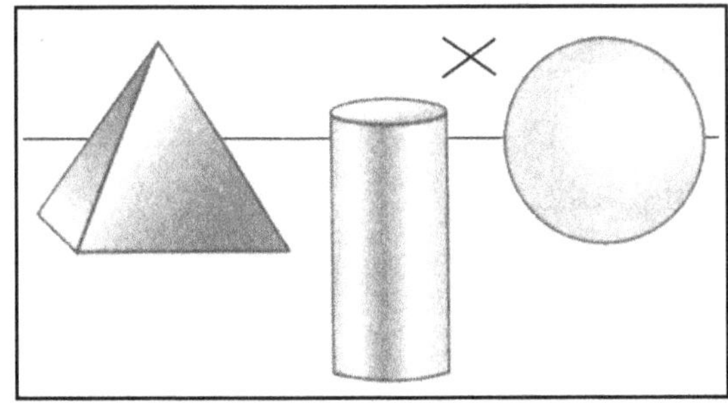
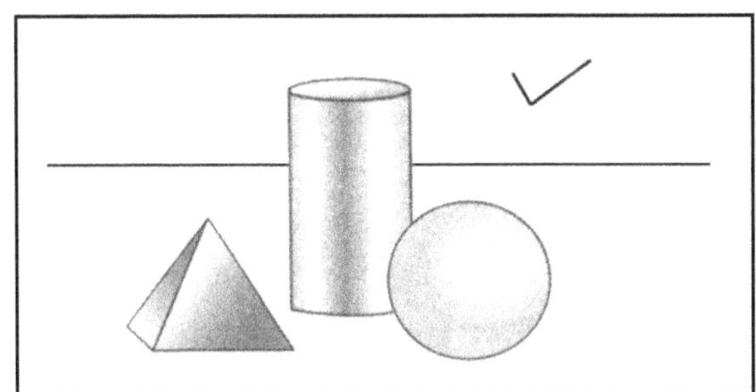

FREE HAND DRAWING

INTRODUCTION

Drawing is the first step to realize one's feelings and thoughts. By practicing the learner can develop his/ her imagination creativity and his/ her skills. The learner should know the methods of drawing such as how to hold a pencil, how to draw lines of different types, seeing different objects in proper proportion placement of the object and sketching from memory. Thus drawing is the back-bone of painting.

EXERCISE:

The drawn by hand without the use of drawing instruments is known as free hand drawing. This is also sometimes known as sketching. Take some old blank sheets & with a pencil draw parallel lines one under the other, from left to right and top to bottom. Try to keep the lines of same length and same width. Keep trying. At the same time., do this with curved lines and with as many different lines as you can think of. Next, you can go on to shapes. Try drawing two equal squares, triangles, circles and keep on changing their sized. You can also try the same experiment by taking ink in a brush.

This practice is not only good for freehand drawing, but will be very useful in any kind of sketching. It will also make your line rendering more polished. You will be able to do better pictures in a shorter time.

TIPS:

1.Use only soft pencils like HB or 2B.

2.Don't hold the pencil close to the tip it will obstruct your hand's movement while drawing.

3. Grab it at least an inch away from the pencil tip and hold it lightly. While drawing move the whole hand from the fingers to the elbow.

4. Don't erase much while drawing a picture otherwise the paper gets torn or its surface spoiled.

5. Keep a white paper or a clean dry piece of cloth under your hand while drawing.

6. Always draw natural things in informal shapes and men made things in formal or perfect shapes.

7. Never draw bold line as out lines. Draw like master strokes in life line.

Freehand drawing : Symmetrical & Asymmetrical

   Symmetrical: If you draw a vertical line at the center (central axis) dividing the figure into two equals parts, the halves on both of its sides are exactly alike, just like the mirror image of each other. This means that you have to draw exactly similar forms on both sides of the central lines. Thus, it is important to be able to draw the two sides contrariwise in symmetrical figure. Draw vertical and horizontal guidelines touching the important protruding curves and points on both sides of the central lines. Now draw the central lines at the center of the paper, which is held horizontally. Using the guidelines, either complete the drawing on one side of the central line and then finish the other side or complete the drawing starting from the top and end it at the bottom. Finally, erase the guidelines with an eraser.

   Asymmetrical means the opposite of symmetrical : The two sides are different in some way. Asymmetrical things are irregular and crooked, and don't match up perfectly when folded in half. Drawing something perfectly symmetrical is pretty hard, so most of your creations are probably asymmetrical. Draw line touching all four sides of the figure on the printed plate. A rectangle will be formed by these lines. Then draw vertical and horizontal guidelines touching the main points and curves in the figure. Draw on the answer paper a rectangle two times larger than the one on the printed plate, or in an enlarged size proportionate to the answer paper. In this rectangle, draw the outer shape of the given figure. Draw all the vertical and horizontal guidelines and accordance with the twice enlarged measurements. Complete the drawing with the help of the basic guidelines. Rubout the unwanted lines drawn in pencil.

DESIGN

INTRODUCTION

Design is backbone of art, design that is a part of art actually a part of our life and personality and influences the enjoyment of everything to do and of everything to select. Design is the creation of a plan for the construction of an object. It has different connotations in different fields. Design is widely associated with the Applied arts.

Art elements include line, direction, shape, size, value, texture and colour. Balance is a restful effect obtained by grouping shapes or colours around a center in such a way that there are equal attractions on each side of that center. Harmony produces an impression of unity through the selection and arrangement of consistent objects and ideas. Proportion is the law of relationship. Designs breaks down the families into categories based on one or more of the following criteria.

Motif: the most important factor in any design, determines the family to which the pattern belongs. This is the basic image –a fish, a square, etc.

Layout: It describes the arrangement of the motif- whether it is spaced widely or closely on the ground, in neat order or apparently at random, or in rows that form stripes.

Colour: designs are so classified when a particular dye- indigo, madder or Turkey red say –is the strongest element of their look.

Requirement of good structural design:
• Good structural design in addition to being beautiful, it be suited to its purpose.
• That it be simple.
• Well proportioned
• That it is suited to the material.

There are four types of design :

1.Design with Geometrical shapes : A beautiful design which is created by using circles, triangles squares, hexagons, etc. drawn with geometrical shapes. This type of design is mainly used in carpets, rugs or woven garments.

2.Design with Natural Shapes: A decorative design created by using various shapes in nature is called a design with natural shapes. Shapes of flowers, leaves fruits, creepers, birds and animals, butterflies, feathers, sea shells etc. are used in this type of design. This type of design does not suffer from the limitations of light and shade. Such designs are especially used in knitting and embroidery.

3.Design with decorative shapes: A design created by using decorative patterns making slight changes in the natural shapes of flowers, leaves, fruits, creepers, birds and animals etc. is called a design with decorative shapes. In this type of design ornamental shapes are arranged in set patterns. These designs are used specially in Rangoli Patterns or Free hand drawings.

4.Design with abstract shapes: A design which does not make use, directly or indirectly of geometrical natural or decorative shapes and which is created by using symbolical and original patterns is called a design with abstract shapes. Such designs are used extensively in saris, curtains, (Printed cloth) etc.

STEPS OF DECORATION

Useful tips :

Outlines are of two types :   (a) Free-hand and   (b) Arranged

Arranged outlines are those where shape is divided into equal parts. Whereas free-hand outlines needs no repetition and allow you the liberty to draw free-hand. There arrangement is so well organized that it gives a transforming effect to the picture.

REPETITION

Decorative effect is created

by repetition of units

INVERSION

Alternatively arrange the units

inversely to create variation.

FACING EACH OTHER

Put two units facing each other.

Repeat them as shown underneath.

FACING OPPOSITE SIDES

Put two units facing the opposite

sides. Repeat them as shown.

OVERLAPPING

Put the units overlapping each other.

DIMENSION

To show the dimension of the units

put them in reducing sequence.

Drawing Method of designing:

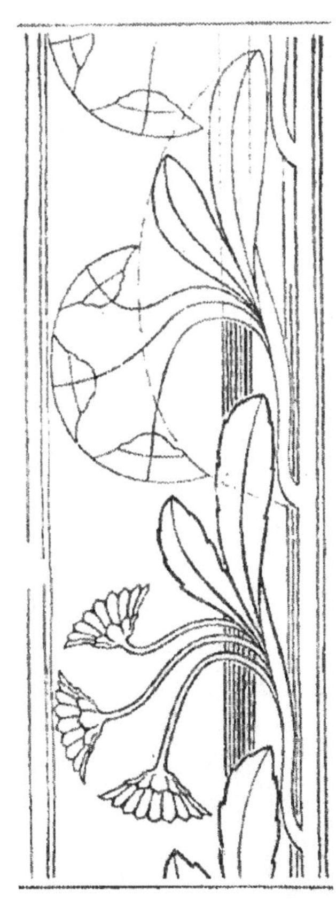

EXERCISE

       Learn to sketch different objects like Vase, Lampshade, Hand fan, Handbag as Outer or External shapes and Compose the design within the given outer shape.(Geometrical,Natural,Decorative and Abstract.).

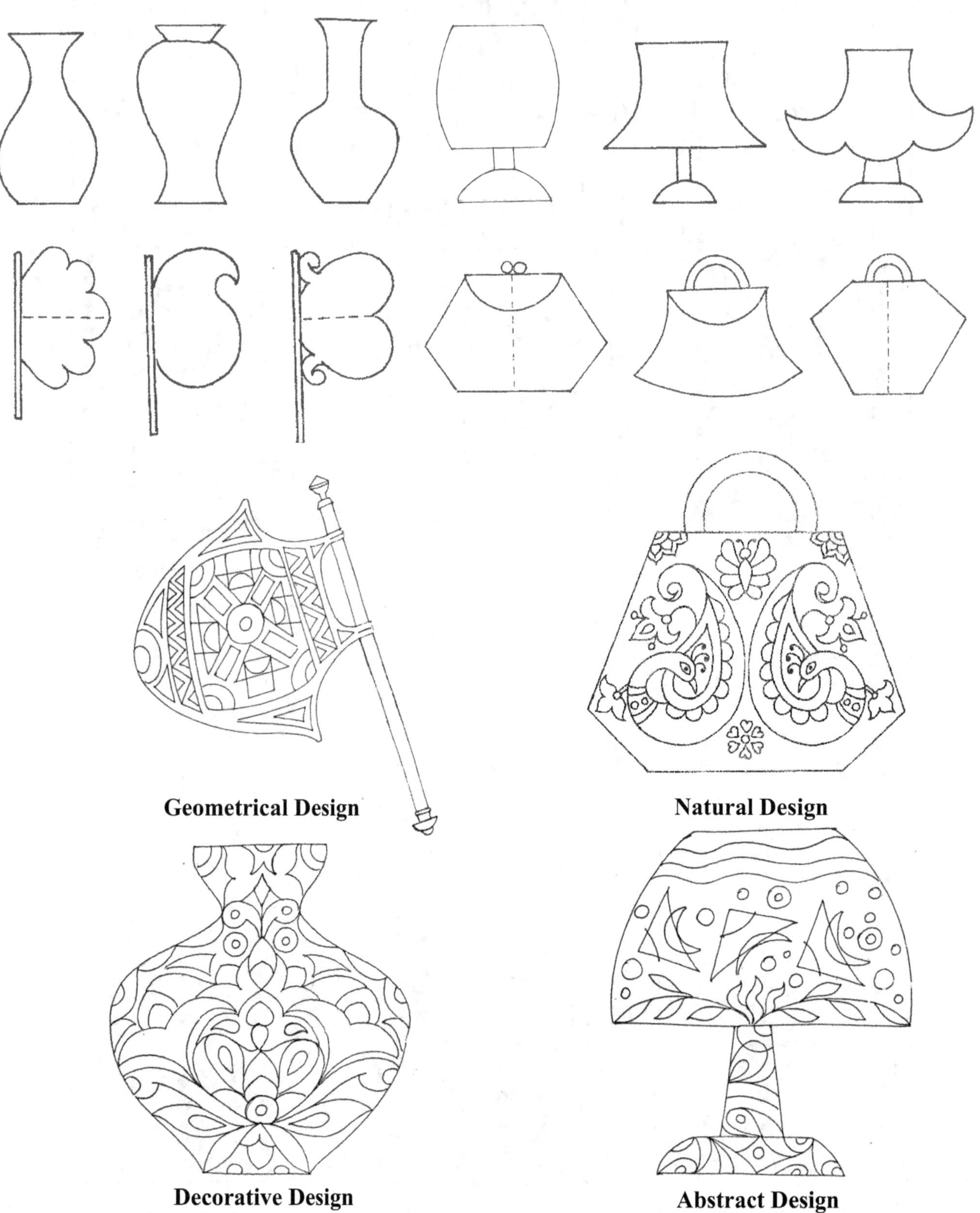

Geometrical Design

Natural Design

Decorative Design

Abstract Design

If you look around, there is design everywhere. Only to those who keep their eyes open. with observation you will also notice that everything around us is connected to design. you will not have to try very hard to find it.

The specimen "Fish" designed in a decorative way. The motif is fish repeated and several compositions and tried out. you can really play with shapes. Here you see some arrangements- you could make hundred different arrangements with just one shape.

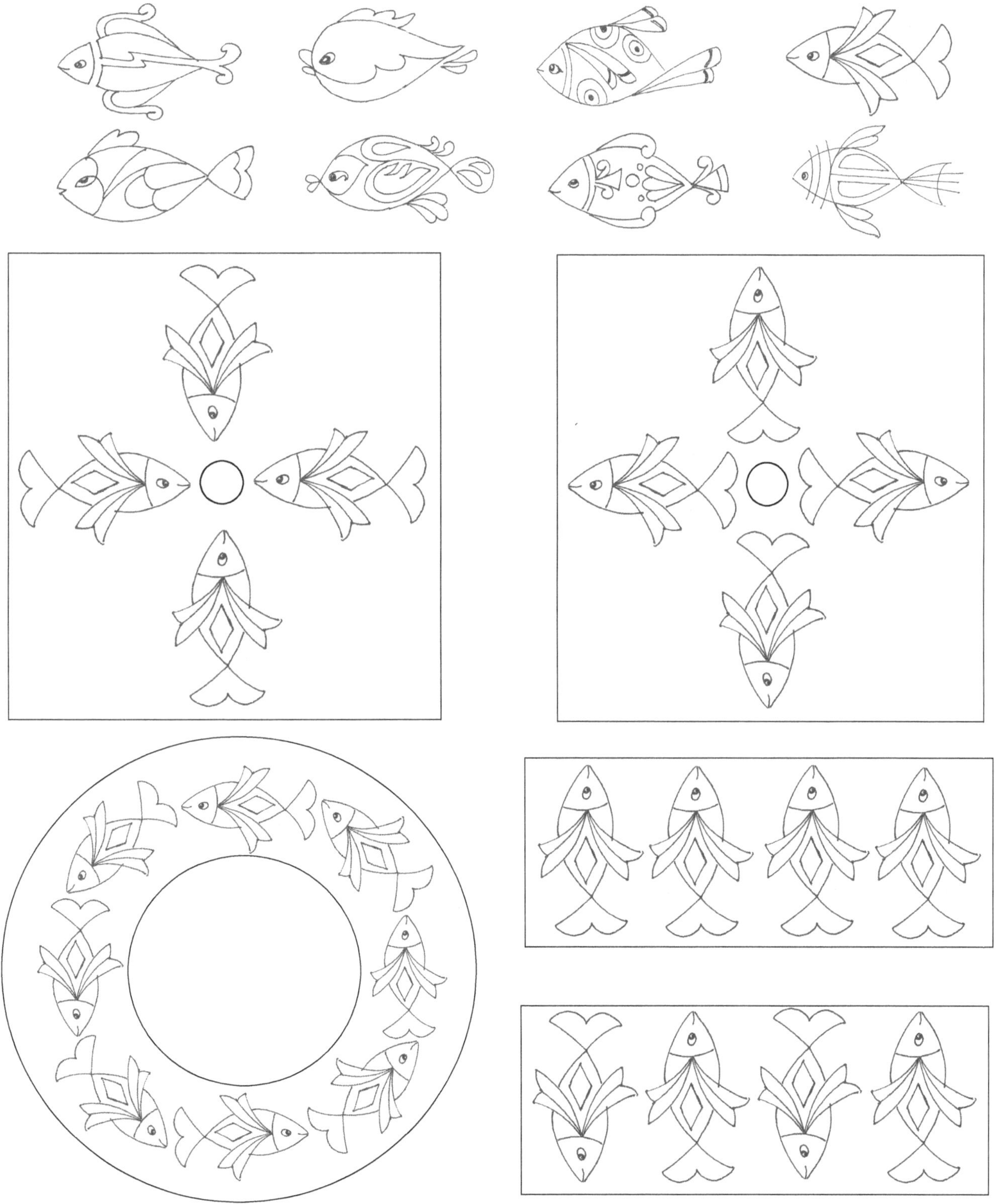

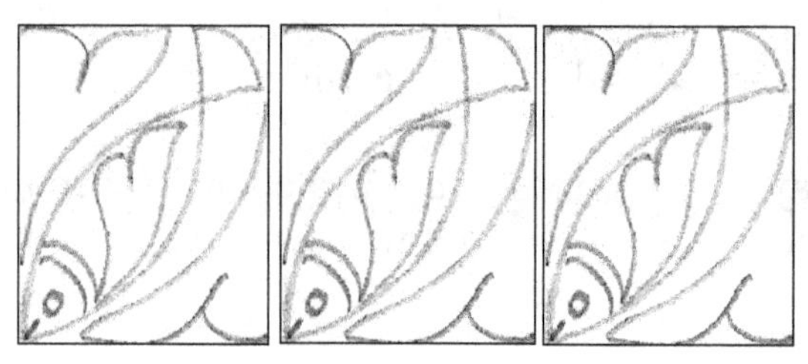
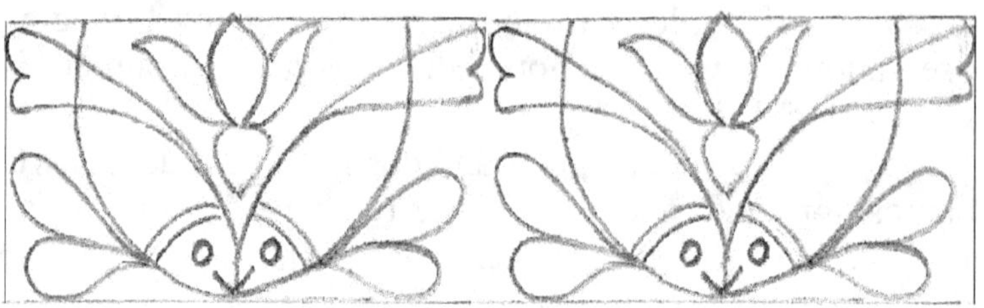

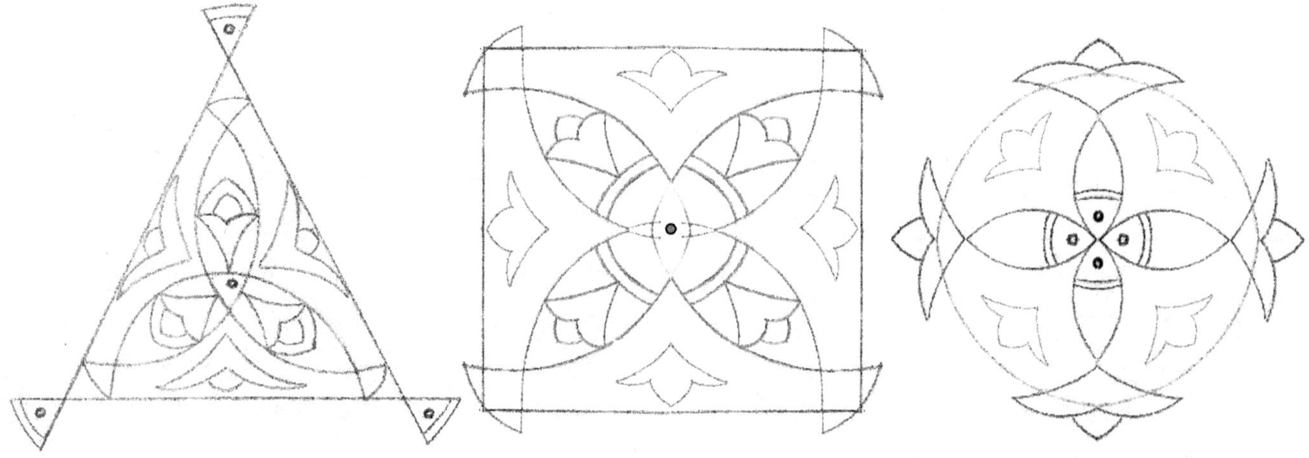

DEPICTION OF SUBJECT

Develop your own awareness about depiction of subject. Collect elements according requirement of subject i.e., The subject is "WATER" we have elements like leaves, flower, fish, crab, turtle, seahorse, conch, masroom etc.

Compose a design with the help of above elements in attractive way. you can observe same example in given here.

Freehand Symmetrical Design: **Freehand Asymmetrical Design:**

Single Sided Repeat Tracing: Trace one part at a time
and go on to complete the whole design.

COLOUR SCHEME FOR DESIGN

Before painting the design, it is important to think about an appropriate colour scheme first. The type of colour scheme to be used is mentioned sometimes in the question paper (e.g., cool colour scheme, warm colour scheme, complementary colour scheme, etc.). However, very often, the choice of colour scheme is left to you. For instance, the question paper may have instructions such as, "Choose a colour scheme of your liking", or "Choose a colour scheme that you consider appropriate", etc. In such cases, the right colour scheme is also an important aspect.

Many students use only the primary and secondary colours like red, yellow, blue, green, etc., for painting. This will make the design look very ordinary and simple.

To make the colour scheme attractive, you should create a new shade of colour by mixing two different colours in varying proportions. You can make attractive colour schemes by grouping three to four different colours, e.g., a few direct colours, and a new shade of created colour that would suit the direct colours.

After making various groups of colour schemes, you will definitely have a fairly good idea about colour schemes and you won't get confused during the examination as regards the selection of a colour scheme.

After completing the drawing, you should decide about the method and technique of colouring. You can select the method and technique based on what you think would enhance the beauty of the picture. While selecting the method and technique, one important thing to be taken into consideration is the time left for painting.

INSTRUCTIONS FOR PAINTING (DESIGN)

It is necessary to take the following precautions while painting design :

(1) If one part of the picture is still damp, do not be in a hurry to colour its adjacent part. There is a possibility of the picture getting spoilt if two wet colours merge into each other if applied side by side.

(2) While painting in flat colour use opaque colours (poster colours) to prevent the painting become cloudy and patchy. Use transparent colours (cake or tube colours) for colour with shading.

(3) Instead of taking the colour straight from the bottle, take it out on the palette. Then, by adding the right amount of water to the colour, it can be applied evenly all over.

(4) While mixing two colours or while adding black or white in a colour to change its shade, take out the two colours in a palette in proper proportion. Add the right amount of water in it and mix them properly to merge the colours. Only then should the mixed colour be applied.

STILL LIFE /VISUAL STUDY
(OBJECTS & NATURE)

INTRODUCTION:

Still life as an art form came into its own in the 16th C and the 17thC.A.D. prior to that time the subject matter was studied primarily as preparation for use in figurative composition.

The subject matters found in object drawing are natural and men made objects of almost any shape and function. An art student has to learn different aspects and technique of drawing like, perspective, sense of proportion, use of proper light and shade and most of all the sense of composition. One must begin by describing the three dimensional form, then developing texture and values. Lot of practice can only develop confidence.

EXERCISE

Still life is an important subject in the Drawing Examination, because it assesses how well candidates can render aesthetically a group of objects arranged before him.

For still life, there would be 2 to 3 men made objects and natural objects e.g. bucket, basket box, vessel etc.. arranged in front of the candidate.

Usually, thus arrangement is done on two levels; the top level and the bottom level on a table coloured drapery (cloth hanging in loose folds) is always used in the back ground so as to make to objects stand out.

(Study given examples in gallery for still life arrangement)

In painting a "Still Life', the group of objects arranged by you is regard not just as a collection of more objects, but as life itself presented in a still motionless condition. With this viewpoint, your aim should be to present a kind of beauty, full of lite and vitality thought the drawing, arrangement and colour -work of the group objects. It is seen in a still life painting, whether they be forms, lines, shades of colour, texture of shade and light, all have been expressed in a thought-provoking. So in still life painting you have full freedom to make necessary changes in the arrangement and colour of the objects in your painting for the purpose of making the picture more beautiful and appealing.

THE LIGHT, SHADE AND SHADOWS

In object drawing, in order to show the right effect of light and shadow, you must carefully observe the direction of light falling on the object. even while drawing a group of objects, the light must seem to come from one side only.

LIGHT:

The light that falls on the object reflects and shows us the object. The part of the object that is facing the light is called lighted.

HIGHLIGHT:

It is the lighted area of the object on which maximum light is directly falling. In other words, it is that part on which the light rays are falling straight. This heavy light comes directly from the source of light. The effect of highlight increases the realism of the object.

SHADE:

It is that part of the object on which the light does not fall directly. In other words, that part on which there is not enough light is called shade.

SHADOW:

When light falls on an object from an opposite direction the object leaves a shadow on the ground. This shadow is darkest on its edges and becomes lighter away from it. The shadow becomes big or small according to the angle at which the light is falling. The shadow takes the shape of the object.

REFLECTED LIGHT:

When the light of a shining object falls on an object next to it, or when the light of the nearby objects falls on the shining object, it is called reflected light.

REFLECTED SHADE:

When the effect of a light or dark object falls on a nearby object, it is called reflected shade.

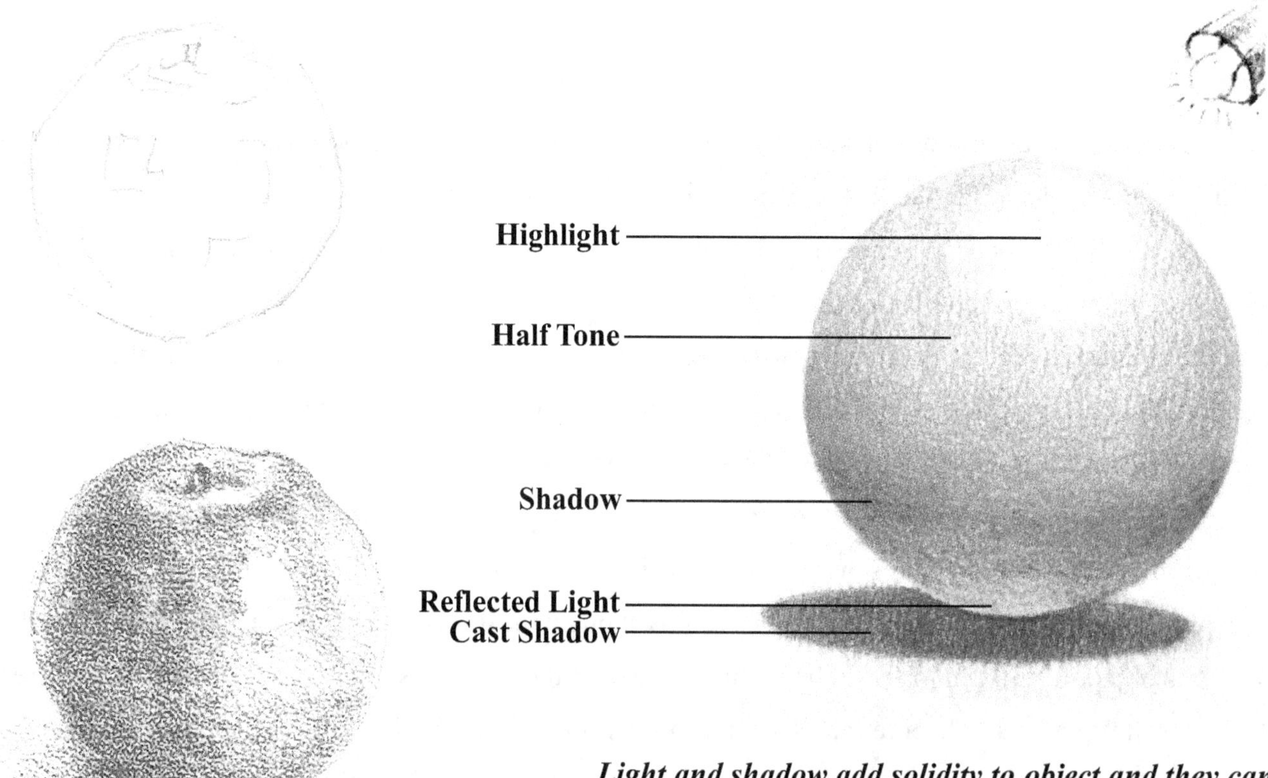

Light and shadow add solidity to object and they can be used as effective elements of the composition.

LINES & TEXTURES

Lines and Texture is another way of defining the objects and using texture is the only way that you can express tonal values of your subject in a drawing. Practice the art of some group of texture that you may need when you come to any drawing in any medium.

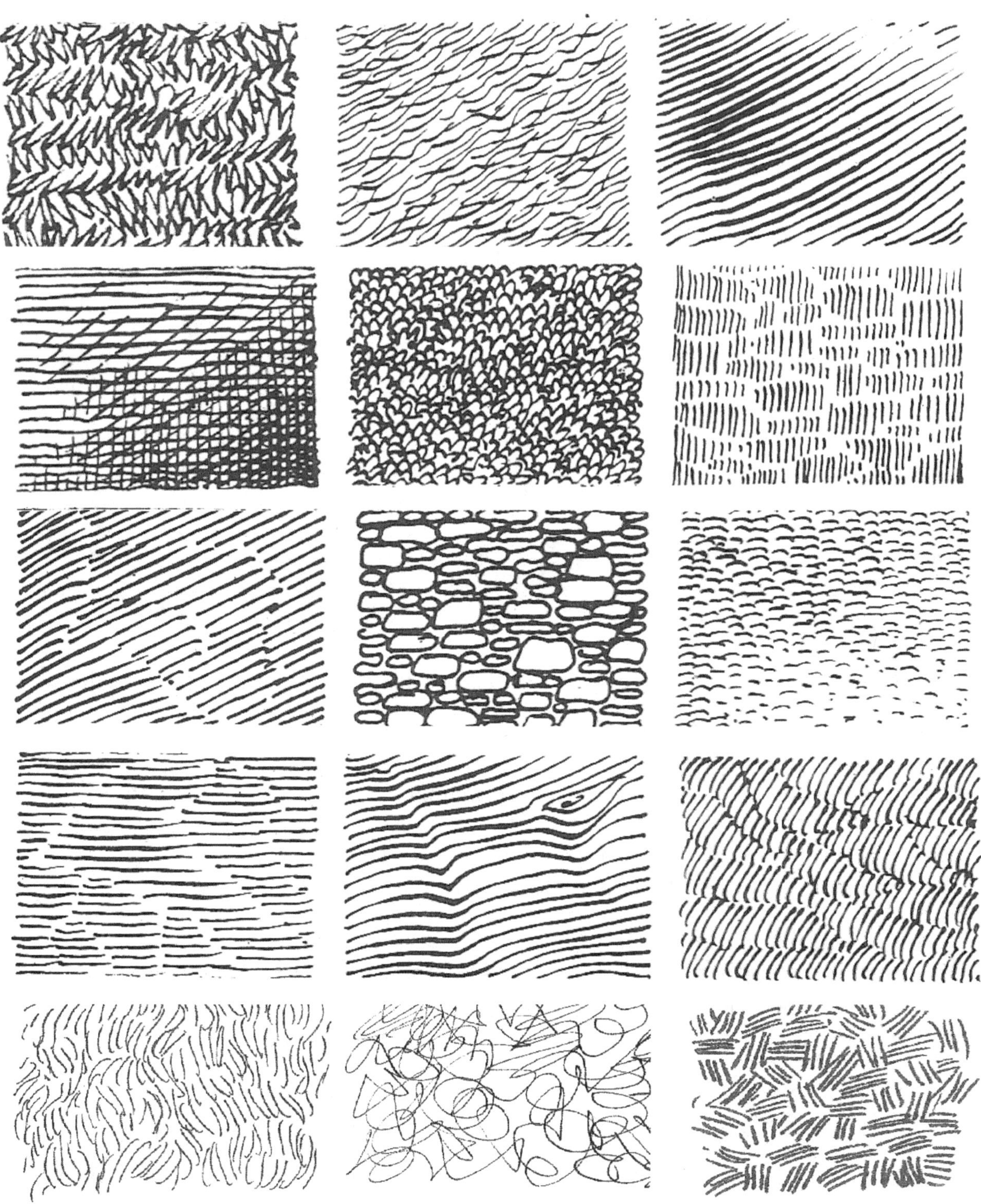

TONE

Besides the varied contours and cross contour lines, many other lines and line patterns. have been developed to create shading effects. Always begin with a soft line with light pressure of the fingers, which makes it easy to erase. Shading gives "tone", that means to an area of colour a value of a particular lightness and darkness. Tone also helps to define the perspective or three-dimensional effect to a drawing. Try to get different values of tone with pencil on a paper. Use your pencil (2B) with very light pressure on the paper to get soft tone. For darker tone, use 4B pencil and put more pressure and you get darker tone. You can use 6B or 8B pencil to get very dark tone.

EXERCISES IN TONE

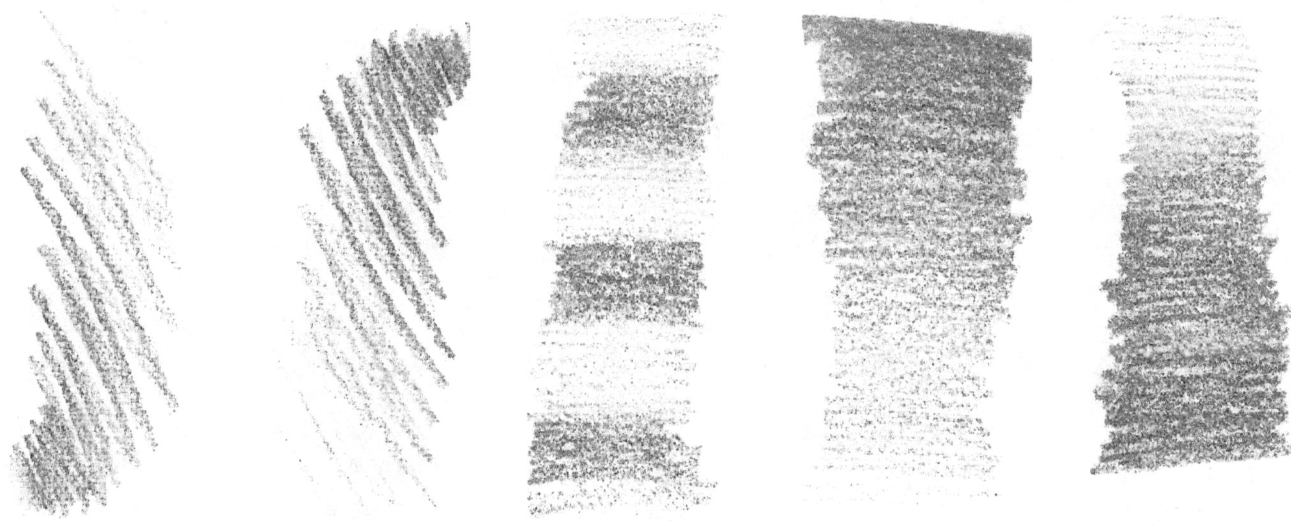

VALUES(GRADIATION)

First understand the various graduations or values is therefore important to achieve the necessary affect. There are five ways to achieve gradiation:

1.Hatching   **2.Cross Hatching**   **3.Scribbling**

4.Smudging   **5.Dots**

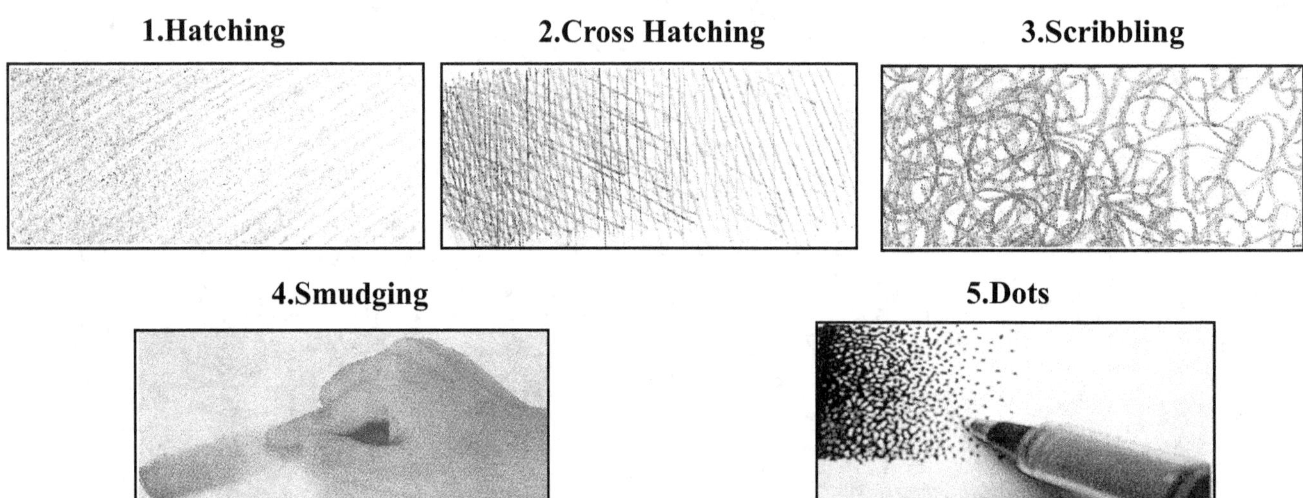

Illusion of Perspective

The rails of the railway are parallel, but they appear to be merging with one another at a particular distance. This is an optical illusion. It has an importance in the study of Object Drawing. While drawing any squarish object like a book or a bag, the side nearer us appears to be big and broad and the other side appears slightly smaller and narrower. Draw the side nearer to you big as shown in the picture. Then only you can create an illusion of distance and flatness.

Consider the level from where we see the object. Find out whether it is above our eye-level, or on the eye-level, or below eye-level, and then draw the object accordingly. Its called Point fo View.

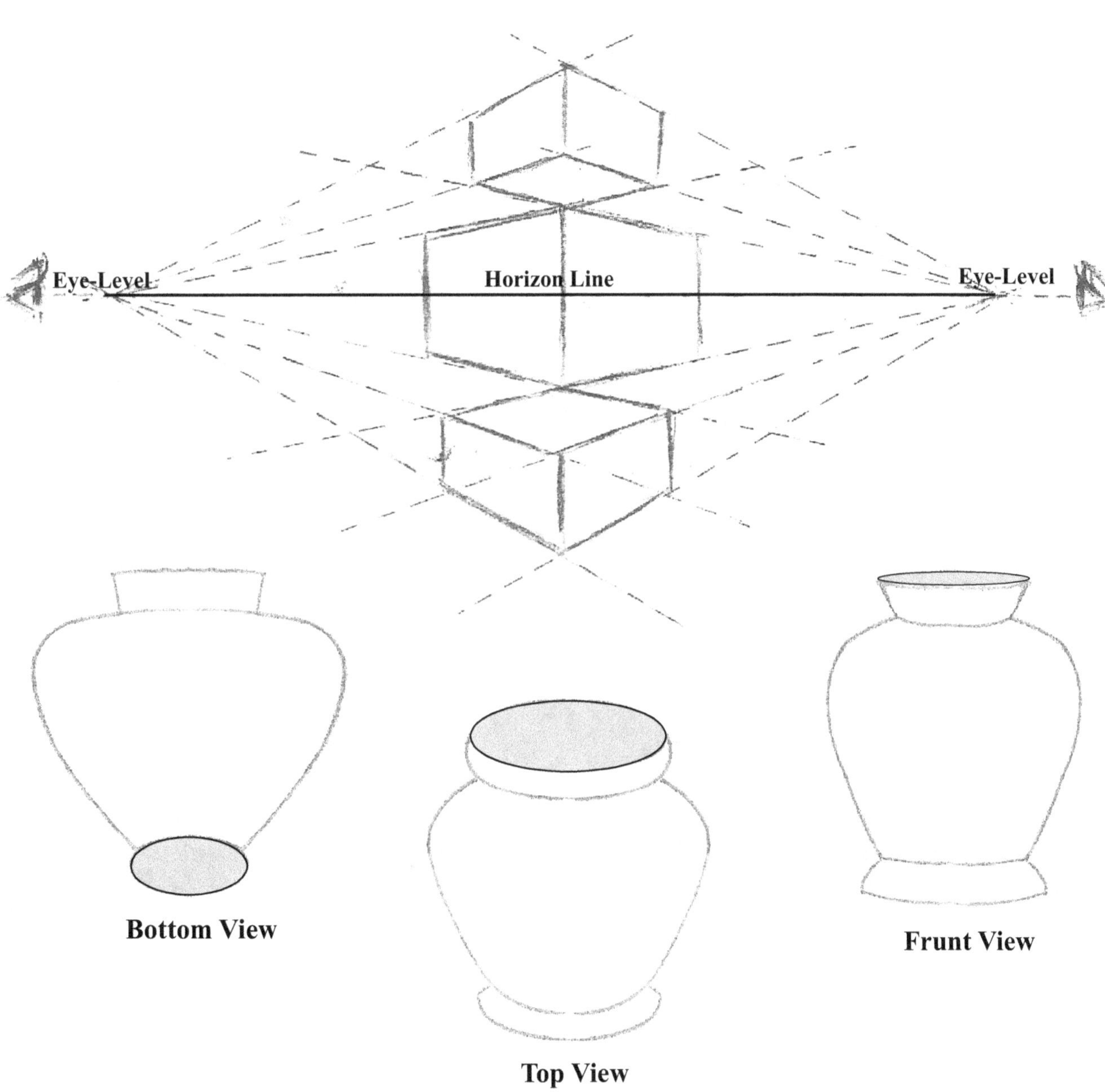

METHOD OF DRAWING

1.MEASURING THE OBJECTS: You can measure the object from distance by holding a pencil vertically with your small finger at the bottom along with other three fingers and the thumb on the top to shuttle it up and down to measure the comparative proportion of the object. Close one of your eyes and now you hold the pencil at arm's length. Measure from the point to your thumb to compare the sizes of other objects. Hold the pencil at arm's length to ensure a fixed distance between your eye and the pencil.

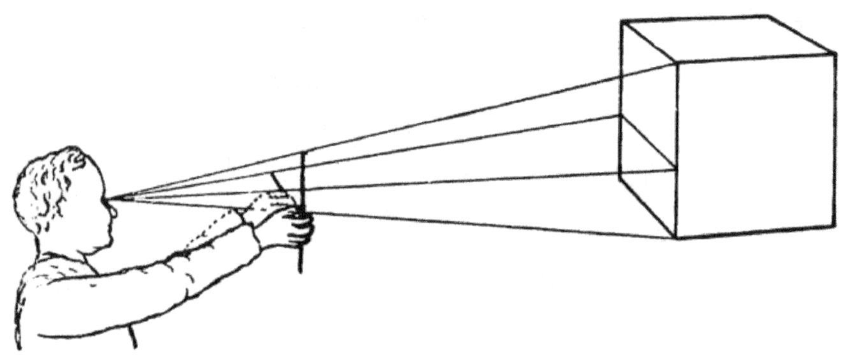

2.USE OF VIEW FINDER : To make a static subject one tan take the help of view finder - like camera view finder. Take a post card size blackboard. Make a 1" X 1.5" hole. This will help you to compose the objects and as you see through the hole, you may move the card right or left, upwards or downwards - keep watching to get a suitable composition.

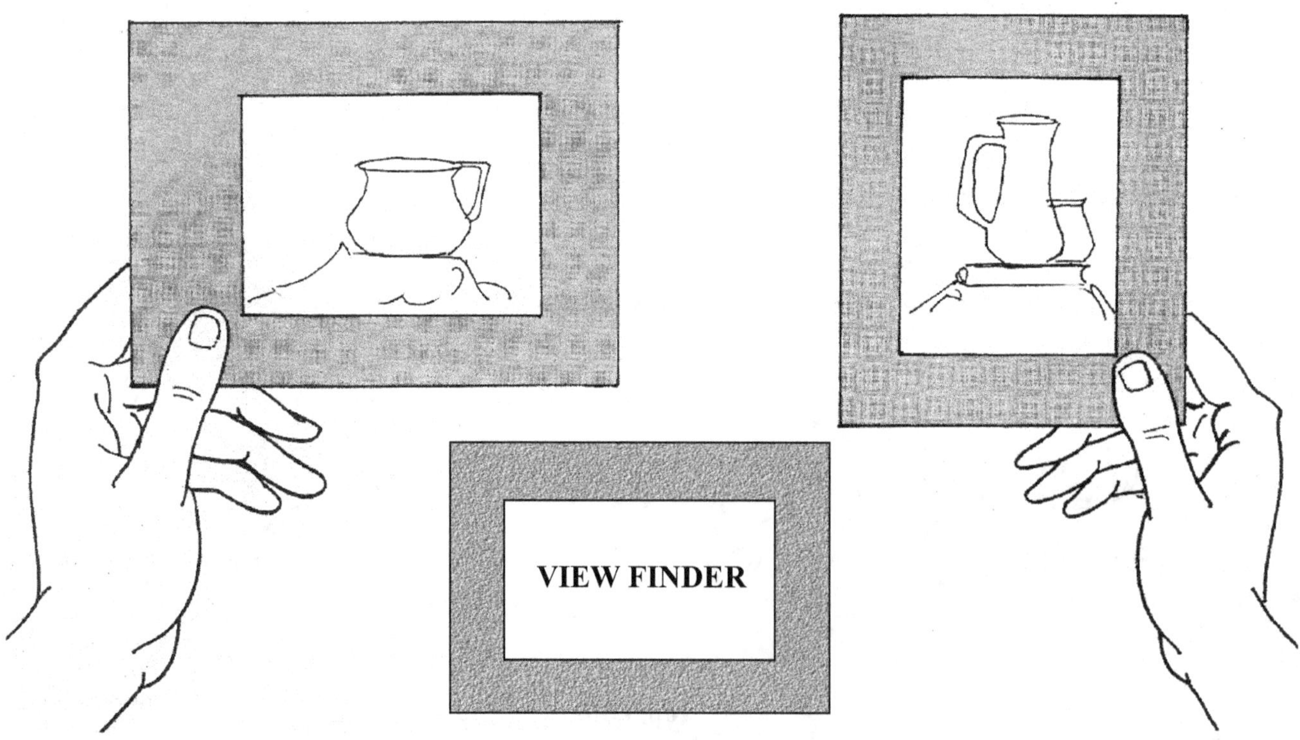

Useful Tips Before Shading

The Responsive Line: When we pick up a pencil ,our first impulse is to make lines. Initially, we use line to define the outer edges of an object or a scene; but then we need to learn how to use internal lines to describe the form of the object and also to give it a sense of three dimensions.

        Different drawing implements will provide different types of line. A pencil can give a delicate, sensitive line if used lightly, and by pressing harder, or using a softer pencil which provides a darker line, you can achieve firmer, more positive linear strokes.

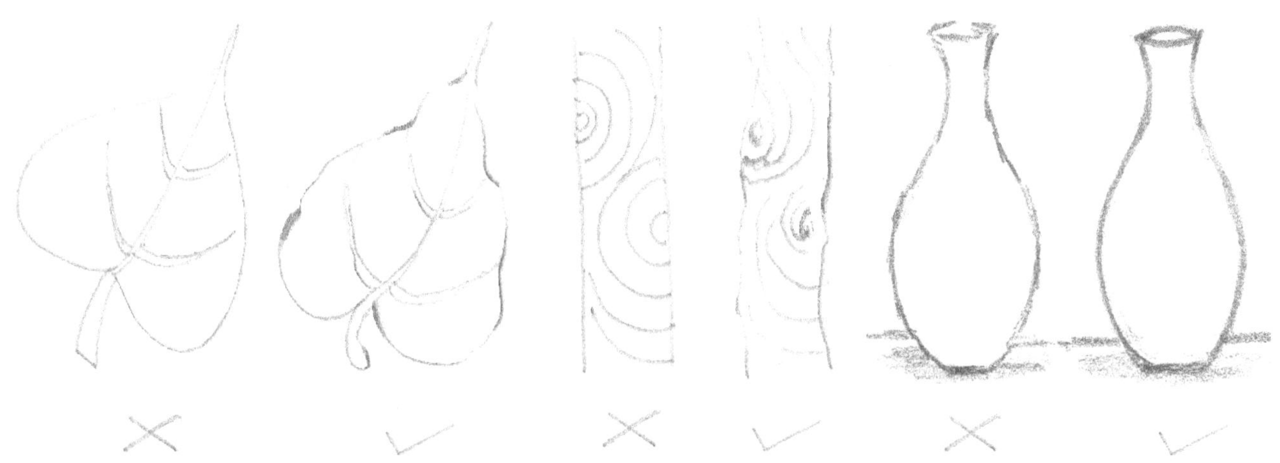

Tone Supports Line: We need to let go to the idea of everything having an 'outline'. Where is the 'outline' of an object or a person? A man- made things may have edges but there are no 'edges' to a natural things. Now let's see how line can, in fact, work against, rather than with, tone.

Pear with outline: Sometimes line and tone used together can work against. The line drawn firmly around the pear in this first step acts like an edge, seems to flatten the fruit, despite the volume shown by the tone.

Pear with tone: This image is much more successful; the tone used to describe the fullness of the pear works well, and we are not distracted by hard outline.

Subtle Forms: If the form is more subtle and changes of plane more difficult to discerns, mapping tones is a good way of analysing and simplifying what you see. Break down your subject into a simple arrangement to positive areas of tone value, ranging for light to dark. Allow five tones at most plus the white of the paper to see the subtle changes of plane. Squinting at your subject will also help, will strong directional light.

Planes: Surface appearance as defined by light and shadow or Changing the direction of lines as per the moudling.

Counterchange: Counterchange or **contrast** is simply 'light against dark, dark against light'.So,when working with a object, look out for light object s against a dark background, near to dark objects silhouette against a light background. it is a great tool to use.

Surface texture: Try to depict tones and reflections of things with pencil, non-reflective objects presents a different problems. To get this right you have to take a very subtle approach with the application of tone.

Glass: Glass is a transparent material. The surface of the glass object is full of reflections and highlights, you need to carefully analyze the reflections that you see and pick the ones that seem important. Transparent object needs to be constructed very well, otherwise the object drawn will look shapeless and foggy. Give special attention to the tonality. Make many sketches of simple glass objects with different lighting. To make the back ground stand out more against the glass, add a touch of dark tone over background. The glass has more volume and depth due to the dark treatment of the background to define a object clearly.

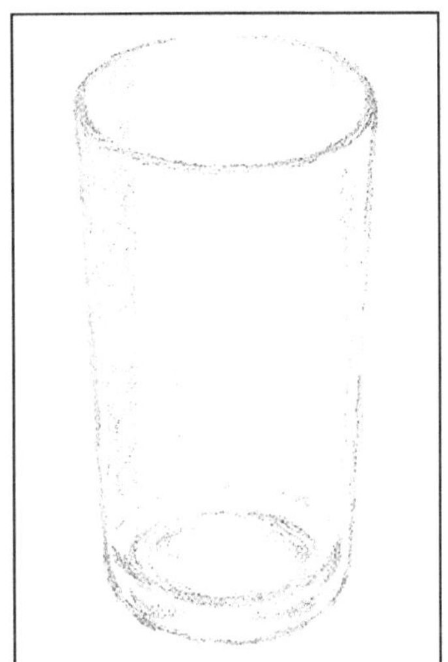

Paper: Screw up a sheet of paper. keep it on to a table lit by a single source of light and draw that. First draw the lines or folds in the paper, paying attention to getting the sharp edges of the creases. Put the main areas of tone. Once you have covered each tonal areas, put in any deeper shadows, capturing the contrasts between these areas.

Wood: In many forms, wood can make an attractive materials to draw. you can practice the natural log or man-made wooden object. Try to depict the original character of hardness or roughness with pencil.

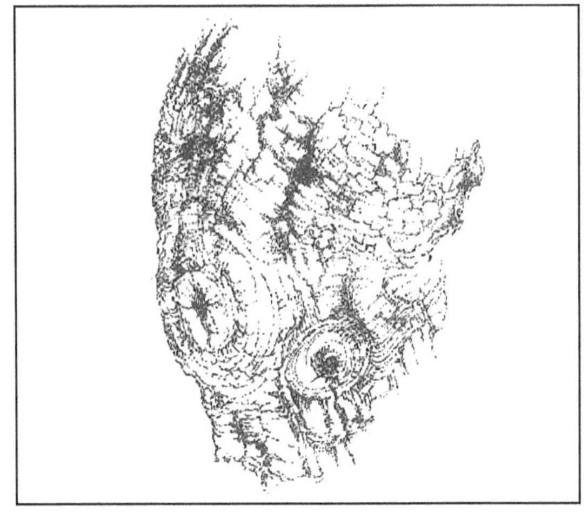

Metal: There is a lot of reflection in metallic objects because they are highly polished, so the contrast between dark and light tends to be at the maximum. It requires quite a bit of dedication to draw all the tonal shapes correctly, your aim must be for viewers to have no doubt about the object`s materiality when you have completed the drawing.

Different Subject Matter:(i) Manmade

Any ordinary set of object that you come across in your house can make a good subject for study, Often you will notice   around you things left in arrangements that you would never have put in place as they are found.

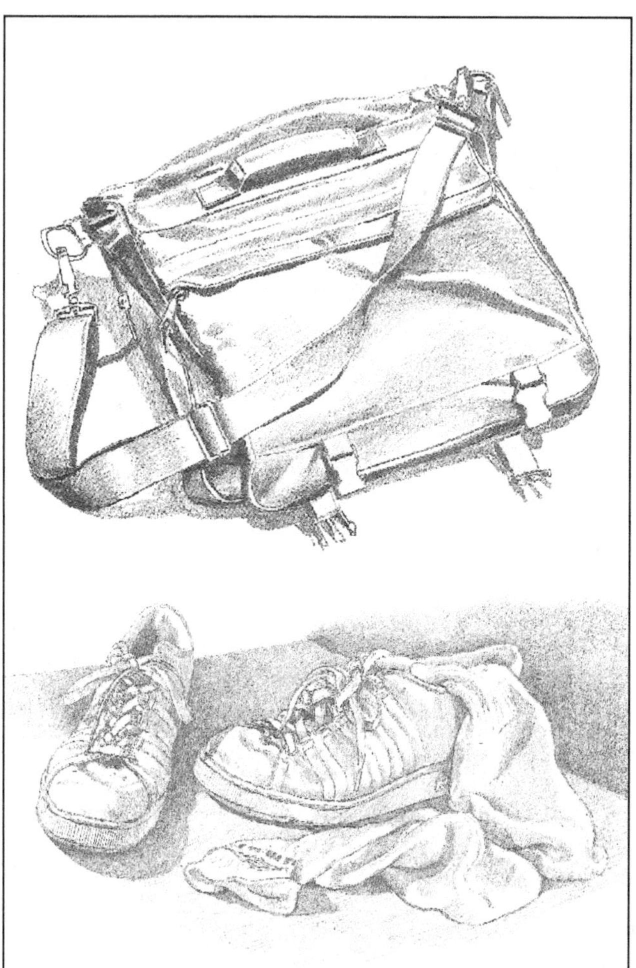

(ii) Natural

Natural materials such as rock, shells, fish, bones, food, leaves are very intrusting types of materiality that you might like to include in some of your composition. It offer the artist practice in the drawing of unusual and often fascinating shapes as well as different textures. It is the textures that convey the feel of the subject to the viewer.

Depicting Cloth Folds: While doing Still Life, a cloth is often hung as backdrop or objects are placed on a board which has a cloth cover spread over it. If you draw with care the cloth or the drape, particularly show the folds on them, the beauty of the picture will be enhanced. You must practice sketching the light and shade of folds ,it is not simple.

1. Begin with a lightly sketched outline Carefully observe the outside edges as well as the major fold shapes.

2. Lightly shade shapes that are in shadow Look for "valleys" in the fabric to add your shadows, try to record the entire shape of the shadow. The tops of your folds will almost always stay white, because the light is hitting them! Use a medium pencil like a HB or 2B to create subtle shadows.

3. Darken the most intense shadows Keep some areas of the lighter shading visible, so you will now have highlights, mid-tones, and shadows Use a dark pencil like a 6B to create dark shadows.

4. If using toned paper, add white for highlights Only record the brightest highlights to allow some of the blank paper to show through and give you more variety of tone! Use a white colored pencil or white conté.

NOTE: THE SAME TREATMENT SHOULD FOLLOW WHEN DRAW CLOTHING WRINKLES AND FOLDS IN HUMAN FIGURES.

Basic Shapes

Squares, rectangles, triangles, cones, cylinders, circles, ovals...these are the basic shapes that will aid you in drawing objects more accurately. This technique can be used when doing a still life, a landscape, and practically any other object or subject you wish to draw. As you progress through this book, you will see how this style of drawing can aid you in producing a more accurate presentation of the subjects. First, examine the object you want to draw, and determine what basic shapes make it up.

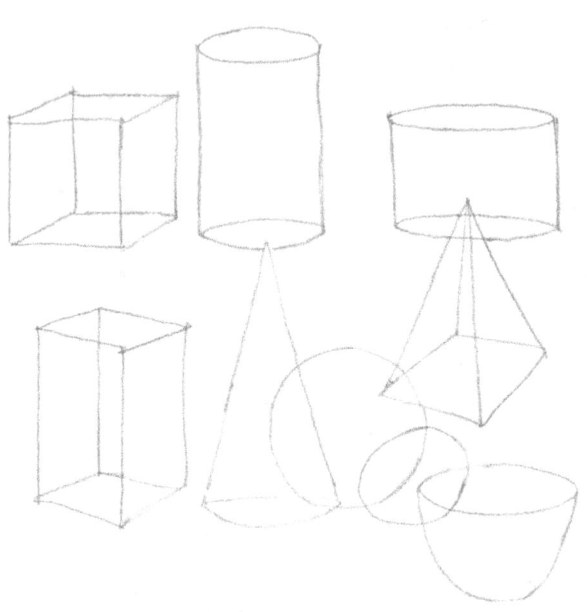

Observe the objects you are going to draw, and reduce them to basic shapes. Then combine the shapes to create the finished objects. Add detail and shading. Shapes can be modified to produce a better drawing. Note that the basic shape of the pear is a round circle with a tapered rectangle.

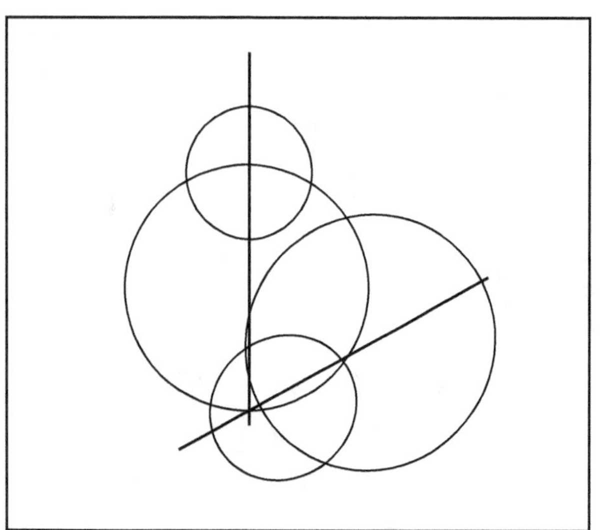

Selecting Basic Shapes:
1. Look at the object you want to draw. Determine what basic shapes are needed to render the object.
2. Start by roughly locating where on your picture plane you want the object to appear.
3. Draw a center line, top line, and bottom line.
4. Place a line where one shape changes to another shape. (see dash rules below)
5. Draw in the basic shapes.
6. Select the lines you want in your final drawing.
7. Draw the complete shape. This avoids connecting the shapes later in the drawing and improves placement.

ELLIPSES

You may well decide to sketch some man-made object. Rectangular and square objects are quite straightforward to measure, but bowls or vases often have circular bases and openings, and there are certain things you need to watch out for, since a circular opening is only circular when seen from directly above. From other angles, circles become ellipses, and you need to bear these points in mind.

Curved forms

Ellipses do not have pointed corners always ensure that your ellipses have rounded ends .

Checking the depth

Check the depth of an ellipses by comparing it with the width, measuring in the usually way. Seen from different angles, ellipses can vary greatly in width, as can the depth of a bowl.

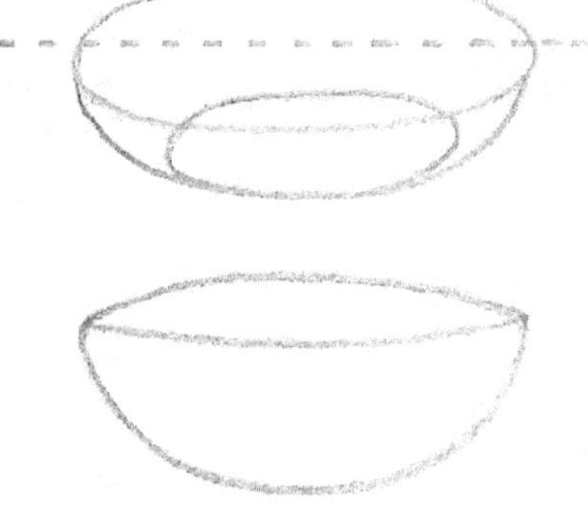

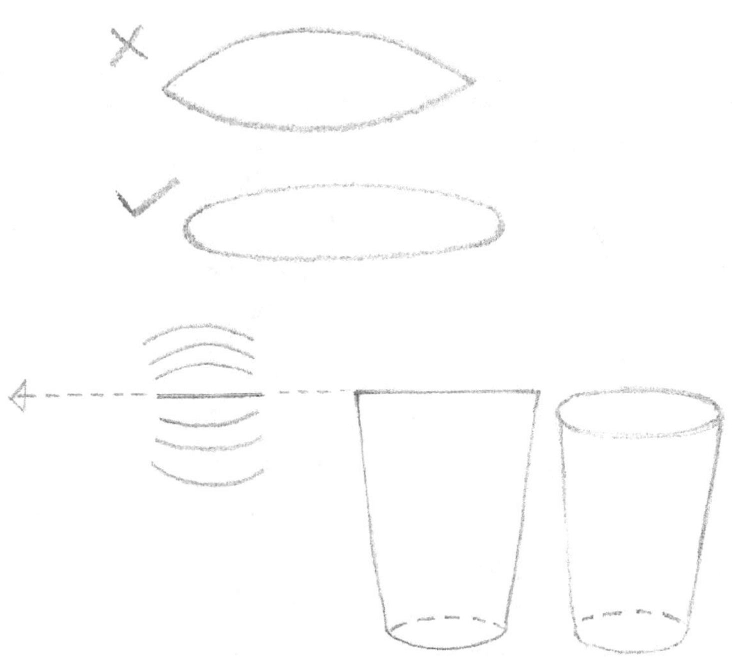

Eye level

Ellipses seen at eye level form straight lines. Above eye level, they curve up.

Curved bottom

A common is to give a pot, or vase, a straight bottom edge, just because it is sitting on a flat table. The bottom must curve more than the lip.

Checking your drawing

To check the drawing of a complex object, place a piece of tracing paper over your drawing ; find the center line, fold the tracing and see if both halves match.

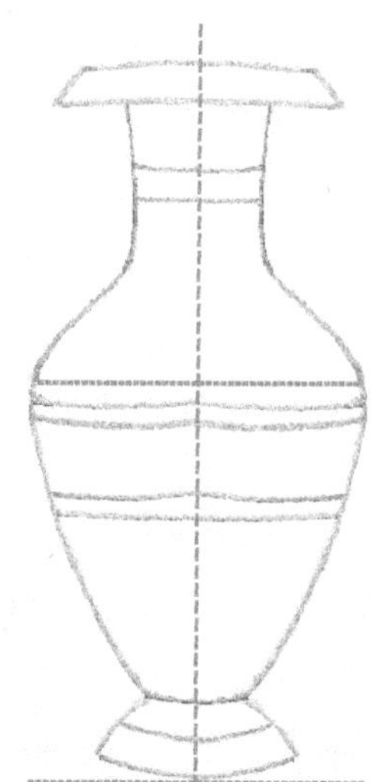

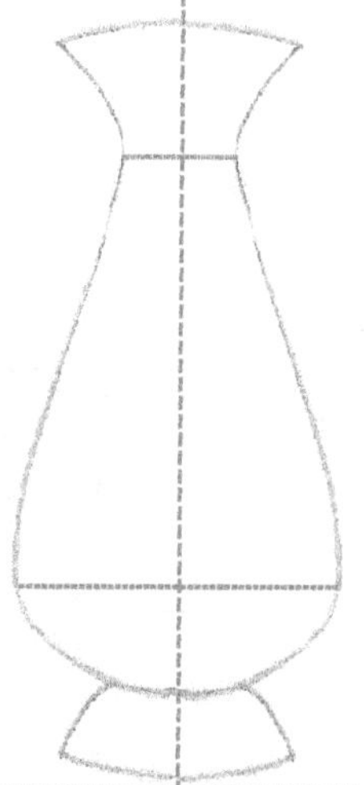

Sketching a Group with overlapping: When sketching a group of shapes, it is best to draw each shape fully. In this manner, all of the curves and straight lines are more accurate, and you don't have to draw the objects to fit into each other. Remember to draw the objects lightly so they can be erased or covered in your final.

 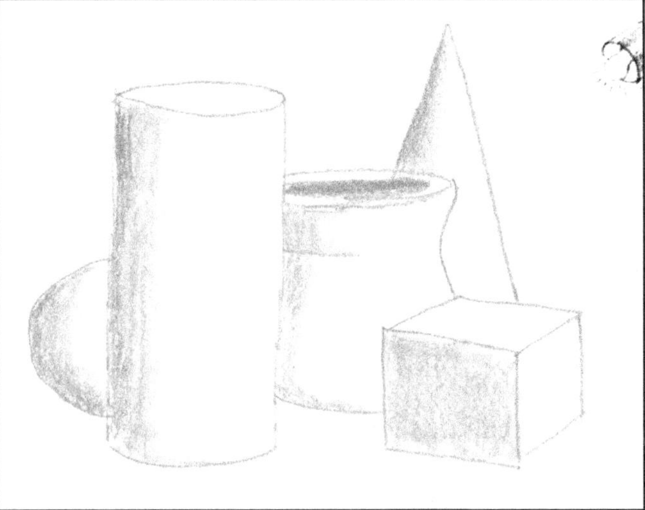

Study of object's shadow: Study of an object's shadow is just as important as the study of the object's shade and light. A beautiful still life painting can be created if shadows falling on the ground or shadows of objects falling on another object or shadows changing their shapes according to the shape of the object on which it is falling on are done properly.

Demonstration:1

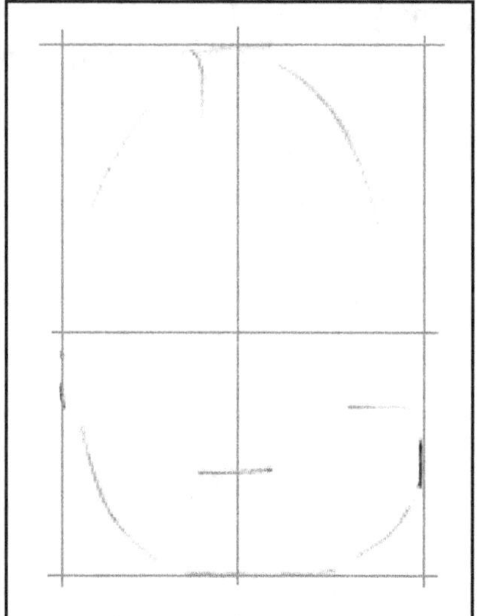 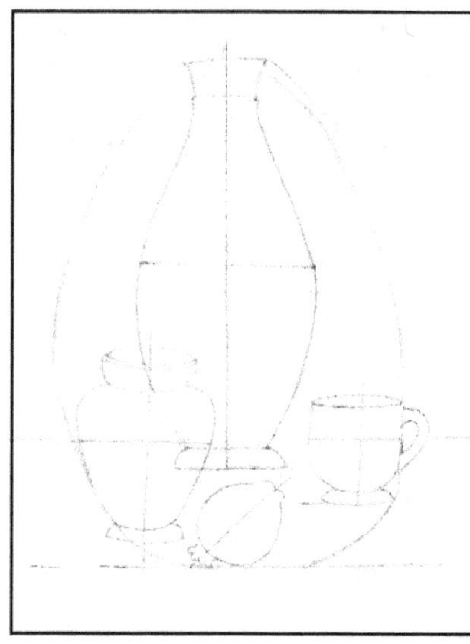 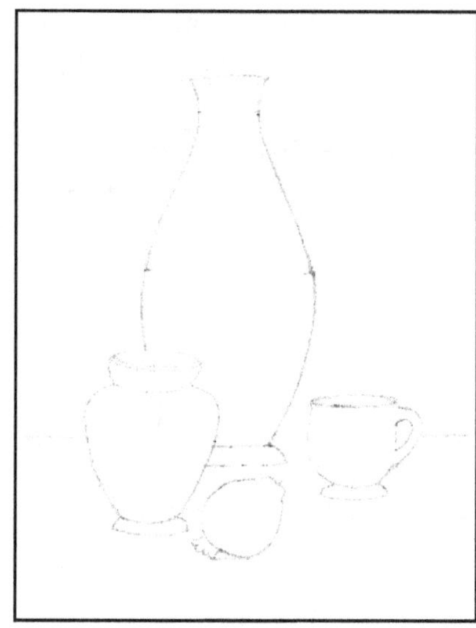

Step 1-The picture should be proportionate to the size of the paper and according shapes of the objects, such as Vertical or Horizontal. Then sketch the entire outline lightly with a pencil. Try to get the rough idea of the biggest object and other small objects in respect of their height lightly. If the drawing is correct, erase the unwanted lines with a light hand. Retain the lines that are correct and make them bold.

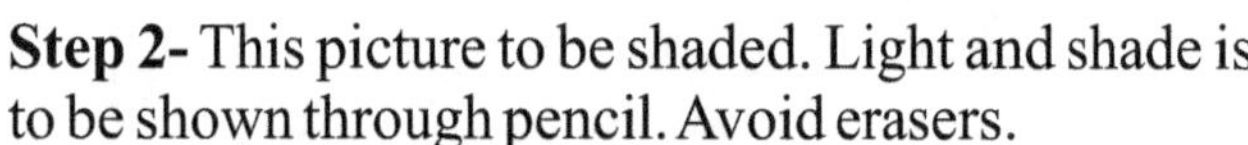

Step 2- This picture to be shaded. Light and shade is to be shown through pencil. Avoid erasers.

Step 3-The last step is to add 6B Pencil to the darkest parts of the drawing under the objects.

Demonstration:2

Step 1- Using household objects, arrange a similar Still Life to mine or choose another theme, but remember to keep the objects simple so that you can draw them. Start with the objects basic structure in light, sketchy lines with HB pencil. To add stronger contrast to your Still Life set up a light on one side of the arrangement.

Step 2- Shading is generally built up from lightest to darkest tone on each item. Use the 6B for the dark shadow and the 2B for the lighter shadow. Bear in mind the direction of the light source and keep highlight areas free of pencil marks. You can create highlights using an eraser too.

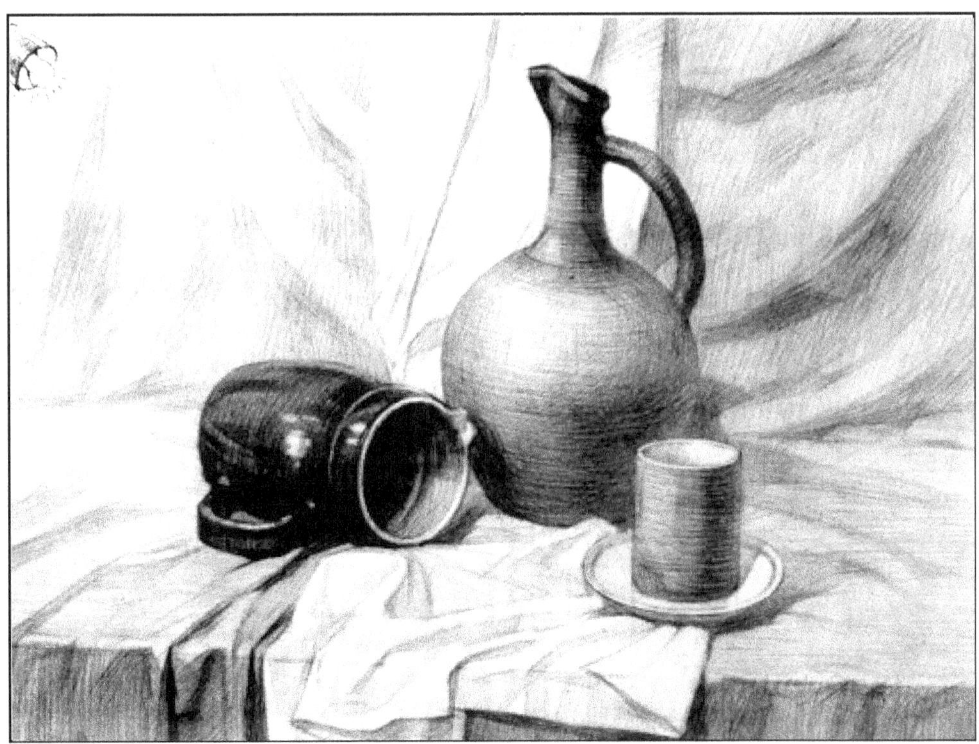

Final Step - Add more shading and highlights and increase individual texture of objects for fine detail. Finally, shade surrounding -foreground and background subjects.

Nature Drawing

In all objects of the nature like flower, vegetable, leaves, fruits and living creatures, you will find colour, texture and shape. Nature can not be put on paper still, with the right combination of lines, tone, space and composition, we can recollect and communicate our experience and make the viewer a participant in our multi sensed response to nature.

You need to train your senses to see and record this beauty. Watch closely, all are different from one an other. Try and sketch this on paper. It should be done softly with a light hand.

While sketching plant, make closely the various leaves and flowers. Study their shades of colour, shapes and the number of petals, etc. Different leaves and petals can be recognized due to such peculiarities of shapes, size and colours. Remember, study of those plants or flowers which are seasonal in that easily available particular region.

Sunflower, Dehlia, Shoeflower (Hibiscus),zinnia, etc., which are easily available, collect and keep in front of you specimens of flowers, leaves to practice Nature drawing.

During practice observe the veins of the leaves have proceeded from one point to both the sides, or have done so alternatively. If any leaf is folded, withered, spotted, rotten or moth-eaten, it has to be drawn as it is.

Specimen drawing of different types of leaves, flowers and stems are shown in here. Copy these drawings accurately before actually drawing the leaves and flowers by keeping them in front of you.

Study the following folded leaves:

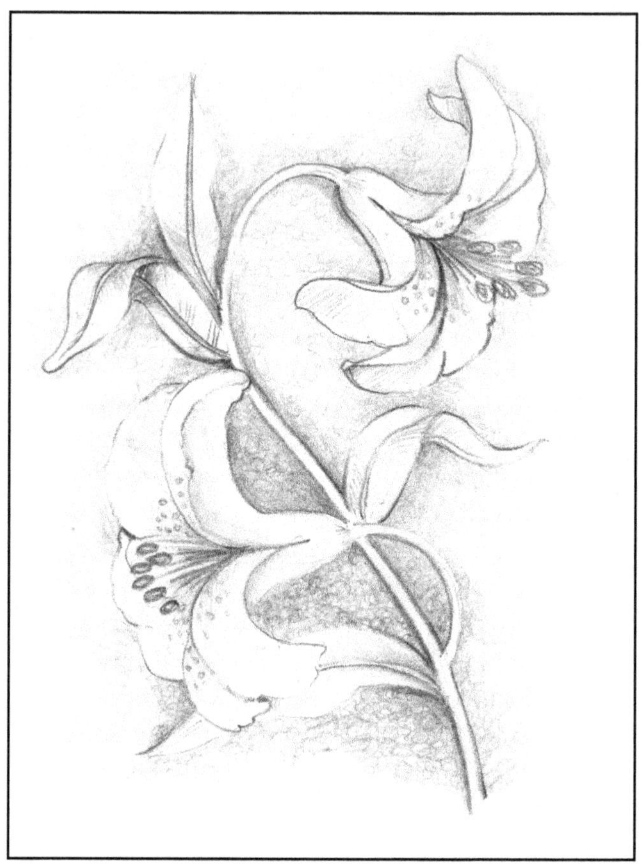

Very often, you find a tub with plant, it should be included in the nature drawing, making it more attractive. When drawing it remove some unwanted, complicated and crowded parts to clarity and beauty of the drawing.

Nature gives us guidance in abundance. We have to accept this gift in our able hands. Sketching a flowering plant exactly is a more beginning.

The play of light and shade on the objects is the main subject. Before employing shading techniques, the light and shade on high and low parts of the object have to be observed closely. That is the basis of your skill in shading. With observation and imagination, as you practice more and more, you can became well-versed in showing the ply of light and shade.

NOTES FOR PENCIL SHADING

1.   Use HB pencil for drawing and 2B to 8 B for shading.

2.   Draw freehand, don't use any instruments.

3.   Draw very light and perfect, with the help of geometrical shapes

4.   Don't hurry or rush while you draw.

5.   Shapes of the picture will be horizontal or vertical according to the requirement

6.   Arrange little group of objects according to the given example.

7.   Study and draw hidden shapes even if it is behind the object before detail drawing.

8.   Practice tones as examples given.

9.   Always shade or paint from top to bottom and left to right accordingly.

10.   Distinguish objects after shading in sure hand.

11.   Must show texture or design of object if required.

12.   Don't forget to work surrounding background base and shadow. Sometimes
        the treatment of the background helps to decline a natural object of clearly.

13.   Reflecting can only be seen in the water or glasslike things. In water, the reflection
        of an object appears directly below and in glass, right in front.
        After you complete shading, Compare your work with the original reference and
        make the necessary changes. Pay special attention to this aspect and try to achieve
        the look (character, surface and smoothness etc.) as per the original.

C

POSTER COLOUR/OILS
(OPAQUE COLOUR)

COLOUR
PENCILS

D

HUMAN FIGURES & PAINTING COMPOSITION

INTRODUCTION

The painting composition some time called memory drawing is liked by the students much and has always remained the most attractive subject for them. To observe things minutely, to retain in memory various incidents, to remember the different positions of the body while performing various movements and to make rapid sketches of the details of all these, are the things necessary to master in composition.

EXERCISE

Suppose if you have to draw a situation from memory, first see it and close your eyes and imagine the shape through the eyes of mind. How it looks? This will improve the observation and unfold your creativity.

While dealing with this subject, many students begin directly with drawing details like the nose, eyes, etc. of the human figure minutely and in bold hand, without considering the size of the given paper. This results in their drawing becoming either too large or too small in proportion to the paper. It may also happen that the head of the figure in the drawing appearing much bigger in proportion as compared to the rest of the body or vice versa. Then, erasing it becomes unavoidable. Drawing very small figures leaves a large part of the paper blank. Some unimportant details such as tree, houses, etc. are then added to fill the vacant spaces. As a result, the main subject of the drawing gets a less important place in the whole composition. This should be avoided. Besides, many students show unnecessary details in their painting. For instance, design on the clothes, lines in the hair, roof tiles on the house, leaves in the trees, flowers, etc. Obviously in many cases, the coloring is left incomplete as too much time is spent in drawing such details.

Draw the main figures of the picture first. Compose the drawings of the main figures in such a way that they are placed in the centare part of the paper. After this, draw the other sketch surrounding also, as background of the picture. Always focus on the subject, avoid background details which is not necessary and study subject from your locality. While showing a huge crowd in a picture, you can just show the faces of the people in the background becoming smaller and smaller. This way the illusion of crowd can be achieved.

Before starting a painting in water colour, oil colour, pastel colour or any other medium " a composition " is must, based on which the painting will be done. Even before thinking about the composition, one should think about the selection of subject/ theme of the painting Namely- picnic, Market place, Bus stop, Village scene, Mother & child etc.

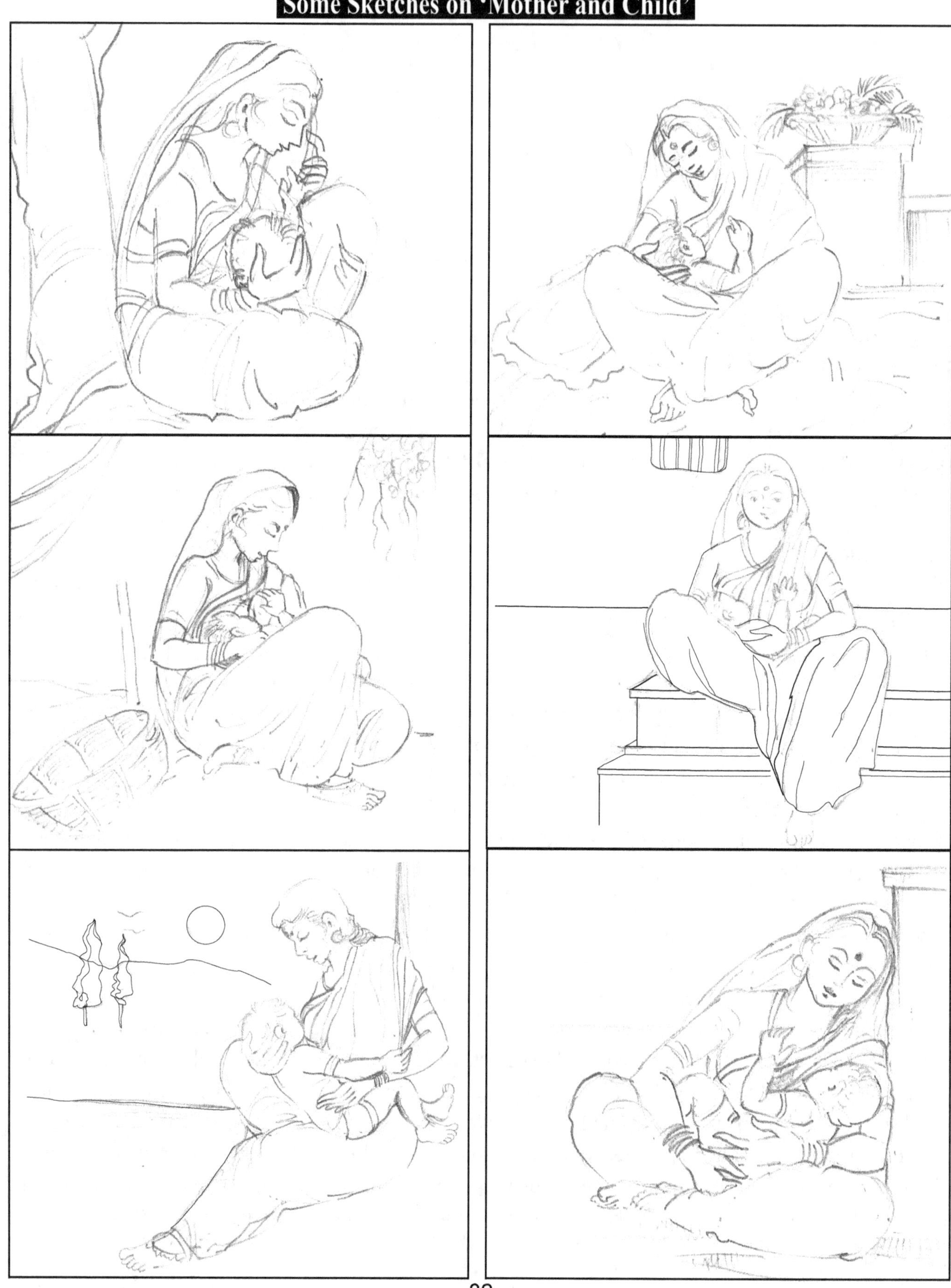

BEFORE START COMPOSITION, MUST STUDY ANATOMY AND METHOD OF RAPID SKETCHING MOVEMENTS OF HUMAN FIGURE:

Draw a light drawing using minimum strokes with an HB pencil. Do not use the eraser for this. Rapid sketching can be done by referring to photographs, printed pictures, reference pictures or even by observing a person in front of you. Practice simplified drawing of Anatomy, e.g.

 ***The Body is divided in three equal parts:** Adult figure- 7&1/4 of head size.

(1) Shoulder to waist **(2)**Waist to Knee and **(3)**Knee to heal. Each part is equal to the height of two head.

Shapes of body: (a) Head like a oval **(b)** Torso (parts from the neck to the waist) like a rectangle and **(c)**Arms and legs like curve line.

*The length of legs are two times of torso.

 *The arm reaches up to the middle of thigh.

*The elbow reaches up to the head in upward and touching the naval level in downward.

*The female shoulder is narrow than male.

*The female body is naturally delicate and short height compared to that of a male.

Study from Mannequin of the Male Female & Child :

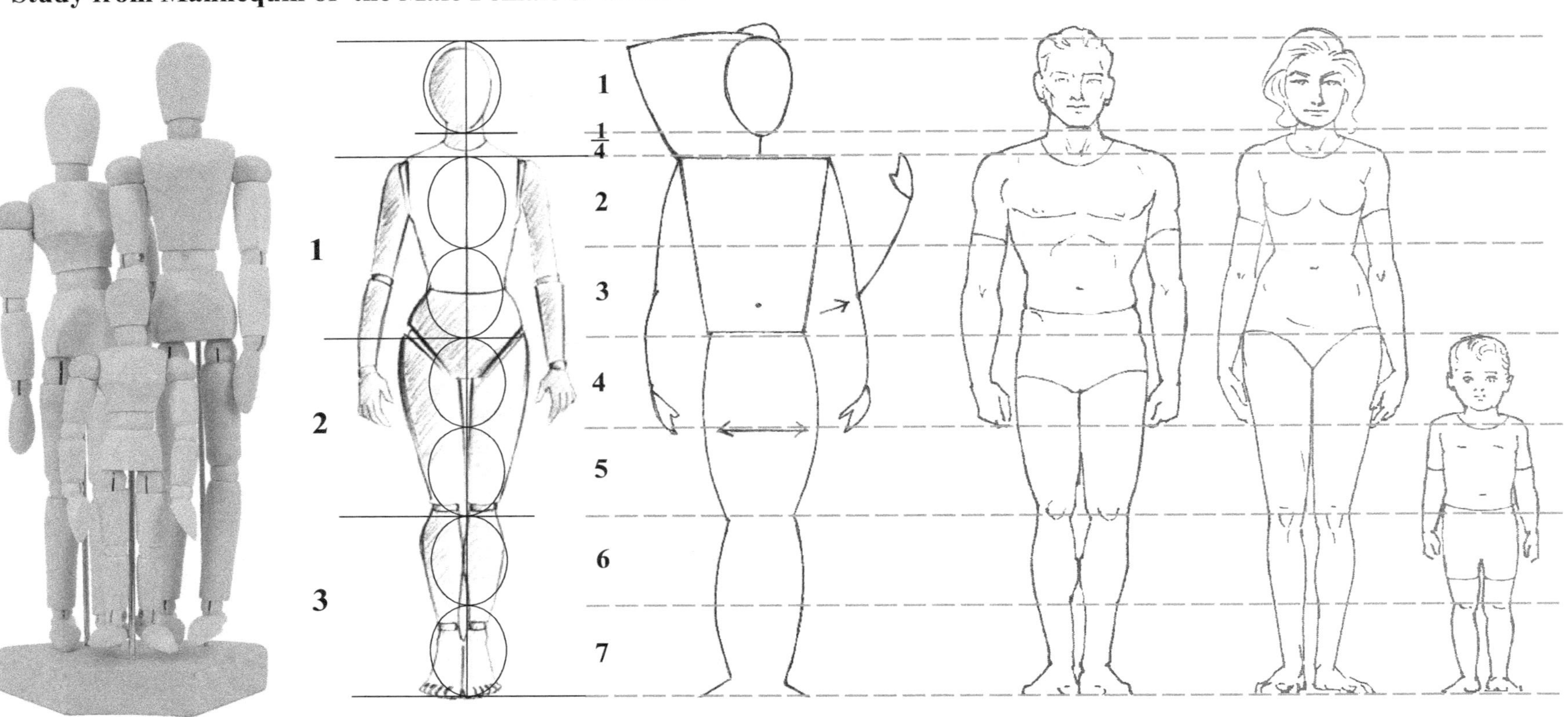

FASHION MODELS & COMIC CHARACTERS ANATOMY

A model figures draw 9 of head size and comic figures 10 & of head size than average guy.

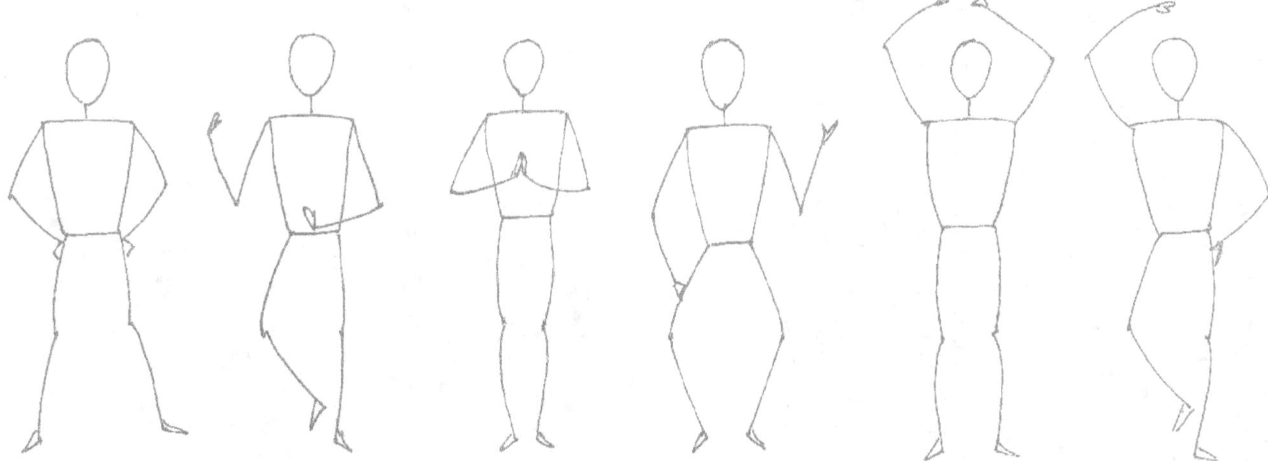

TALL BODY AND HEAD THAN NORMAL PERSON   **SMALL HEAD THAN BIGGER BODY**

QUAKE SET UP IN ACTION: First draw figure in action and add detail character and costumes as require. Observe carefully the given example and practice yourself.

Basic Simple Form

Different action in basic simple form

Drawing Folds in Clothing and Drapery with Shadows and Light

Clothing is drapery arranged around a body that is beneath it. To express the multitudinous forms it takes, one should learn to express in a direct way the different characters of folds, for each one plays its individual part as distinctly.

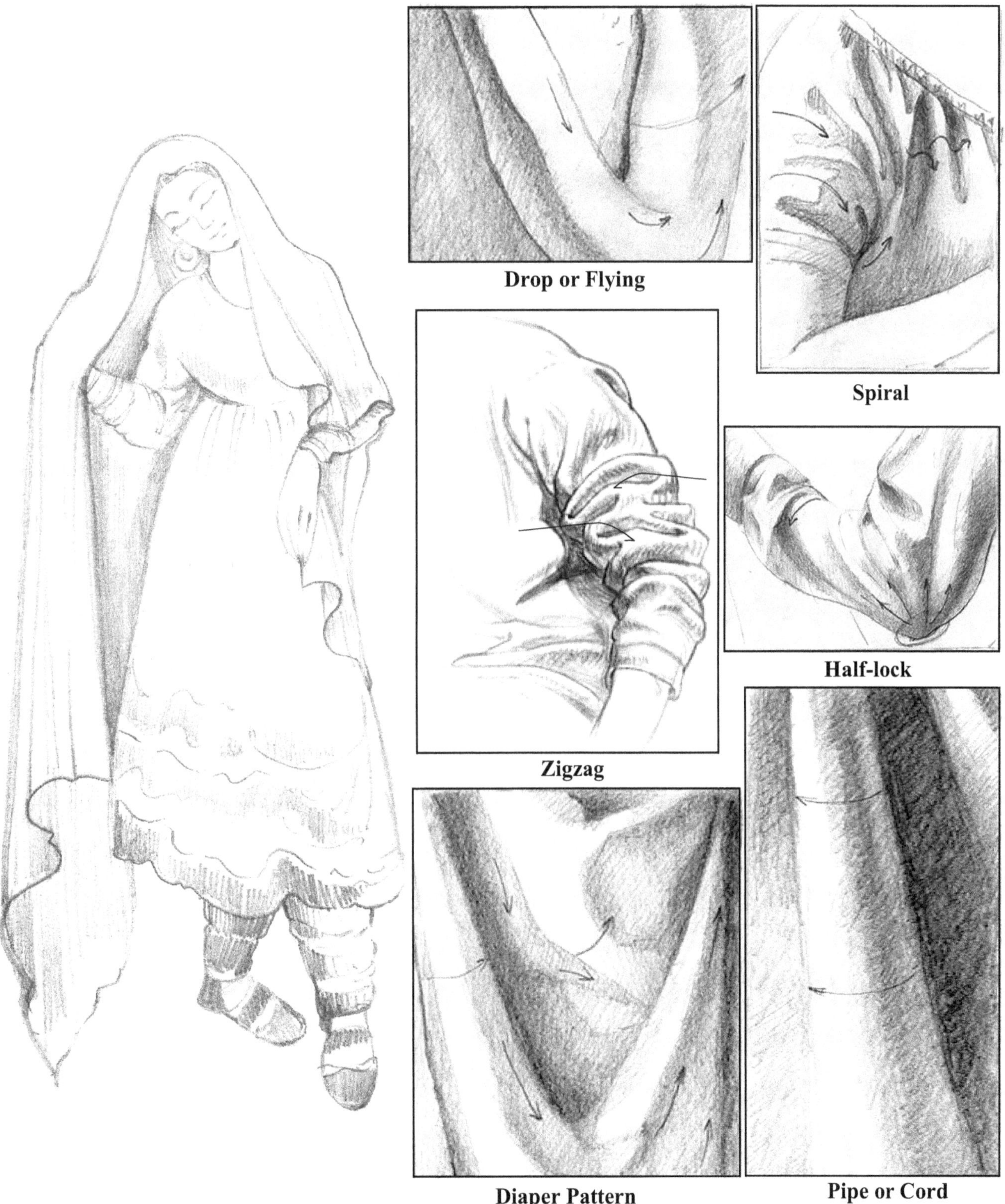

Drop or Flying

Spiral

Zigzag

Half-lock

Diaper Pattern

Pipe or Cord

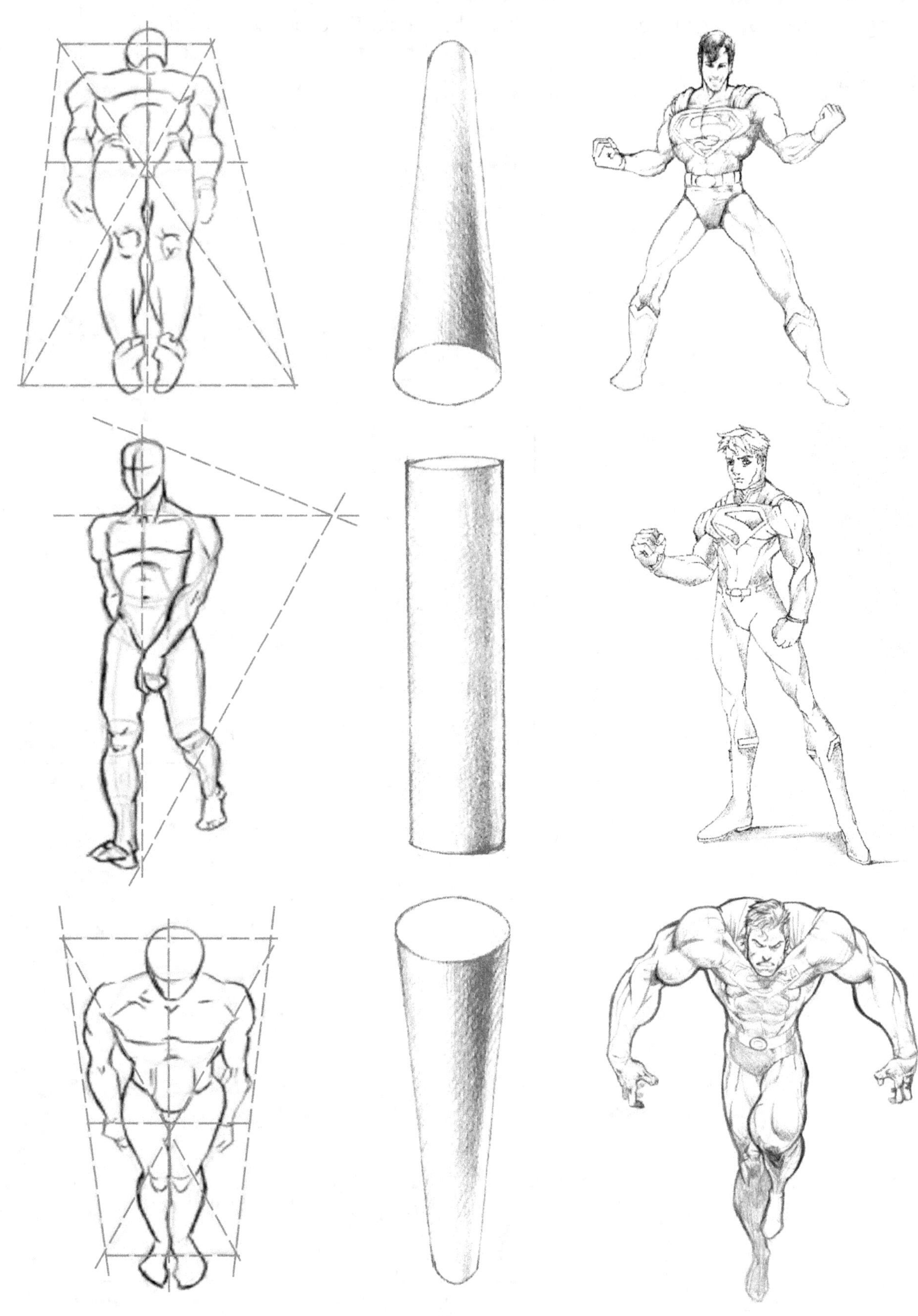

First draw a rough sketch, then by adding essential details, make it complete.

FIGURES DRAWING- STEP BY STEP
(Demonstration: 2)

PARTS OF THE HEAD

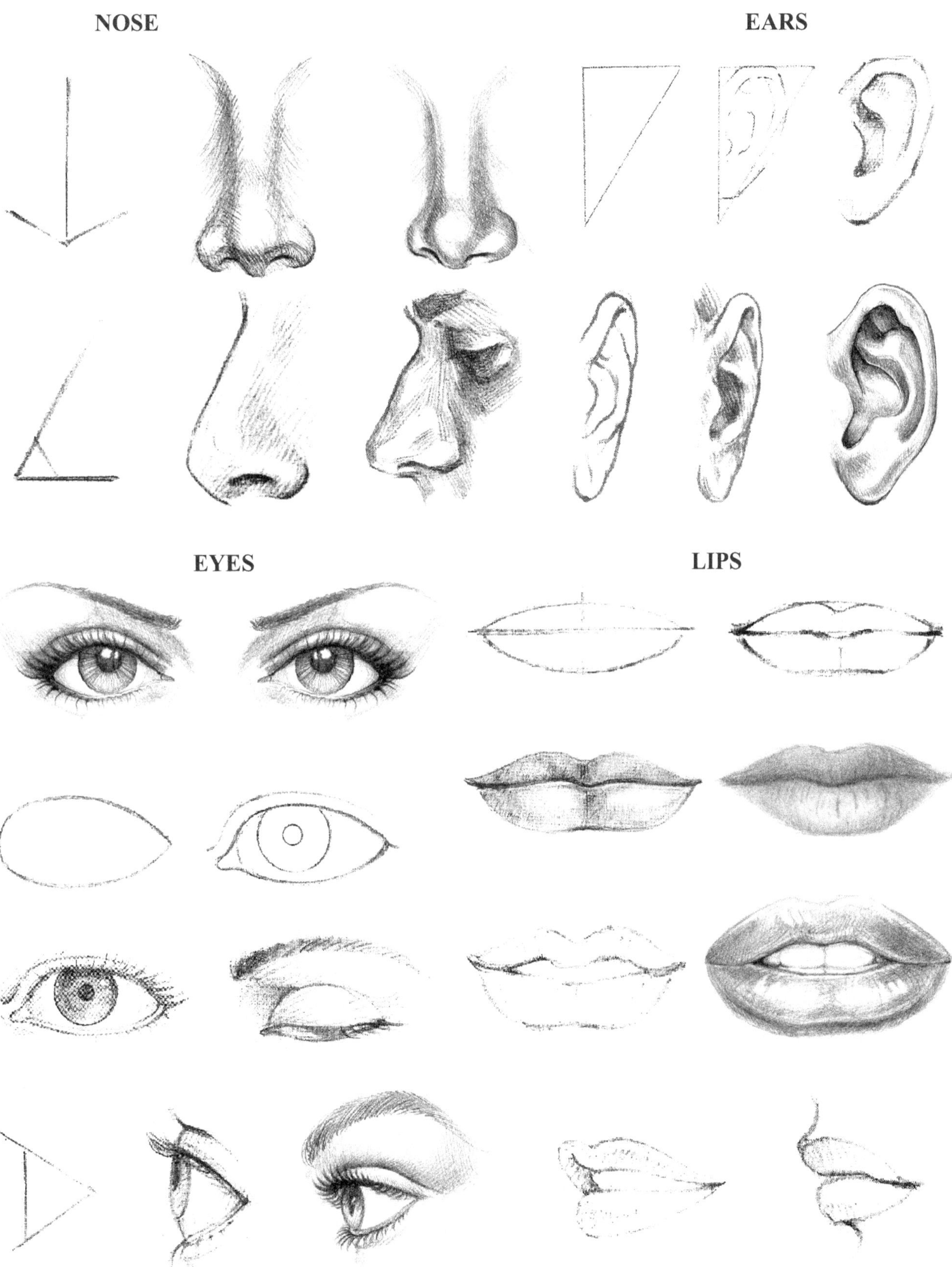

Head study: Points to remember

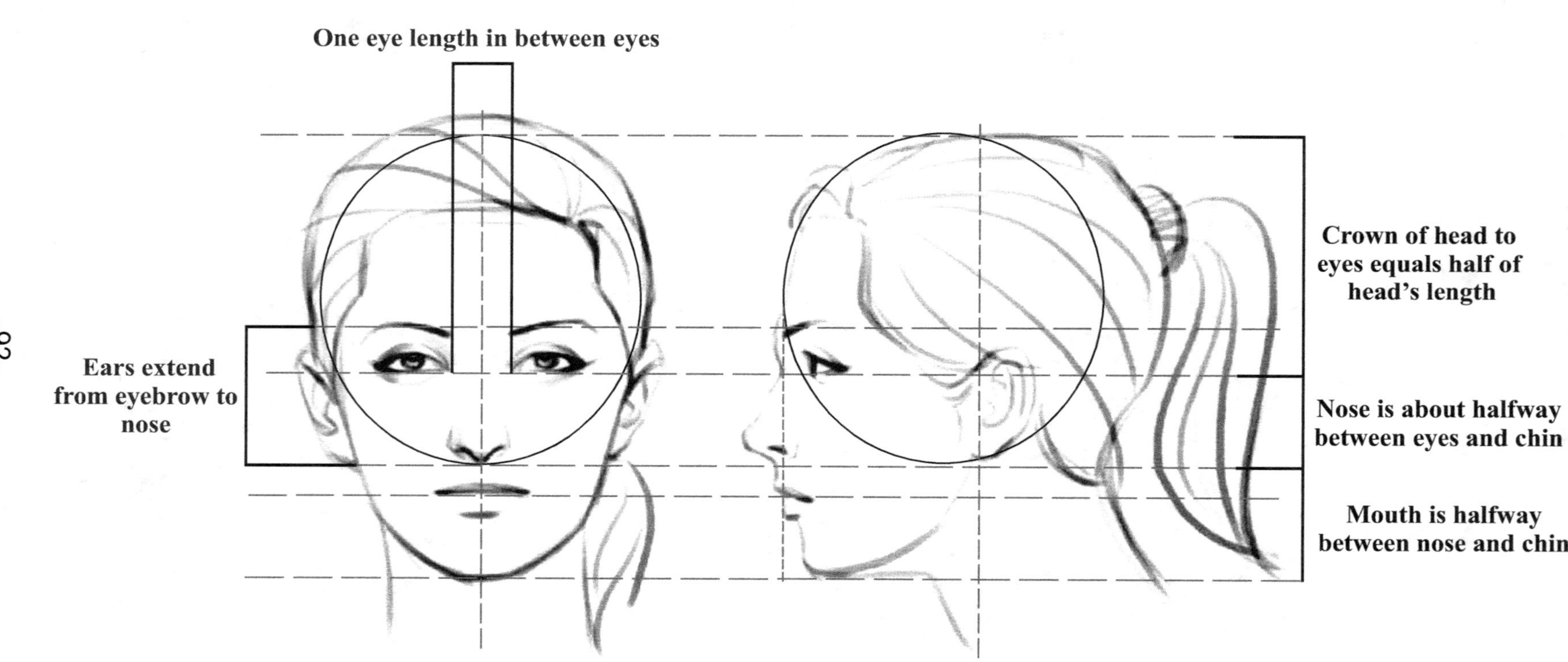

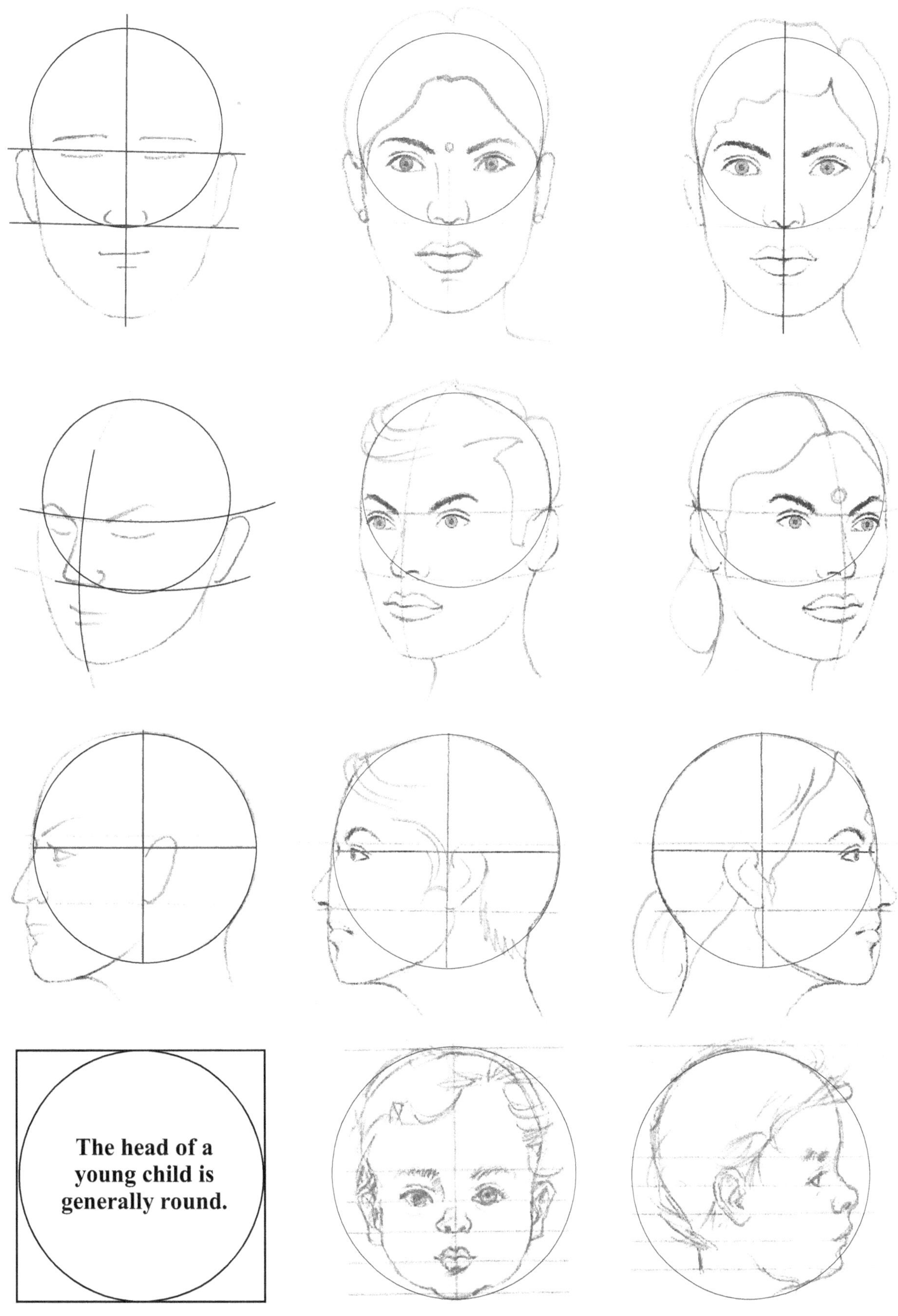

The head of a
young child is
generally round.

FACIAL EXPRESSION

Learner should try to bring proper expression in the gesture and body language of the figures in co-ordination to in organic elements. You must try to create a composition which bears the distinct mood and emotion.

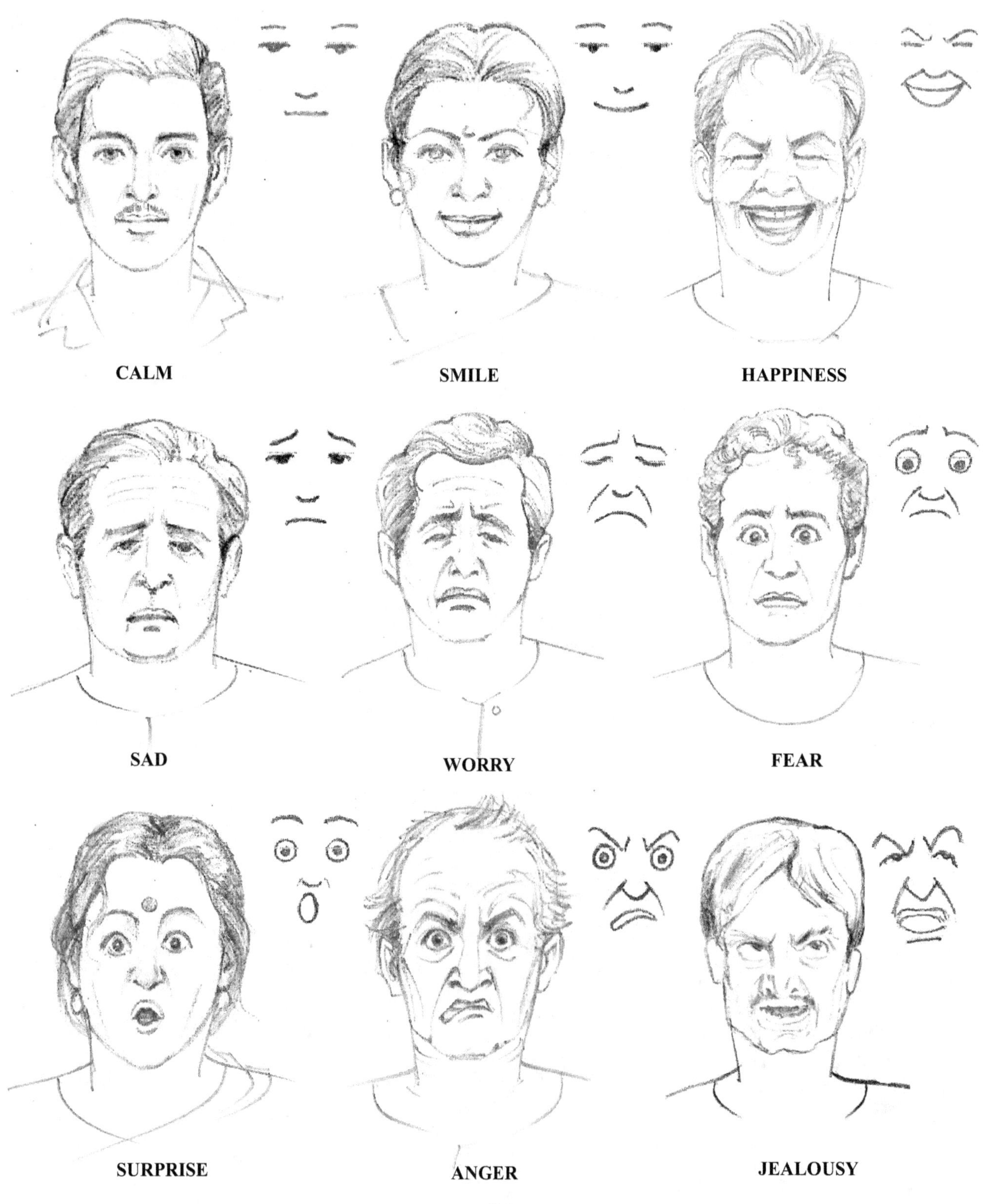

ARM & HANDS

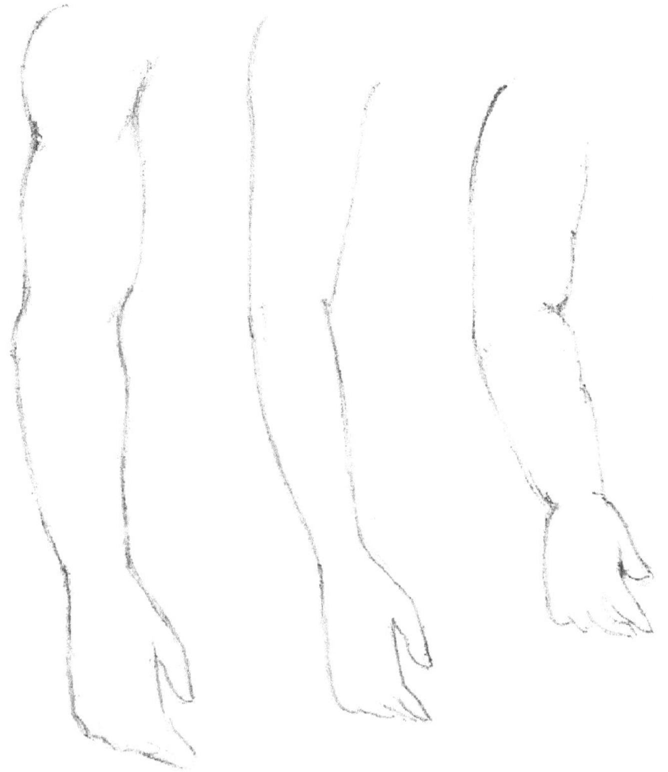

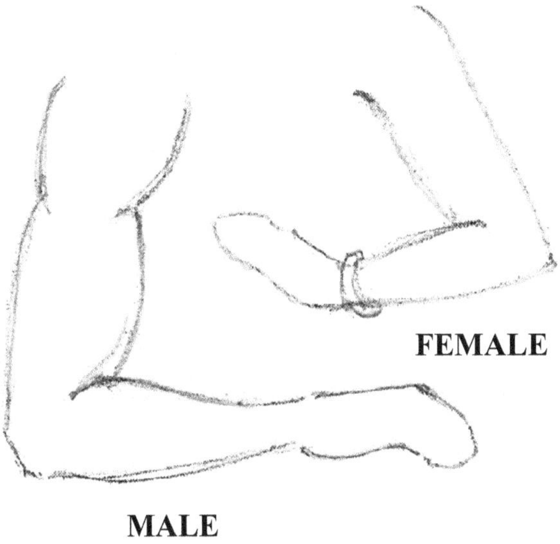

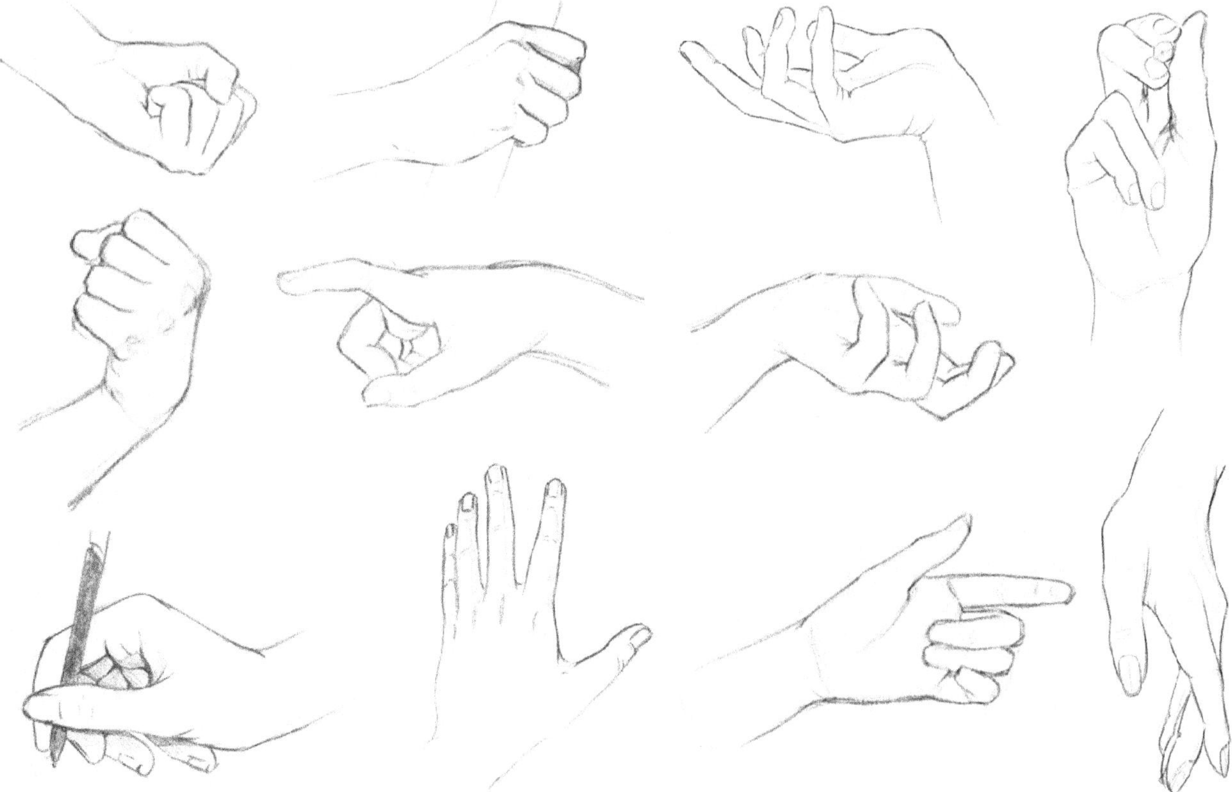

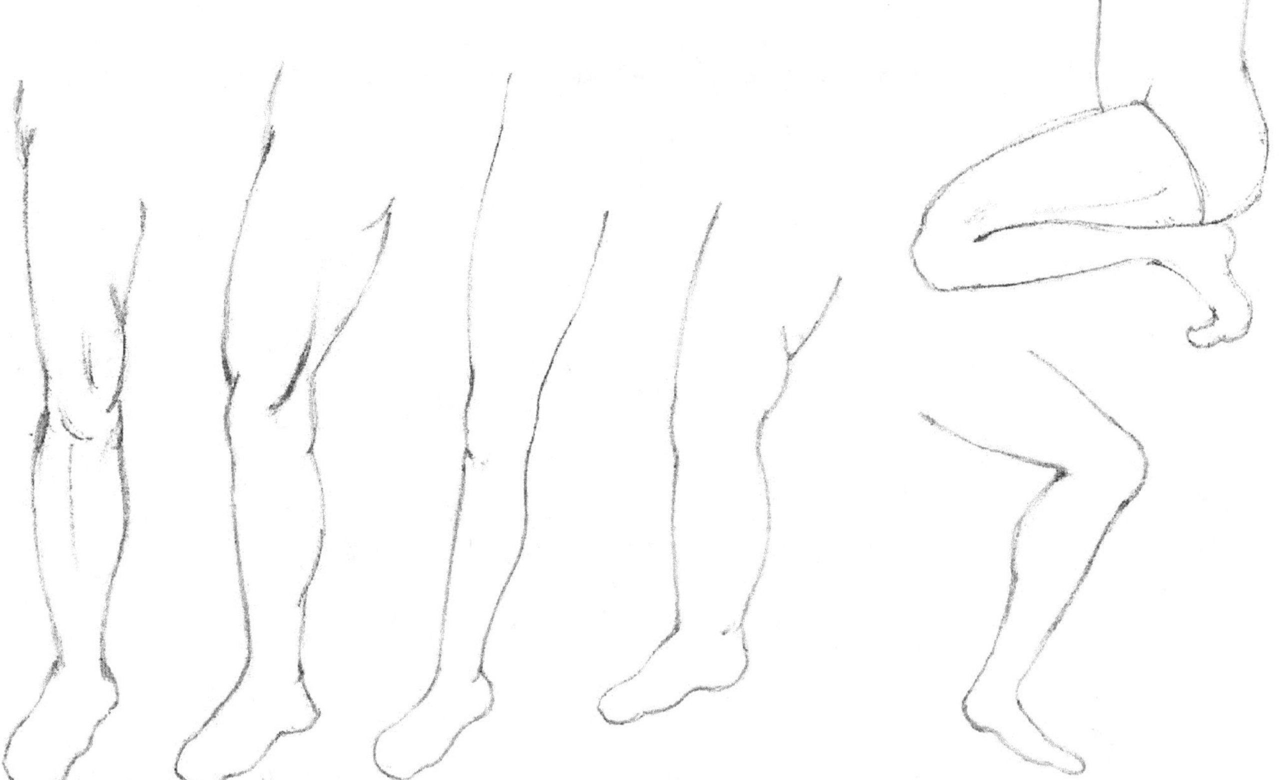

FRONT   SIDE MALE   FEMALE   CHILD   BENDING MOVEMENT

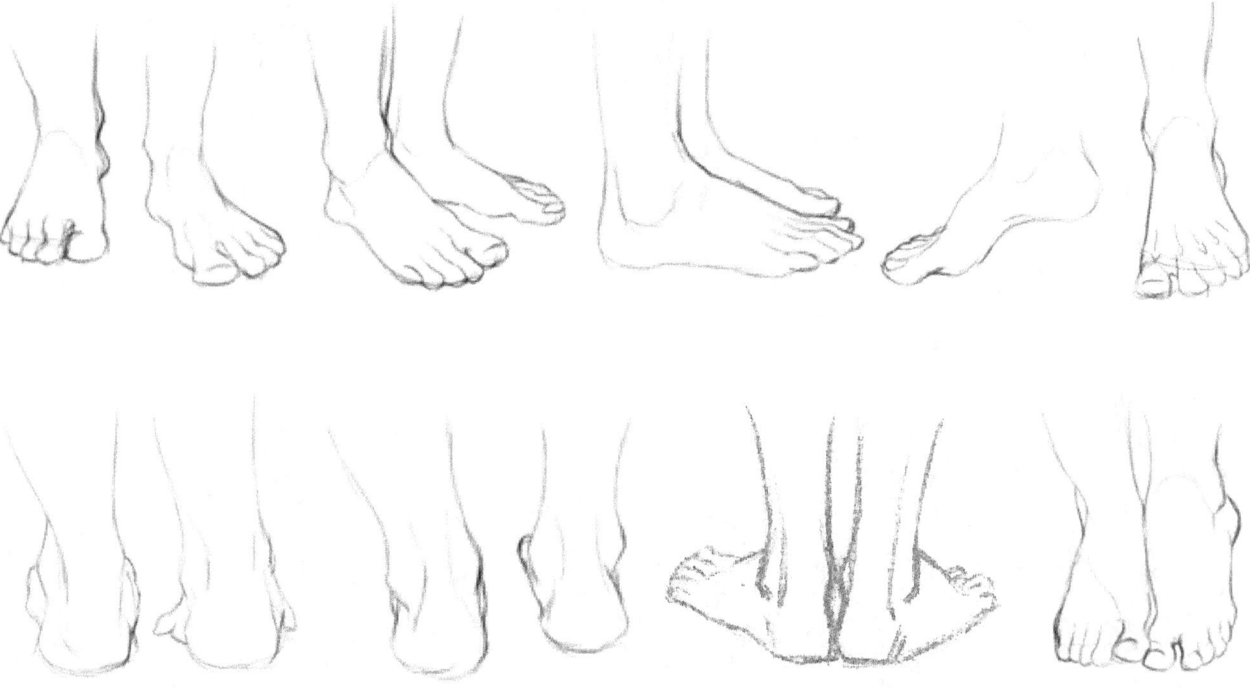

SUPPORTING ELEMENTS FOR PAINTING COMPOSITION

In composition study any activities of human life. What we see in surrounding-Trees,Houses,Birds,Animals,River,Hills,Clouds,Boats on river, Rocks etc. Learner is suggested that he/she can compose the above subjects according to his/her idea or imagination. Before going for final he/she should go to for rough pencil drawings. Then go to final drawing on an art paper for water colour /pastel colour or canvas for oil colour painting.

Simple drawing of Trees:

Simple drawing of Houses:

Simple drawing of Birds:

Simple drawing of Animals:

Simple drawing of Vehicles:

DURGA PUJA

VILLAGE KITCHEN

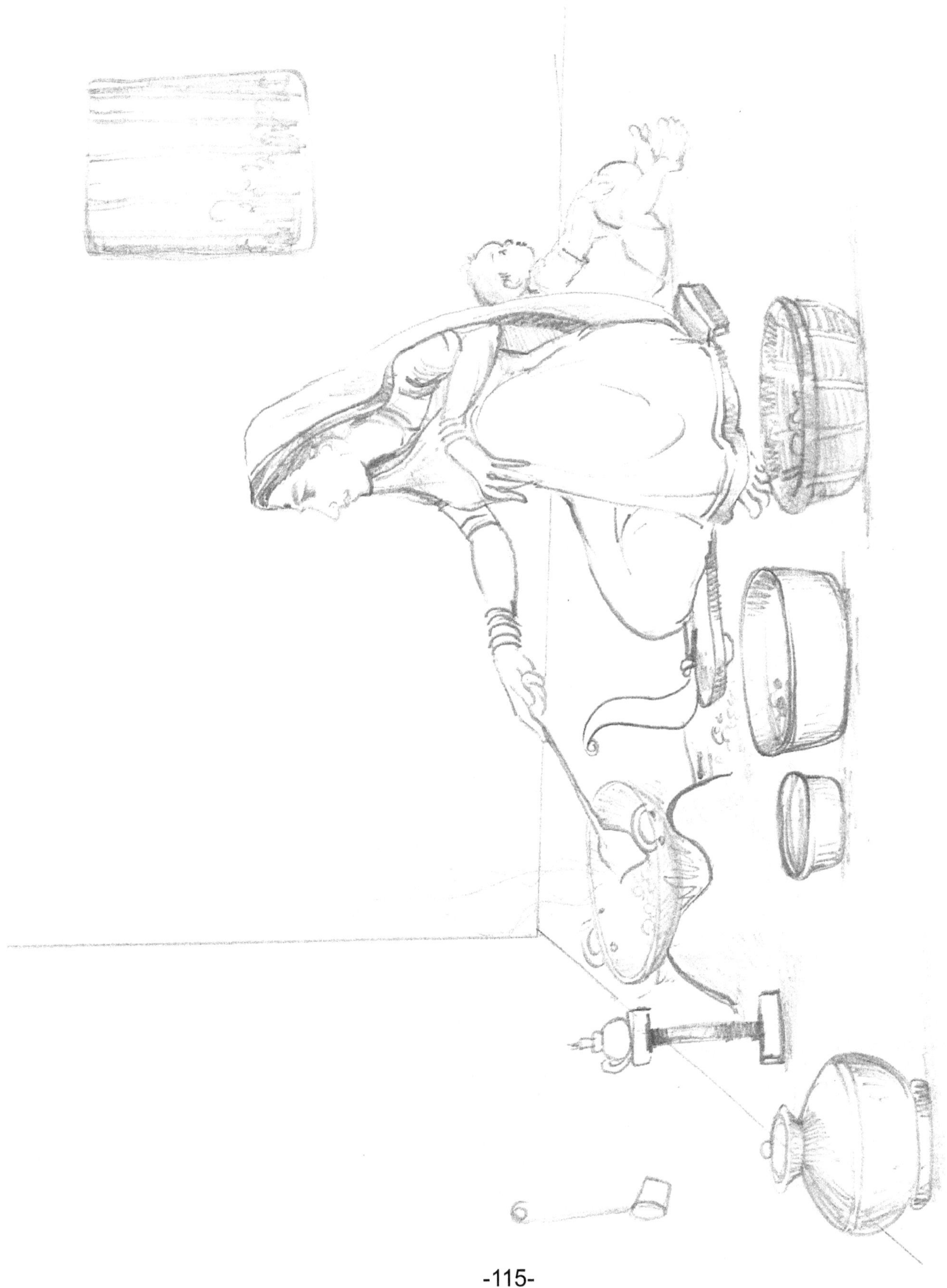

BUS STAND

An **illustration** is a displayed visualization form presented as a drawing, painting, photograph or other work of art that is created to dictate sensual information (such as a story, poem or newspaper article) by providing a visual representation graphically. The earliest forms of illustration were prehistoric cave paintings. Before the invention of the printing press, books were hand-illustrated. Illustration has been used in China and Japan since the 8th century, traditionally by creating woodcuts to accompany writing.

The illustration generally have to describe and explain the subjects to a nontechnical audience. Therefore the visual image should be accurate in terms of dimensions and proportions, and should provide "an overall impression of what an object is or does, to enhance the viewer's interest and understanding".

Today, there is a growing interest in collecting and admiring original artwork that was used as illustrations in books, magazines, posters, etc. Various museum exhibitions, magazines and art galleries have devoted space to the illustrators of the past.

LORD BUDDHA

LORD KRISHNA LIFTING MOUNT GOVERDHANA

METHODS OF PAINTING USING DIFFERENT MEDIUMS

MEDIUMS: A drawing can be paint using various methods and mediums. You can select the methods of colouring by choice.

1. Colour pencils.
2. Oil pastels or Wax crayons.
3. Transparent colours - Tube or Cake colours
4. Opaque Colours - Poster colours/Oils (Bottle/Tube colours)

(1) Painting with Colour Pencils

One who is able to show light and shade with pencil, will not find it difficult while using colour pencils. Use pencil colour set of 24 shades. Colour the subject with light hand by applying short strokes. First use transparent colours to apply flat, light tones of that particular colour on the entire picture, medium and dark tones apply gradually. Finishing touches can be applied with a sure hand.

(2) Painting with Pastel

Use oil pastels of 24 or 48 shades set. Colour the light areas of the object with a light coloured pastel and the dark area with a dark coloured pastel and merge them into one another. If there are more shades in the pastels, colours the subject with light, medium and dark tones and merge them into one another.

Colour the dark tones and the shadows with a dark shade. By varying the pressure on the pastel, you can make the tone either light or dark painting can also be done by making short strokes (hatching) as done in pencil shading. Similarly, colouring can also be done by applying forceful strokes with pieces of pastel held horizontally. It is better to leave the parts of the figures to be highlighted paper-white. This is because a white-coloured pastel is not seen properly when applied over other shades.

(3) Painting with transparent colours

Transparent colours should be applied in a thin or medium coat. In order to make the colour light, add water to the colour. Colour the main figures first and then other parts. While painting, apply a light toned wash on the entire subjects. Apply the dark tones on the figure while the previously applied wash is still damp. Merge the two tones. By applying the dark shade when the previous wash is damp, the colours of course merge into each other to a certain extent. Leave the portion to be highlighted paper-white.

Finally, the finishing touches can be applied with a pointed brush. During the painting, dip the brush in the other colour only after cleaning water should be clean and change the water very often. Don't fill in minute details while painting the picture (e.g. design on clothes, details of the leaves and flowers on trees etc.). The outline of the picture should not be too thick.

There should be a difference in the colours and shades between the background of the picture and the main figures of the picture. If the background is coloured with dark tones, then the subject matter or the main figures should be coloured with light and bright colours. If the background is coloured with light tones. then colour the main figures of the picture with dark tones or its opposite colour scheme. Use a bright and attractive colour scheme to colour the picture.

(4) Painting with opaque colours

Opaque colours should be applied in a medium and thick coat. Add white to the colour in order to make the colour light. Similarly, the highlights can be coloured using white colour. Use small brush for fine work and bigger brush of higher number for painting larger parts.

Do not put the cap of one bottle on that another and clean your brush before dipping in the colour bottle, Otherwise the original colour will spoil the colour in the bottle. Your colour work is over add 4-5 drop of water in the colour bottle before fixing cap, so that the pigment inside not dry up.

✳✳✳

PAINTING COMPOSITION & ILLUSTRATION

POSTER COLOUR/OILS (OPAQUE COLOUR)

WATER COLOUR

OIL PASTEL
COLOUR
PENCILS
F

CALLIGRAPHY/LETTERING
(THE ART OF FINE WRITING)

INTRODUCTION

Lettering or Calligraphy is beautifully formed of writing. It is one type of freehand drawing. It leaves an individualistic impression of your personality on the people you are communicating with. It is possible only if you know how lettering or the method of lettering.

The essential materials needed to practice lettering are writing tools like different types of Pens, ink and a writing surface. Crow- Quills are among the oldest writing tools. Brushes are also used for writing, and for filling in outlined letters and painting decoration.

Every letter has its own unique form and its own beauty. One must be able to draw the shapes of letters in beautiful forms. We come across lettering a variety of items such as sign boards, banners, advertisements and greeting cards, etc. Students generally draw English letters in Roman and Hindi letters in Devnagari script. There is ample scope for creative imagination in the world of lettering. An artistic touch should be given to the letters. The meaning or characteristics of the world should be expressed through letters.

Writing Tools

EXERCISE

1.Draw the top line and the bottom line of the letters so that the letters will stay in one line and the height of the letters will remain constant.

2.In lettering correct spacing both between letters and words is most essential for a well balanced and overall effect.

3.To make the thickness of the letters constant everywhere, decide upon the thickness or breadth of the letters. for the thick part of every letter. To make the thickness of the letters constant, mark that thickness on a paper ruler. Transfer these marking on the rough sketch of the letters wherever it is thick.

4.If you want the arrangement of the letters to appear in the center of the given outer shape, first draw a vertical center line lightly with a

pencil. Then decide upon the height of the letters and mark the top and bottom horizontal lines in the center with a pencil. Now count the letters so that half of the letters will come to the left side of the center line and half of the   letters to the right side of the center line. First write the letters on the left side of the center line in reverse order meaning from right to left with the pencil. Then draw the letters on the right side of the center line so that the balance of the given word will be properly maintained.

5.keep the height of the letters straight in one line.

6.Keep the balance of the word in lettering. Divide the portions of the words properly.

7.After completion of the final drawing in pencil, draw all the vertical, horizontal and diagonal outlines of the letters with the help of a ruler and a black microtip pen. Afterwards, colours all the curved lines with black colour and a pointed brush. It is better to colorur the letters in black so that the colouring of the letters would look neat.

8.If a symbol is included, colour it with black or grey colour. Remember that mechanical instruments can be used for this subject.

Beautiful arrangement of the meaning of the word in a design form and neatness in drawing are the elements for success. Keeping this in mind, do a lot of practice. It is the only secret to success.

X

X

✓

Standard most common font :

Arrus	Comic Sans	**Myriad Pro**
AvantGarde	**Cooper**	Old English
Arial	COOPERPLATE	Ravie
Arial Black	Courier New	STENCIL
BANKGOTHIC	Century Gothic	TRAJAN
Bauhaus	Futura	Times New Roman
Brody	Garamond	Times Bold
Brush Script	Helvetica	UNITED STATES
Bookman Oldstyle	Impact	WHiMSY

LETTERING WITH THE HELP OF GRIDS

Those who find it difficult to fit letters within the top and bottom lines, will find it easy to draw letters with the help of grids. lettering done with the help of grids turn out to be neat and uniform. However, the drawing of grids should be accurate. Otherwise the letters would look thick or thin.

For English letters, divide the height of the letters into 5 equal parts and with the same measurements of the divided part, draw vertical lines. Draw all these lines light. Construct the letters with the help of these lines as shown below.

For Devnagri letters, divide the height of the letter into six equal parts.

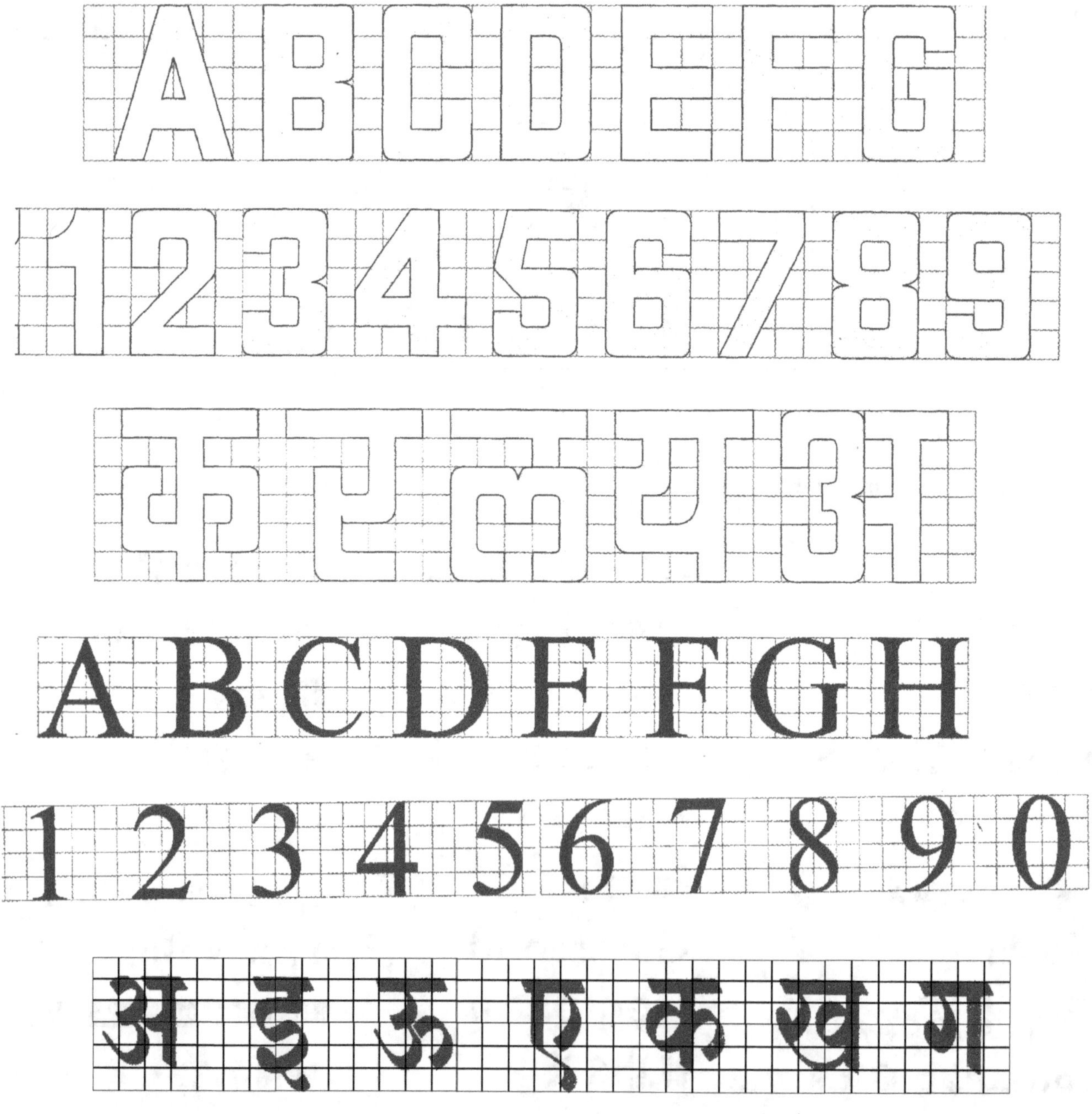

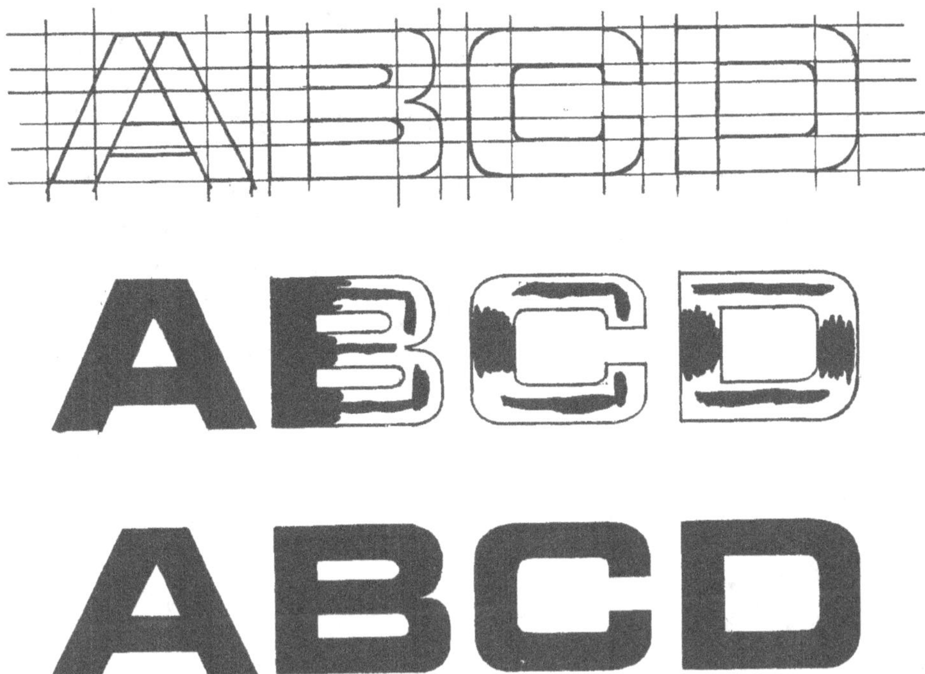

SPACING

Adjustment applied to a block of text or paragraph, to increase or decrease the average distance between letters. In 'proportional letter spacing,' the horizontal space between two characters is adjusted according to the contours of their shape. For example, the letter 'I' will take less space than the letter 'M' in the word 'main.'

letters can be divided in three parts.

1. Regular-**E-H-I-M-N** and **U.**
2. Irregular-**A-F-J-K-L-P-T-V-W-X-Y** and **Z.**
3. Circular-**B-C-D-G-O-Q-S & ?.**

In addition to above we can dived Alphabets in three groups according to Shape and Proportions.

Narrow or Condensed-**BEFIJLPSTY?**

Normal-**CDGHKOQRUVXZ&**

Wide or Extended-**AMNW**

***Always use Optical space and avoid Mechanical space for beautiful lettering.**

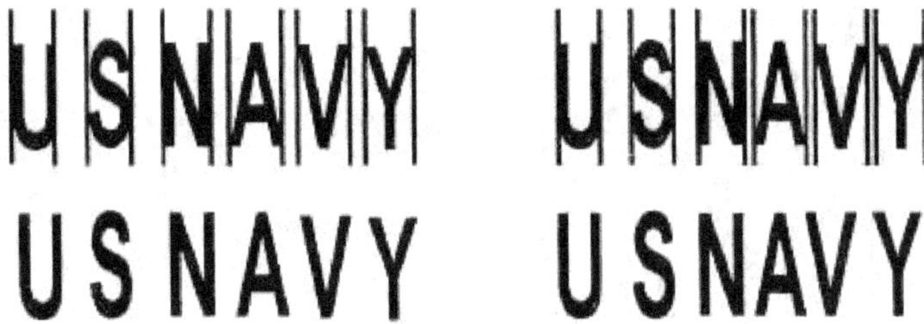

Typography: Sometime lettering used as artistically or aesthetically   to makes text more effective. The Typography means, arrangement of type involves selecting typefaces, point size, line length, line spacing, letter spacing and adjusting the space within letters pairs. The beautiful and positive typography supports and reinforces the message.

COLD
Electric
WET
SPEED
Ribbon
Look
RADIO
HOT
HEIGHT
FEAR
STAMP
POWER
MORE
FURY
Frooti
Cracked
MOTHER

POSTER DESIGN

INTRODUCTION:

Posters are way of communicating your information in the benefit of the society at large. They are best used as an aid to a discussion and should only represent the essence of your topic.

In the same way Advertisement or Ad is another a means of communication how a company encourages people to buy their products, services or ideas. It is usually performed through a variety of media. Ads appear on television, as well as newspapers, magazines and as billboards in streets and cities. The talented and creative minds of designers create visually impactful and memorable designs.

EXERCISE

Technical guidelines: Layout, Colour, Text size and Font type & Visuals.

Before start designing your poster, there are a couple of things you need to do first. Planning your poster is extremely important. The subject of the poster should be meaningful and clear.

\# Start by writing down everything you would like to have on your poster, keeping in mind who your target audience is.

\# Draw your poster on a piece of paper, adding all the different sections and headings you would like to cover in your poster as well as the text. Let someone proof read for grammatical and spelling mistakes.

\# Eliminate any poster " noise" Remember you have less than 3 seconds to draw the attention of your audience to your poster. Poster noise happens when you add irrelevant or unnecessary information to your poster, e.g. information your audience might already know, etc. this will depend on your target audience (colleagues, other specialists in this field, general public, etc.)

\# Have some attention grabbers on your poster. Seeing that you don't have a lot of time to get the attention of your audience you need to make a quick impact, e.g. a catching and interesting statement, photographs, graphics, colours, layout, etc. all of these play a role in attracting your audience.

What you have to do now is to design a new poster on any subject i.e. literacy, Birth control, blood donation, save trees, anti smoking ads etc. Choose your subject and start. you can make this poster by any technique or medium i.e. Line, poster, abstract or cartoon.

Example for headings are:

# title (the audience will view this first)	# introduction
# problem statement	# method
# results	# recommendations
# conclusion	

Your drawing might look something like this:

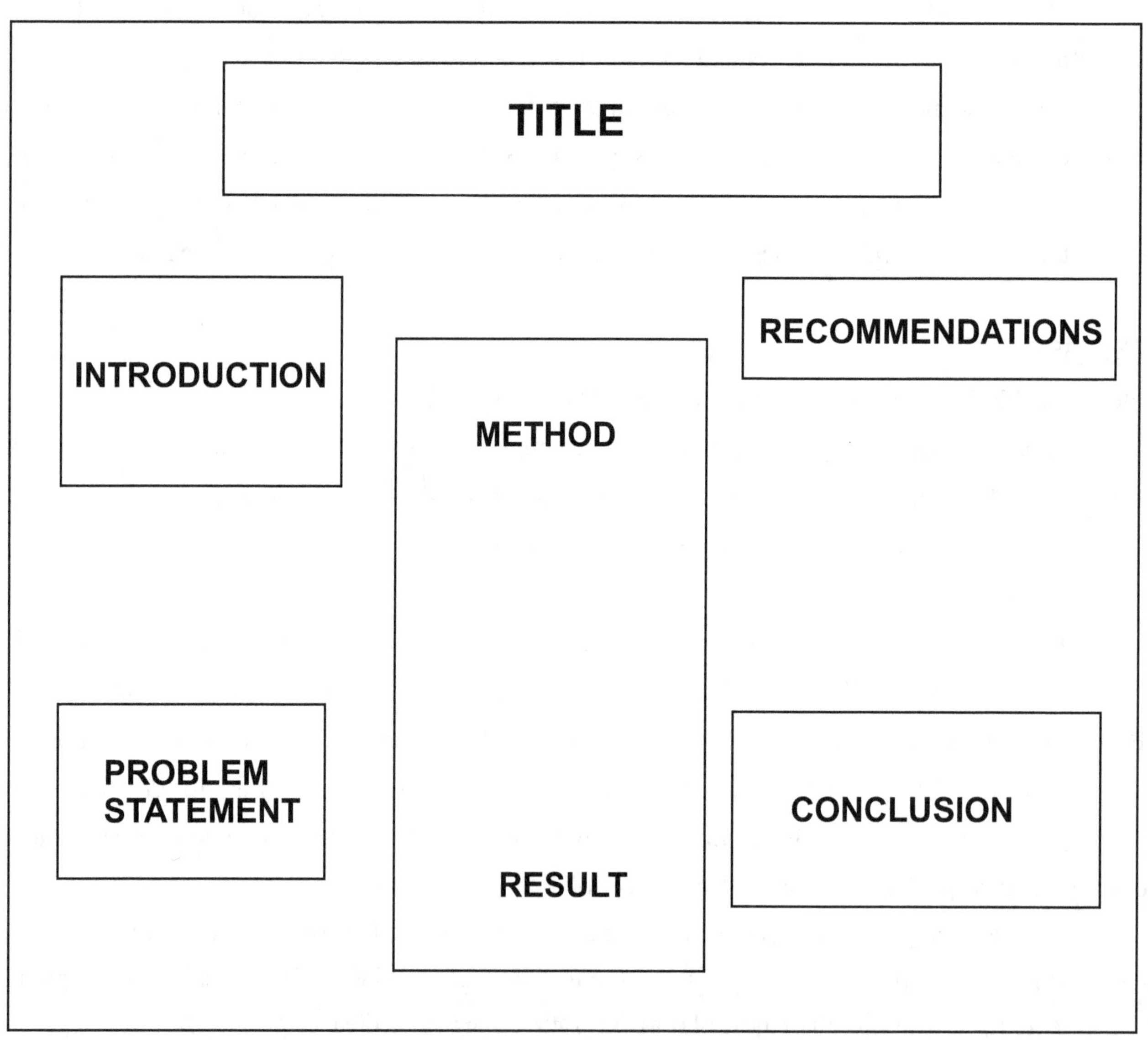

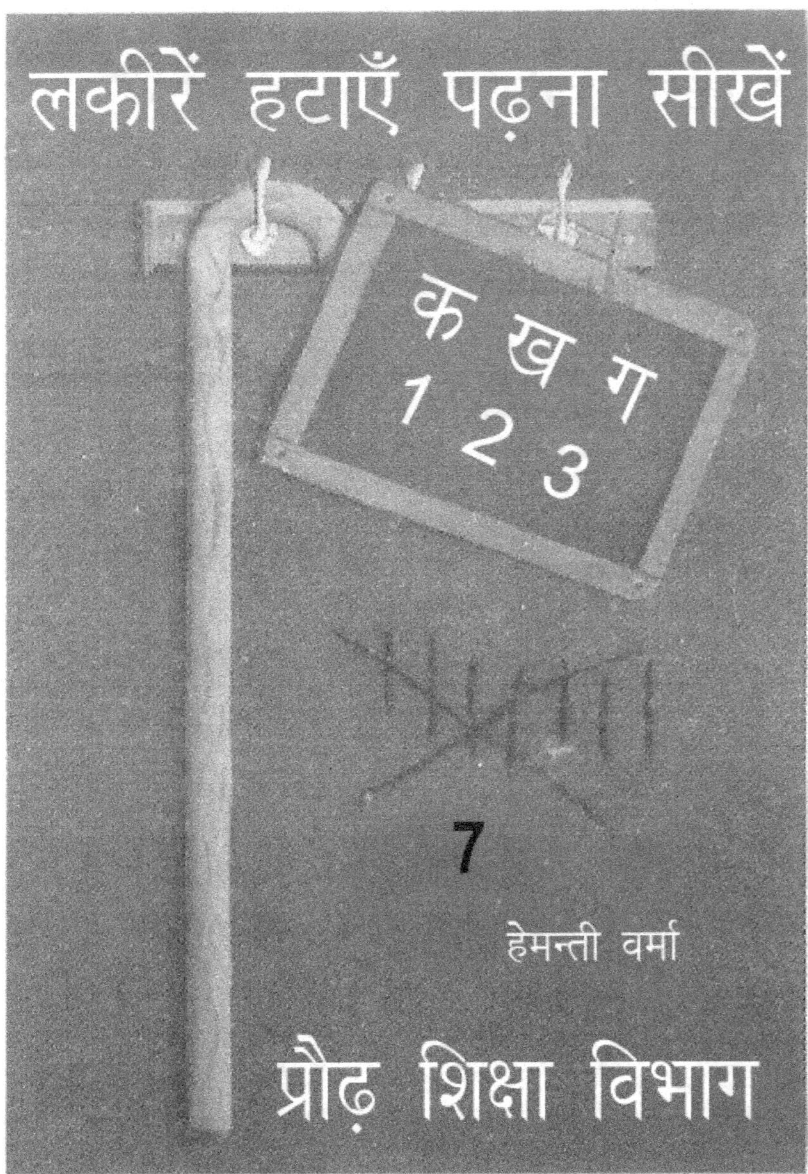

लकीरें हटाएँ पढ़ना सीखें
क ख ग
1 2 3
हेमन्ती वर्मा
प्रौढ़ शिक्षा विभाग

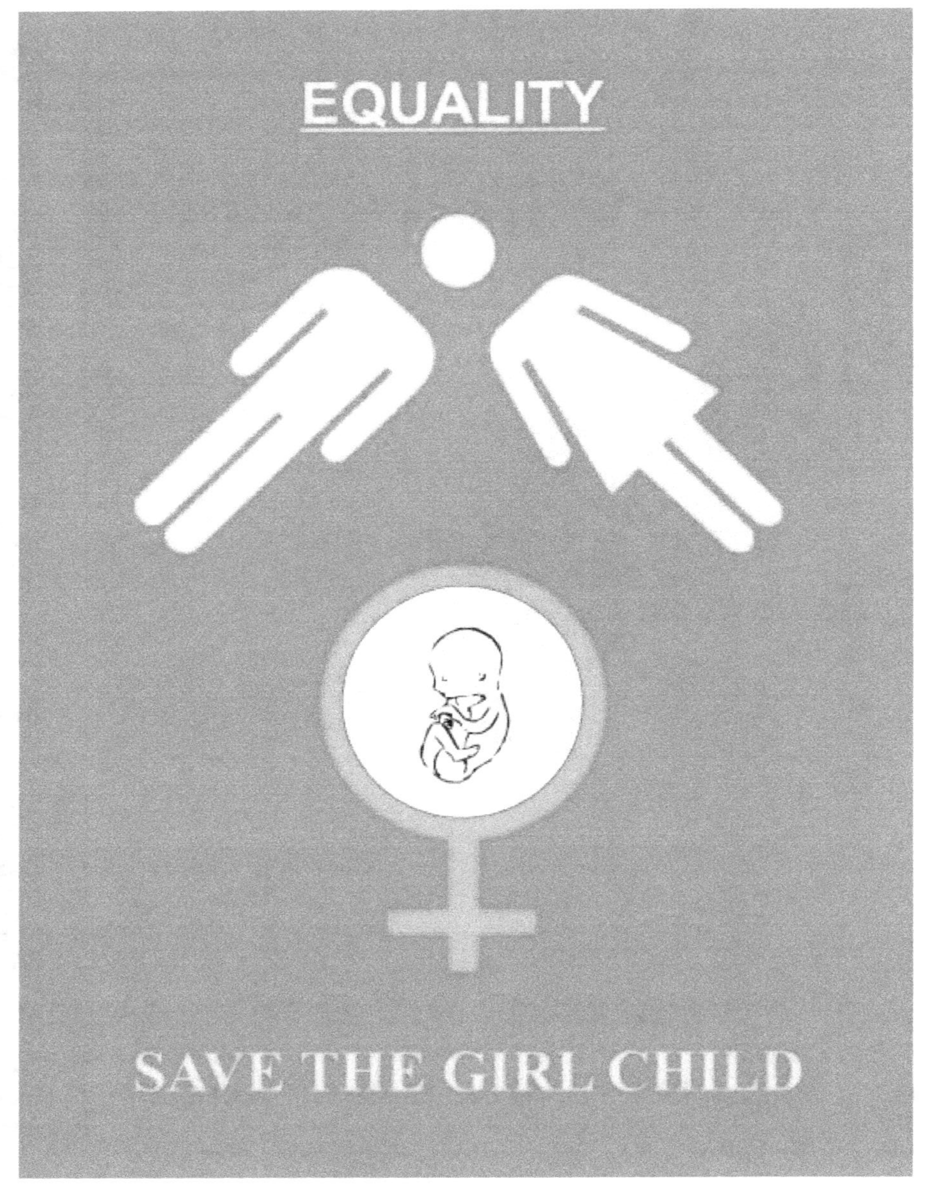

EQUALITY
SAVE THE GIRL CHILD

THE GUN & THE CIGARETTE
Both are dangerous
NO SMOKING
STOP BURNING YOUR LIFE

BEWARE DIRTY GAMES
CAN KILL YOU
PREVENT
AIDS

Just let it
go!
STOP
TERRORISM
'live and let live'

PLASTIC DOESN'T DIE.
BUT MARINE ANIMALS AND BIRDS DO.
100,000 ANIMALS AND BIRDS ARE KILLED EVERY YEAR FROM PLASTIC WASTE.
START RECYCLING YOUR PLASTIC WASTE TODAY.

Melania
charity Fashion Show
new
from
OLD
Date: 9 June 2015 (Thusday)
Start Time: 10 A.M.
Venue: City Centare
La Place, 4th Floor
Free Entry
croyanshop
illustration & concept art
www.xyz.com

Healty
Fresh
Tasty
Freshing Your Day
just with 'One Drink'
Orange Juice
www.abcd.com

BOOK COVER DESIGN

INTRODUCTION

The main goal of every book cover is to **generate excitement**. The front cover is the front of the book, and is marked appropriately, by text and/or graphics, in order to identify it as such, namely as the very beginning of the book. The **front cover** usually contains at least the title and/or author, with possibly an appropriate illustration.

Before you start designing the book cover, you must study the subject of the book thoroughly. It is imperative you select on art method, out of the many, according to the need of the subject. For illustrating we can make use of any kind of colours -water of pencil. While designing the cover, our main motive should be to make the subject matter prominent and clear. Make it a point to not that in cover designing the typography is as important as the picture or illustration is. Therefore, the type also, according to the requirement of the subject, should be properly designed. Design temporary books like magazines are in stylistic text and brilliant colours ,next permanent books in very simple.

EXERCISE

The left page called (*verso*) and right page called (*recto*) are of the same size and aspect ratio, and are centered on the gutter where they are bound together at the spine. Shown below a layout of book cover designed. I strive to create unique eye-catching book covers with attention-grabbing graphics and compelling titles and subtitles. As a result, each book cover appeals to the right audience. A basic unit in book design is the page spread.

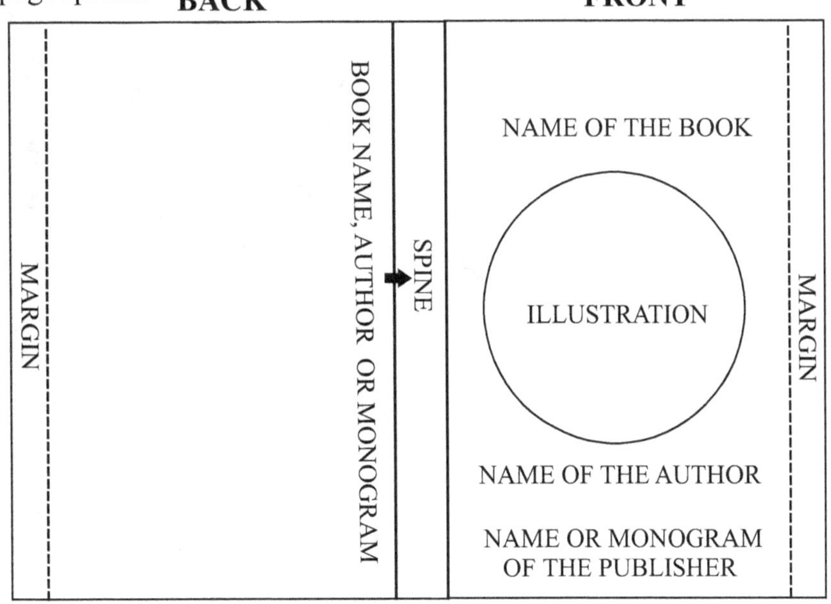

HINDU
PHILOSOPHY
DIJAN PRASAD

लक्ष्मी देवी
औरत

POSTER DESIGN

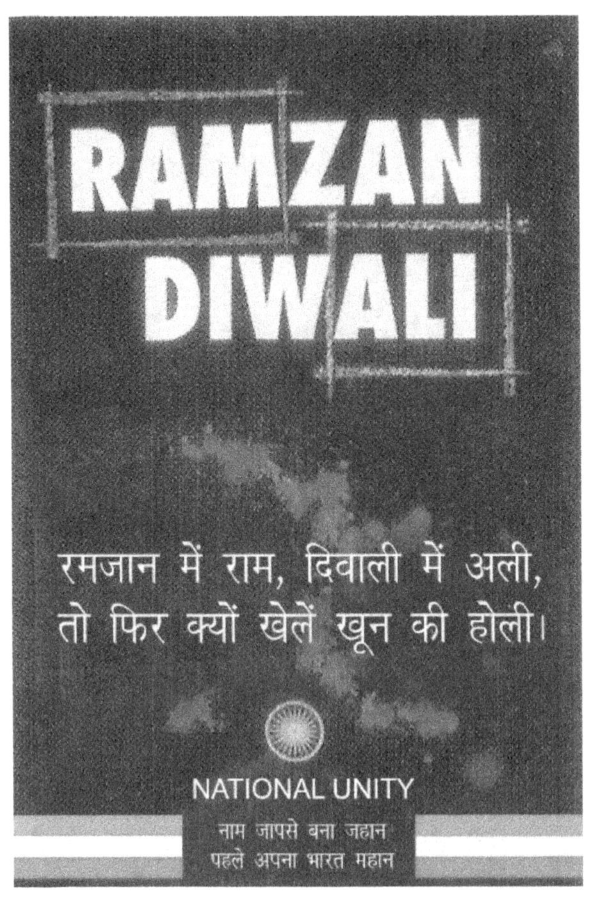

ADVERTISEMENTS

G

TECHNIQUES FOR PRINT MAKING AND CREATING TEXTURES IN DESIGN

Prints and textures make the composition of the design look more attractive. Print making done by taking impressions from objects like leaves, vegetables fingers, textured cloth, crumpled paper, thread stuck, stencil ,toothbrush spray and other articles.

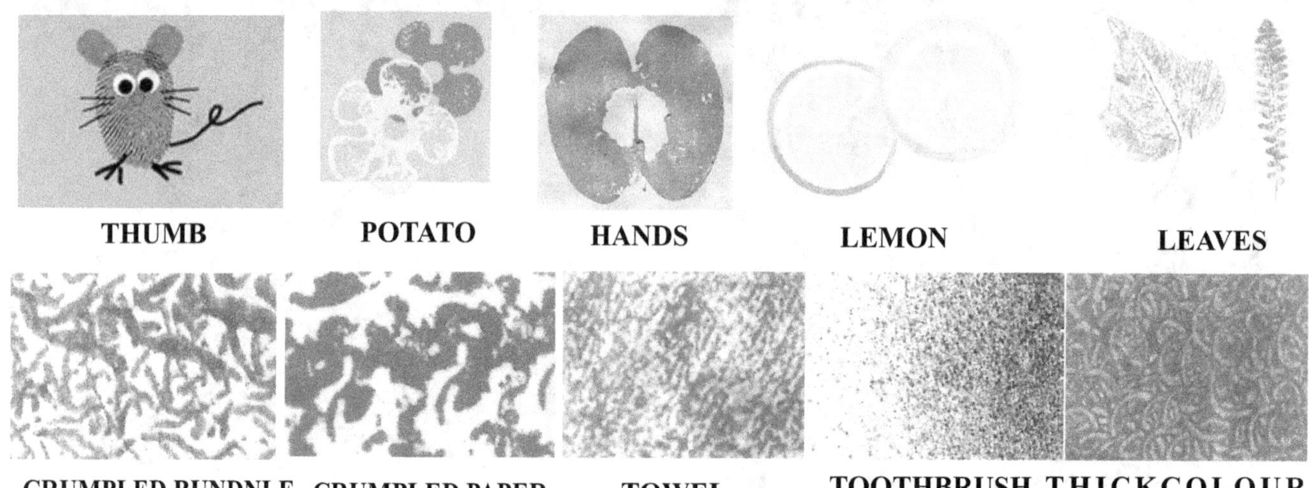

| **THUMB** | **POTATO** | **HANDS** | **LEMON** | **LEAVES** |

CRUMPLED BUNDNLE OF THREAD **CRUMPLED PAPER** **TOWEL** **TOOTHBRUSH SPRAY** **THICKCOLOUR & WOODEN STICK**

HAND PRINTED DESIGNS

Experiment with different types of paints and surfaces. Watercolors, acrylics, inks, even oil paints can be used for printing. You will generally get a clearer print on a smooth surface, but canvas or textured watercolor papers will also work.

Some objects will print with thick paints, others require the paint to be thinned. Sometimes you will press the object into the paint, then print the surface; other times you might apply paint directly to the object to make the print. Try different ways of printing each time you use this technique to be sure you get the effect you want. Use prints to add finishing details, such as textures on walls or trees, or print lightly in a background to suggest distant foliage behind your subject.

Silhouette/Shadow Painting

A silhouette or shadow painting is the image of a subject or scene represented as a solid shape of a single color, usually black, with its edges matching the outline of the subject. The silhouette is typically presented on a light background, usually white, or none at all. The silhouette depicts the edge of an object in a linear form, which appears as solid shape. Silhouette images may be created in any visual artistic media, but was first used to describe pieces of cut paper, which were then stuck to a backing in a contrasting colour, and often framed. Ther artists drew an outline on paper, then painted it in, which could be equally quick.

BATIK (TEXTILE DESIGN)

Evidence of early examples of batik have been found in the Far East, Middle East, Central Asia and India from over 2000 years ago. In Java, Indonesia, batik is part of an ancient tradition, and some of the finest batik cloth in the world is still made there. The word batik originates from the Javanese tik and means to dot.

Batik is both an art and a craft, which is becoming more popular and well known in the West as a wonderfully creative medium. The art of decorating cloth in this way, using wax and dye, has been practiced for centuries. With the help of batik method ,can make new attractive designs on clothes in a short time. Women should specially learn this art.

It is very simple to make batik designs on clothes and very few things are needed for this method. One container is required to heat wax, along with a heater or stove. One plain table or plank of hardboard. A wooden frame on which the cloth is to stretched for waxing. A stencils/pencil, charcoal or coloured chalk for drawing and a brush for blocking og drawing. Paraffin wax for waxing and colours or dyes for colouring the clothes.

To make a batik, selected areas of the cloth are blocked out by brushing or drawing hot wax over them, and the cloth is then dyed. The parts covered in wax resist the dye and remain the original colour. This process of waxing and dyeing can be repeated to create more elaborate and colourful designs. After the final dyeing the wax is removed and the cloth is ready for wearing or showing.

Batik is historically the most expressive and subtle of the resist methods. The ever widening range of techniques available offers the artist the opportunity to explore a unique process in a flexible and exciting way.

TEMPERA AND FRESCO

Tempera: The term Tempera is applied to any paint in which pigment is tempered (mixed) with a water-based binding medium-usually egg yolk. Egg tempera is applied to a smooth and dry surface such as vellum(for illuminated manuscripts)or more commonly to hardwood panels prepared with gesso-a mixture of chalk and size (glue).Hog hair brushes are used to apply the gesso. A layer of gesso grosso (coarse gesso) is followed by successive layers of gesso sotile (fine gesso) that are sanded between coats to proved a smooth, yet absorbent ground. The paint is applied with fine sable brushes in thin layers, using light brush strokes. Tempera dries quickly to form a tough skin with a satin sheen. The luminous white surface of the gesso combined with the overlaid paint produces the brilliant crispness and rich colours particular to this medium. Egg tempera paintings are frequently gilded with gold. Leaves of finely beaten gold are applied to a bole reddish-brownclay) base and polished by burnishing.

Fresco: Fresco is a method of wall painting. In burno fresco (true fresco), pigments are mixed with water and applied to an intonaco (layer of fresh, damp lime-plaster). The intonaco absorbs and binds the pigments as it dries making the picture a permanent part of the wall surface. The intonaco is applied in sections called giornate (daily sections). The size of each giornata depends on the artist's estimate of how much can be painted before the plaster sets. The junctions between giornate are sometimes visible on a finished fresco. The range of colours used in Bruno Fresco are limited to lime-resistant pigments such as earth colours(below).Slaked lime (burnt lime mixed with water), bianco di San Giovanni (slaked lime that has been partly exposed to air, and chalk can be used to produced fresco whites. In fresco secco (dry fresco), pigments are mixed with a binding medium and applied to dry plaster. The pigments are not completely absorbed into the plaster and may flake off over time.

Tempera Painting

fresco Painting

COLLAGE AND MOSAIC

Collage: Collage means an abstract form of art composition. We can utilize waste material such as photographs, pieces of black and white and coloured papers, stickers, coins, match-sticks etc, by pasting on a surface. The world famous artists picasso and Braque prepared paintings with this technique created interesting art pieces.

For a collage composition you have to select pictures from newspaper, magazine cuttings. You have to paste them in such a way that the original pictures no longer remain the same but are transformed into new kinds of images. The original pictures should be cut or torn in a haphazard manner so that the original meaning of images is completely lost. Now paste these pieces side-by-side or overlapping each other to create an abstract composition. In creating collage art proper balance should be maintained and colour scheme should be bright.

You also can use pieces of wires, thread, coloured glass bangles, wool, playing cards, stones and other waste materials by applying fevicol any other type of adhesive, natural or synthetic.

Mosaic: Mosaic is the art of making patterns and pictures from tesserae (small, coloured pieces of glass, marble, and other materials). Different materials are cut into tesserae using different tools. Smalti (glass enamel) and marble are cut into pieces using a hammer and a hardy (a pointed blade embedded in a log). Vitreous glass is cut into pieces using a pair of nippers. Mosaics can be made using a direct or indirect method.

In the direct method, the tesserae are laid directly into a bed of cement based adhesive. In the indirect method, the design in drawn in reverse on paper or cloth. The tesserae are then stuck face-down on the paper or cloth. the tesserae are then stuck face-down on the paper or cloth using water soluble glue. Adhesive is spread with a trowel on to a solid surface-such as a wall and the back of the mosaic is laid into the adhesive. Finally, the paper or cloth is soaked off reveal the mosaic. Gaps between tesserae can be filled with grout. Grout is forced into gaps by dragging a grouting squeegee across the face of the mosaic. Mosaics are usually used to decorate walls and floors, but they can also be applied to smaller objects.

Collage Art

Mosaic Art

Collage: A Ride in a Donkey Cart

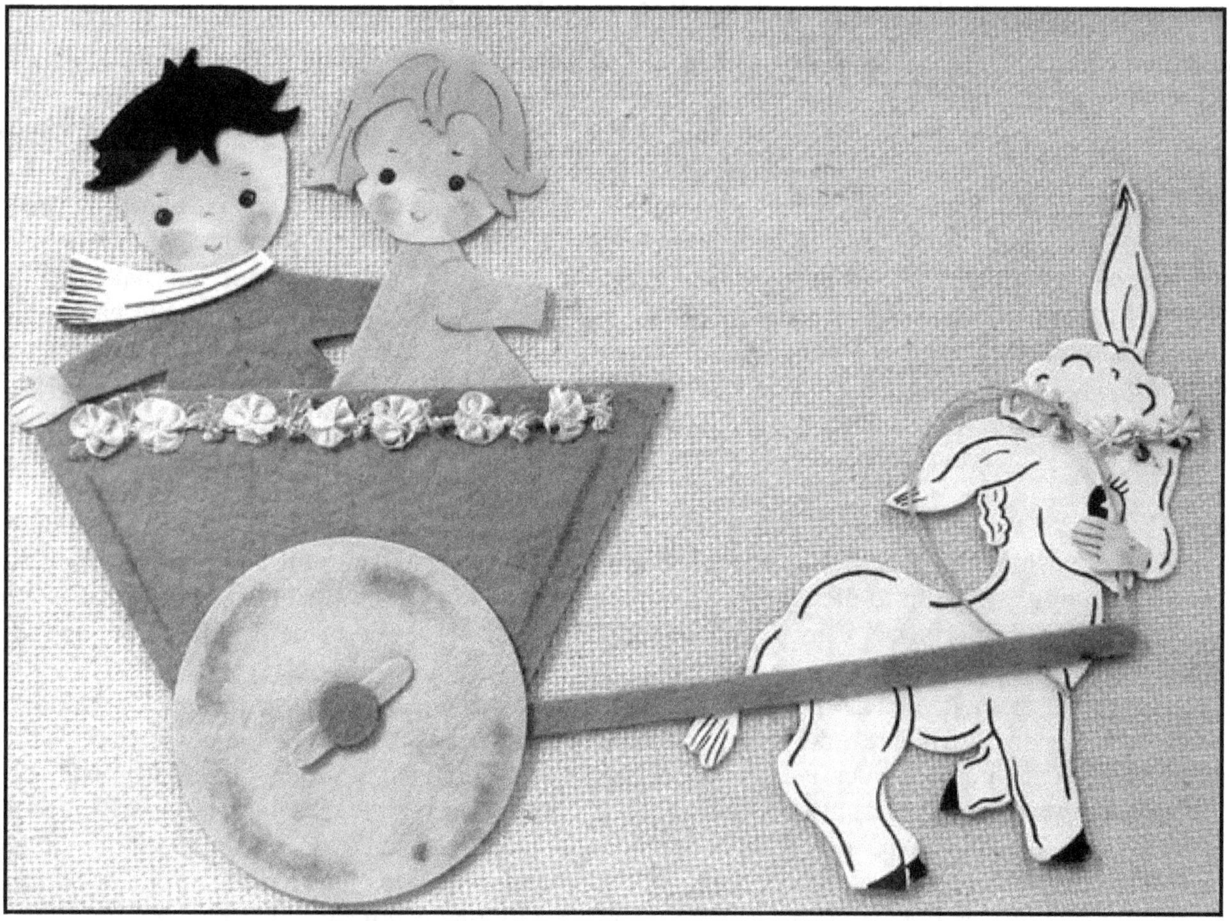

Photo Collage

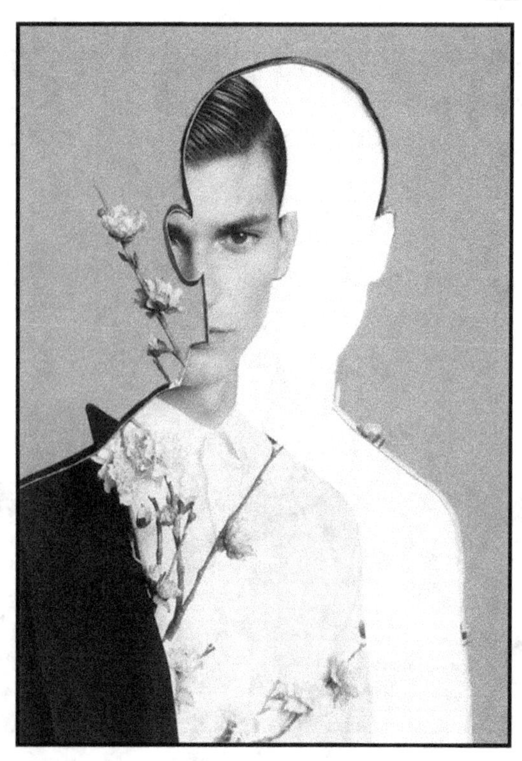

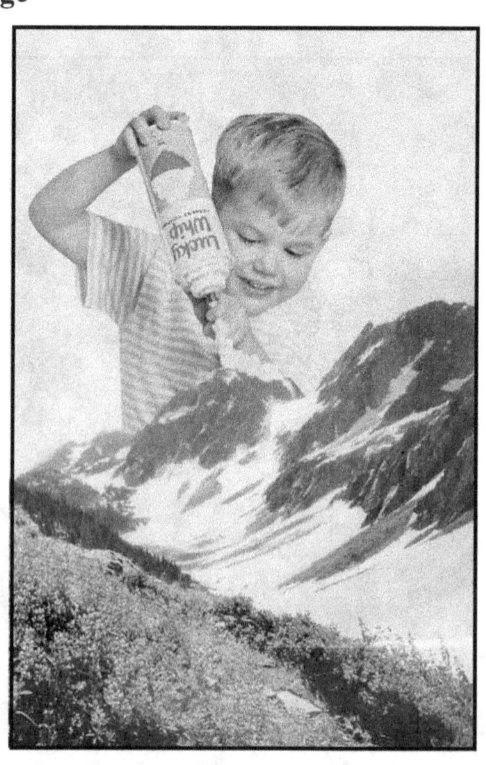

MASK MAKING: Making a mask is a fun, easy and inexpensive way for adults or children to prepare for play or a masquerade party. The masks can cover your entire face or just a small portion over your eyes. The materials required-paper pieces, sometimes textiles, bound with an adhesive, such as glue, starch, or wallpaper paste. After you create your mask, you can attach a ribbon, string or dowel to make it wearable.

PAPIER MACHE` (SCULPTURE)

You can make big, bright sculptures with a simple process called papier mache`. It is easy, but it takes a long time. Moistened paper pulp mixed with glue and other materials or layers of paper glued and pressed together, molded when moist to form various articles and becoming hard and strong when dry, suitable for painting and varnishing .They used to make boxes, trays, or ornaments etc.

Materials you need: container, newspaper, wallpaper paste or flour and warm water, papier mache clay, glue, paintbrush, tempera or acrylic paint, varnish, etc.

1.SOAKING OF PAPER   **2.PULPIING OF PAPER**   **3.MIXING WITH FLOWER & GLUE**

4. MAKING ROLLS   **5. MODELING**   **6.PEST PARTS OF MODEL**

7.COVERINING WITH PAPER

8.PAINTING AND INSTALLATION

GREETING CARD DESIGN

INTRODUCTION

The custom of sending greeting cards are very popular, who exchanged messages of good will to celebrate the New Year, Festival, Birthday, Valentines etc. There are both mass-produced as well as handmade versions that are distributed by hundreds of companies large and small. Greeting card is printed on high-quality paper (such as card stock), and is rectangular and folded, with a picture or decorative motif on the front. Inside is a pre-printed message appropriate for the occasion, along with a blank space for the sender to add a signature or handwritten message. Some cards and envelopes feature fancy materials, such as gold leaf, ribbons or glitter.

EXERCISE

If you've photos or your paintings and a color cartridge paper, you can make your own Greetings cards. Collage, texture print and stencil techniques are also try to card making. Make simple and attractive design and text should be ornamental, calligraphic style. Depict the pictures and colour scheme according to the occasion. Colour harmony is very important for the same.

These instructions show you how to set up the page you're going to make so that when it's folded, everything is where it should be. You can design your card horizentlly or vertically on choice.

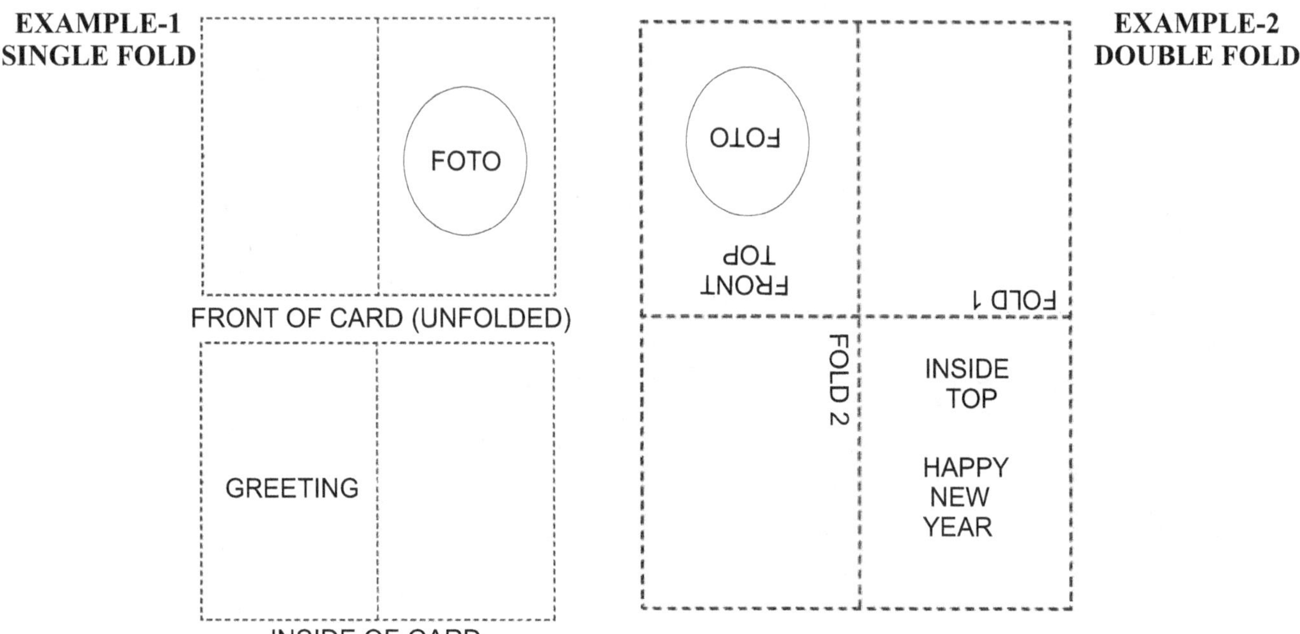

PEACE LOVE LIGHT
Shubh Deepavali
Wishing You a Happy Diwali and
Prosperous New Year

Happy
Birthday

INDIAN FOLK ART

INTRODUCTION

Folk art is traditional art. It is the priceless treasure of any country. These are part of every event, celebration and rituals of our life, viz- Marriage, Birth Festival etc. Folk art is however not restricted only to paintings, but also stretches to other art forms such as pottery, home decorations, ornaments, cloths-making, wood, clay and so on.Other than folk art, there is yet another form of traditional art practiced by several tribes or rural population, which is classified as tribal art. The folk and tribal arts are very ethnic and simple, and yet colorful and vibrant enough to speak volumes about the country's rich heritage.

These folk artists are ordinary people and use very simple method without training(self Taught).These artists create beautiful art effects, paintings and toys. They make use of locally available materials and prepare their own colours and brushes. Twig or bamboo sticks are used as
brush for fine lines. A piece of cloth or cotton is wrapped on the tips of the twig to draw broad lines.

Colours are made from vegetation and locally available minerals. Folk paintings are pictorial expressions of village painters which are marked by the subjects motifs chosen from the epics as well as daily village life, birds and animals and natural objects like sun, moon, plants, trees and symbols. Folk paintings use very vibrant and papers, clothes, leaves, earthen pots, mud walls, etc., are used as canvas.

Various folk paintings of India that have been practiced since ancient times. *Phad paintings, Warli paintings, Madhubani paintings, Patachitra, Kalamkari, Jadupediya, Pichwai , Kalighat* paintings etc. are some of the famous folk art paintings in the country. Folk art in India apparently has a great potential in the international market because of its traditional aesthetic sensibility and authenticity. The rural folk paintings of India bear distinctive colorful designs, which are treated with religious and mystical motifs.

Traditionally in Indian villages, front yard, walls and floor, some drawings are specially prepared during religious festivals or during vratas. Usually, the drawings are made in powder of rice flour is being used for this purpose.

The practice of decorating floor is known with different names as *Alpana* or *Alpona* in Bengal, *Aripana* in Bihar, *Jhuniti* in Orissa, *Mandna* in Rajasthan and Madhya Pradesh, *Salhiya* in Gujarat, *Rangoli* in Maharashtra, *Muggu* in Andhra Pradesh and *Kalamezhuthu, Kolam* in Karnataka, Tamil Nadu and Kerala and in Uttar Pradesh it is known as *Chowkpurna* or *Aripan*.

Main characteristic features of folk painting:
*used strong or fluent outline.
*space are filled with limited range of colours.
*mainly done on cloth and earthen wall.
*colours are very sober.
*no space left vacant in composition.
*depiction more then one figures in painting.

some motifs are shown in the following. These are both floral and geometrical. You can draw and paint these designs on greeting cards, cushion covers, sarees etc., try to innovate new designs combining different motifs.

EXERCISE

To put your paint on the brush is called 'loading the brush'.Put some Red Earth on your wet palette and load some paint on your round brush. Hold your brush on an angle and gently push it down onto the paper, the tip should spread slightly, drag the brush down then slowly lift to get a nice tail. Wipe off the excess paint.

Let's have some more practice at different borders.

Elements of folk painting:

Madhubani or Mithila Painting- Bihar
Background totally covered with flower and leaf motifs. bright colours Red, yellow and blue are used in the picture. Big eyes and long chin are special features of this painting style.

Patachitra-Orissa and West Bengal
The "pata-chitra" means painting on cloth for pilgrims who visited to Jagannath temple in Puri or Kali temple in Kolkota. colors are used white, black, red, yellow, blue, and ochre.

Kalamkari - Andhara Pradesh
A kalam (Pen) kari blocks are used to print the design on the cloth in batik painting. Both for dying and painting, vegetables colours are used.

Worli- Maharastra
Human figures are simplified into trangles and few straight lines. The painting is more a statement of Human and Nature relationship than religious sentiments.

Phad -Rajasthan
Generally depicts the royal and secular theme. Paintings are painted on flat ground. All the colours like red, yellow, green, black are very warm and decorative. Human figures are drawn in a very simple manner, thought appear to be short.

Tanjore- Tamilnadu
The figures are large and the faces are round. Theme-Hindu deities. The rich vibrant colors, dashes of gold, semi-precious stones as well as the relief work which gives them a three dimensional effect.

BIRDS & ANIMALS DRAWING

INTRODUCTION

While drawing human figures we can have models before us. But to draw sketches of animals and birds it is not necessary to roam in forests. You can find some of them in a zoo. You can observe their shape, movements, appearance, mannerisms, gentries, etc. Domestic animals and birds are not difficult to find in your neighborhood. You should have as many sketches as possible, catching them in different poses and moods.

EXERCISE:

BIRD

Circles and ovals are the basic shapes to draw any animal. The difference and variation among them lies in the formation of the head and legs. Always start the day with drawing a number of circles free hand on a rough page.

When drawing birds you have to place the circular shape meant for head more close to the egg shape of the main body. Also mark the correct place of the eyes in relation to the beak.

After placing the basic shape, add the line suggesting neck. Now define the major parts of the birds ignoring the fine details. Your bird will start appearing on the paper. Add main shadows and major dark areas and texture of the feathers. The only thing left now is the fine details around the focal point.

Flying Birds

Watching birds in flight is thrilling. The wings of small birds flap too quickly for the eye to catch. There are three elements to block in before adding any details: posture proportions, and angles. Print out a bird model and practice sketching angles in flight with bent wings.

Some other Animals:

LANDSCAPE

INTRODUCTION

Since times immemorial man has lived with nature. Thus nature's influence on mankind is immeasurable. Man has found solace under natural environments. In leisure moment's man captures nature's abundant beauty in his drawings. Landscape is one of its forms, which undoubtedly is the most talked about subject of the Art World. Whatever man sees around him he tries to capture it by drawing in the form of a picture in his drawings. Landscape is one of its forms, which undoubtedly is the most talked about subject of the Art World. Whatever man sees around him he tries to capture it by drawing in the form of a picture.

EXERCISE

Basic Thing of Drawing: To create a sense of distance in picture, you need to be familiar with the technique of perspective. A common type of perspective used in drawing landscapes is central perspective. Central perspective is straight forward, requiring a single vanishing point, from which an array of vanishing lines are drawn. If you show nearby objects larger and those distance as small, and due to atmosphere effect closer objects looks clearly and sharply .On the other hand, distant objects appear a little hazy, indistinct and bluish. By adding shading gradations to the foreground vs. background, the effect of depth is enhanced. You can use a viewfinder to make better compositions by accurately viewing the subject as through a camera and choosing the right components vertical or horizontal.

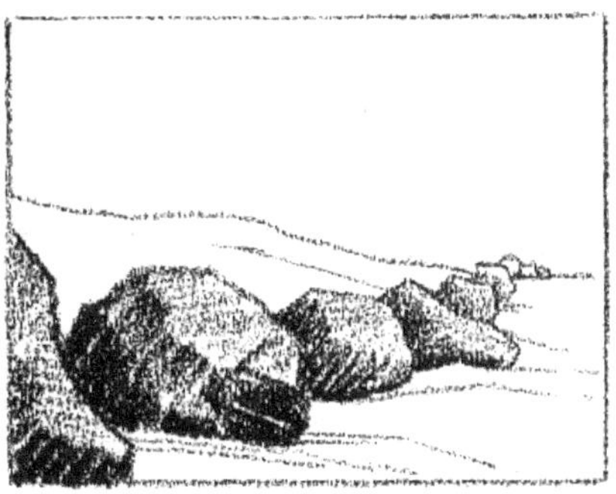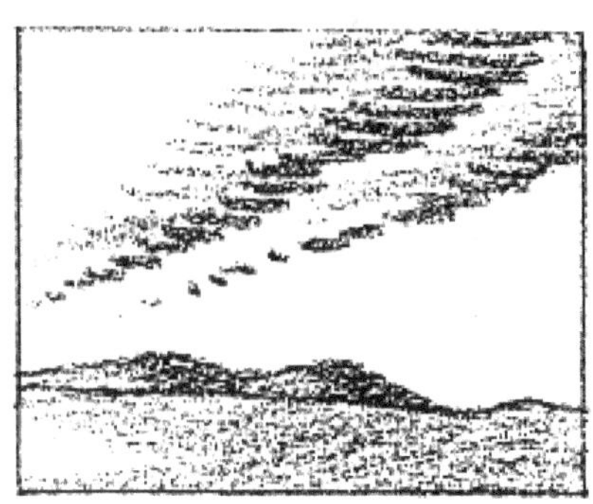

Viewfinder: It is allows the viewer to see and select a certain part of picture more effectively in landscape study. You can move it all over the picture until you find the most suitable part to draw. You always need some way of limiting the parameters, so that the final picture doesn't become too broad for your drawing base.

In the large picture below, there are three outlines superimposed on the general landscape, and you might decide to use one, two or three in your final composition. Each has possibilities but you can choose for yourself the one that is most satisfying to your aesthetic sense.

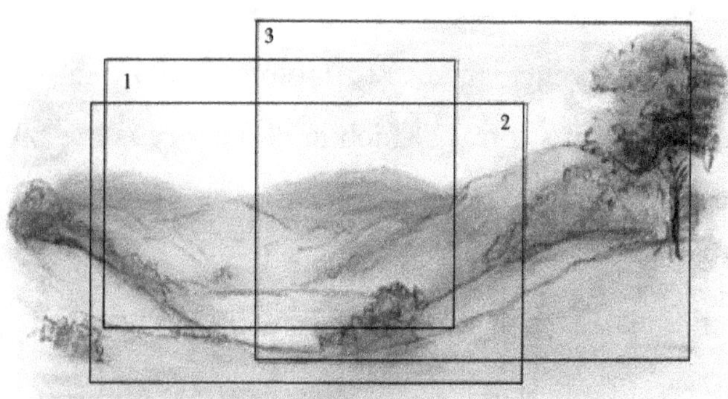

TREES: It is an essential part of any landscape. Every tree is different, and each will present its own challenges. Before making the drawing of any tree or plant, observe it carefully. This kind of drawing can be made easy with the help of the basic shapes or simple forms.

The trunk of trees are various types; some are thick, rough and smooth. After sketching the trunk, make its branch and leaves. Give special attention to the joints of branches and the natural bend of the branches.

In the same way the leaves come out of the branches. It is never necessary to draw each and every leaf to show the trees. It is enough to give the complete feel of the huge tree.

Add in the main areas of tone, shading the dark areas and leaving brighter areas clear. Drawing from life is important, so that the highlights and shadows all make sense, depending on the angle of the sun.

Pencil Drawing

SHRUBS AND BUSHES: When shrubs and bushes are seen individually, in isolation, differences in size and scale are not apparent.

Often, it is better to see shrubs and bushes together, in groups as found in gardens-shape against shape, texture, size against size. shrubs are often soft-edged, but should be seen at first as solid, hard-edged shapes, either light against dark or dark against light look for different contrasts before you start drawing.

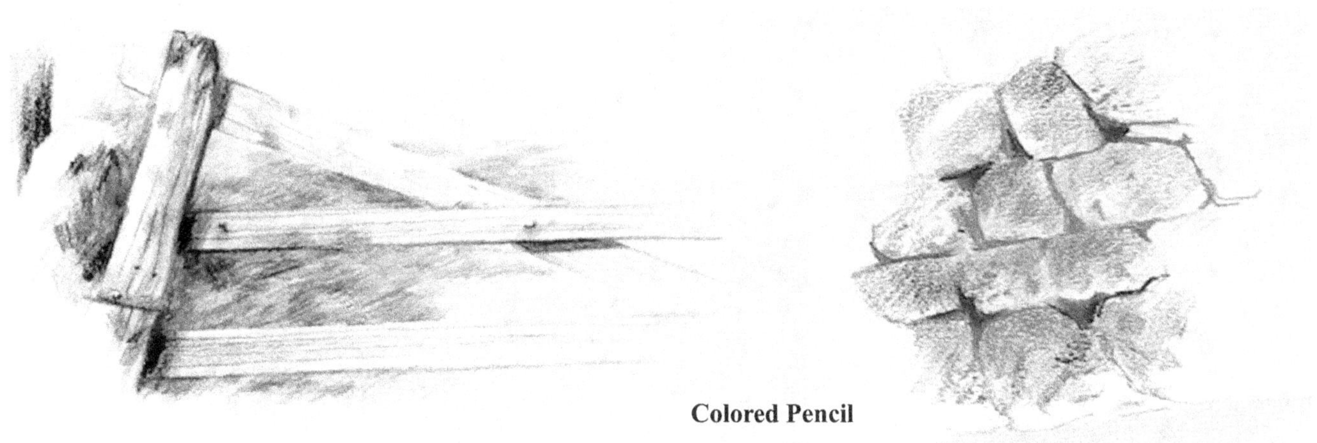

Pen Drawing

Fence and Walls : Knowing how to draw different materials such as brick, stone and wood comes in handy when you want to draw a Fence and wall. These elements add a range of textures that make your drawing more interesting.

Colored Pencil

Clouds: When painting clouds, start by sketching the outline, but use subtle value changes to show the shape and depth of their forms. You can achieve value changes by varying the type of pressure of your pencil strokes or shades of colours. Be particularly conscious of the location of your light source.

Sea and Waves: To draw the sea you need a lot of patience, Capture some moods and motion of waves which change continually. Here are informality and looseness with interesting positioning of wave crests. Analyze the various phases of angry and peaceful waters wave.

Water falls: Here the direction lines of the pencil are showing waterfalls. Falls of all kinds present a challenge to the scenic artist. They are refreshing to watch and gratifying to capture on paper.

Pencil Shading →

Rocks and Mountains: You can make the drawing more interesting by varying the shapes and sizes of the rocks This appears to be a simple drawing, but its subtle value changes make it challenging The outer shape of some of the background rocks is defined by the shading behind them. The rocks are described in values without line being used. Both line and tint and shade may be used in combination.

Desert: Deserts make excellent landscape subjects because they provide a variety of challenging textures and shapes. This drawing is unique because the shading in the foreground is darker than the shading in the background. This effect is caused by the position of the light source (the sun); it is to the right of the main rock formations, creating shadows on the left side of the rocks.

Reflection and shadow: There are some simple sketch and guidelines which may be helpful to study of reflection on water, a highly varnished floor or a wet street. Study careful about still water reflects, running water reflects or night time or moonlit night reflections. Every time you, the reader, are around reflections, make your own observations as to what is happenings.

Charcoal

sunrise and sunset: Learn to draw sunrise or sunset is much better position to paint such a scene in other media. In fact, by mastering black and white drawing, the value in colour painting will vastly improve. This is said with the realization that proper value judgment be made with regard to a particular colour (value being the darkness or lightness of a given colour).

The evening twilight (dusk) and morning twilight (down) have the same problems when it comes to pencil drawing. But, both cases, the sun is below the horizon. When sketching in front of a sunset or sunrise, do not attempt to capture an entire scene at a sitting; the sky changes too rapidly for that. Sketch portions quickly and make indicates of the "theme" of what you see. The cloud arrangement may stay with you, but their exquisite "mood" are only seconds long. Fleeting observations may be recalled easier when fragments and details have been duly noted on a small sketch pad.

Water Colour

**Pencil
Shading**

Snow and Ice: The snow and ice highly reflective surface make a beautiful pattern. When you go out to do winter sketching, look for a pattern such as a plowed field, or shapes like rolling hills to create a design. Create abstract shapes with landscape elements such as fields, trees, houses and winding roads. After sketching, blending the pencil mark into soft gray tones and add more dark to accenting the separations, the snow is the white of the paper.

TIPS FOR LANDSCAPE DRAWING / PAINTING

When painting a landscape, it is essential that you are able to illustrate a visual "sense" of depth, through your brush strokes, colors, and composition. consider the most effective ways to describe a sense of distance and atmospheric perspective in your landscapes—and it doesn't matter whether you're using a brush, pencil, or pastel.

1. Overlap various elements within your composition so that some are forced forward or backward in the scene.

2. Use less detail, texture, and definition when painting objects in the mid-ground and background of the landscape.

3. Paint with lighter values and less contrast for distant elements.

4. Use cool colors to push elements farther into the background.

5. Use warmer, darker colors to bring elements forward into the foreground.

6. As elements recede in the distance, paint them at a much smaller scale than objects in the foreground.

7. Man made structures, animals or human figures will further enhance the center of interest. They take the role of main actors.

8. The subordinate and surrounding elements should direct or lead the viewer to that center of interest by means of pointers and visual paths. It should not be placed in the center nor halfway in the picture, preferably in any of the 1/3 portions.

9. This area should not be blocked, not even partially. This will diminish its importance. An effectively designed center of interest will grasp and hold the viewer's attention.

HOUSES & BUILDINGS

INTRODUCTION

A house or Building often enhance a scene. It makes the area look lived in. A farm or little village has been included in thousands of landscapes. Before we add countryside around these unpretentious structures, we need to sketch them in their simplest form. Building attachments, such as porches, steps, steeples, windows, doors, etc.,may be lightly indicated in the next step. Having done this, the setting and surroundings remain to be added. As they are planned, think of the larger shape into which the entire conception may fit. The scene needs to possess a feeling of unity.

Buildings are rigid. Rigidity seems to invite the use of the mechanical ruler. For drafting purposes and architectural renderings this is all right. For the scenery artist it is suggested that he seek to express himself without the aid of edging tools.

EXERCISE

Draw lightly with your pencil. This makes it easier to erase mistakes and other marks that change slightly in later steps. When you have finished, use a pen or fine felt-tip marker to darken the pencil marks that make up the finished drawing. Then gently erase any remaining pencil marks.

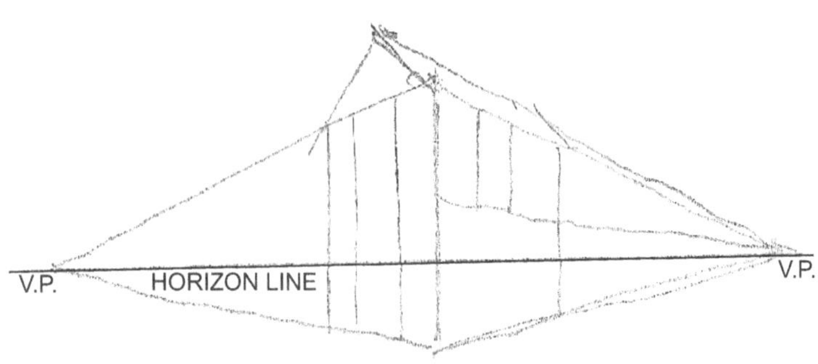

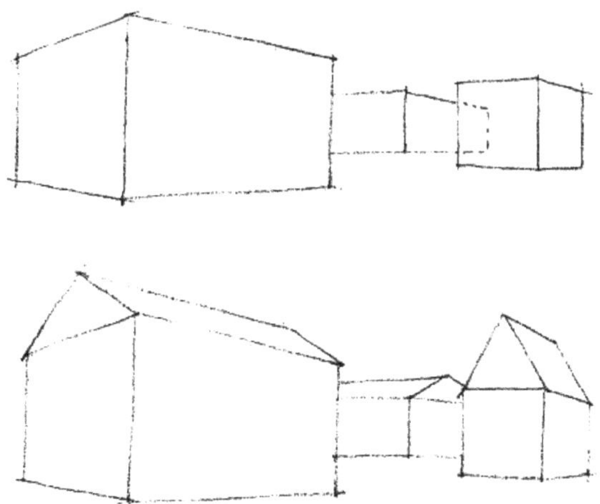

POINT OF VIEW

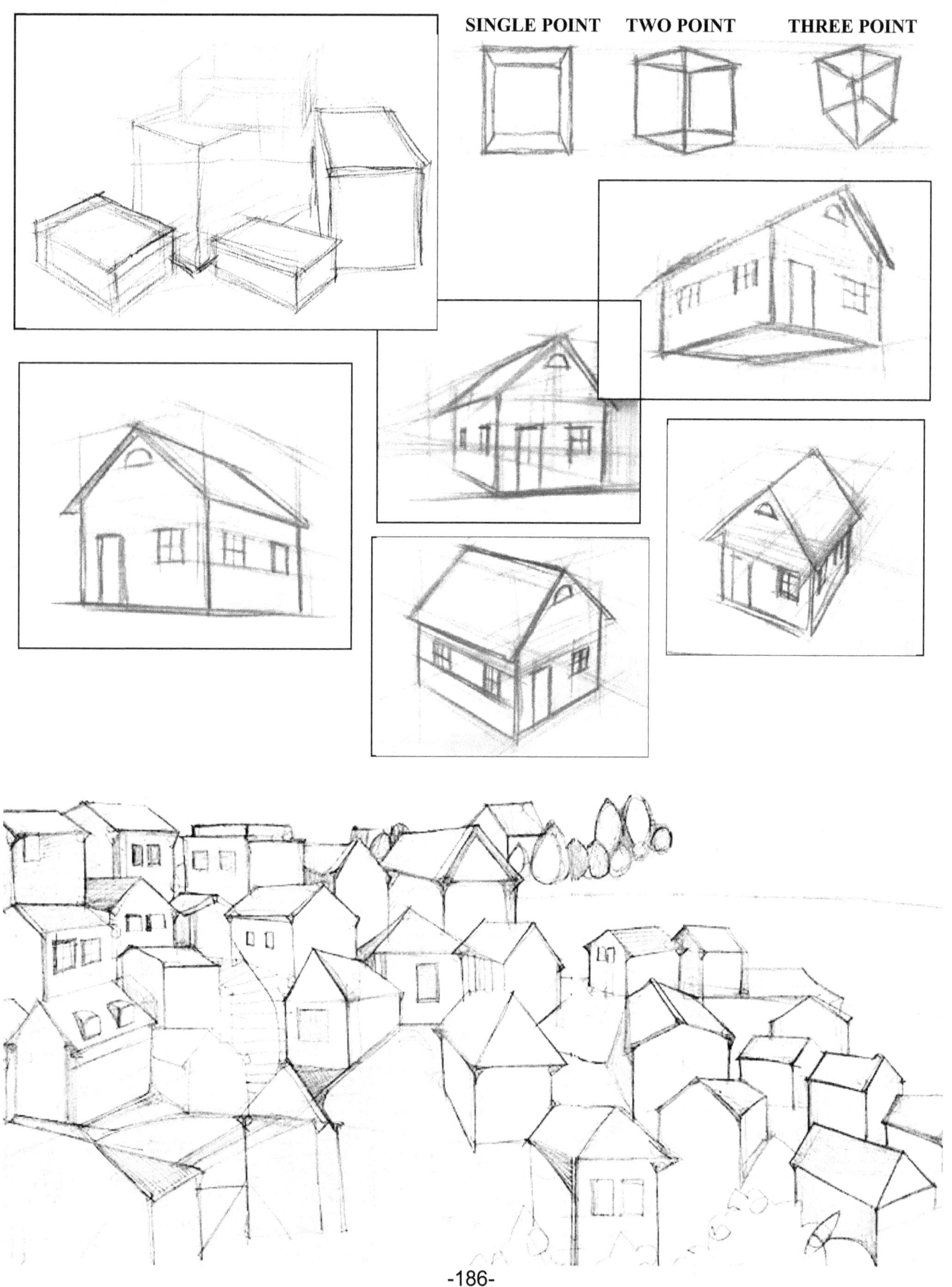

Besides the buildings themselves, some of the most entertaining and rewarding objects to draw in streets and towns are items of what are called 'street furniture'. These include pillar, street lamps, poster hoarding, notices and road signs, seats, tubes of plants, etc.

Also, try drawing from your own home- the windows, garden, yard or balcony can all be of interest. The height from which you look at your subject, knowledge of perspective is more important.

A great advantage of drawing from your home is that of choosing your weather and lighting conditions. Strong shadows can also add interest and character, particularly in early morning or afternoon. try making several drawings of the same subject under different lighting conditions.

Sometime drawing of old buildings is you will come into contact with the past with understand their nature and character. Learn, also, the clues which will help you to identify their date and construction.

Drawing buildings in free hand , the lines of most buildings are broken by protuberances, while plants, trees, lampposts and other objects interrupt and soften then.

FINISHING

INTERIOR STUDY-1

INTERIOR STUDY-2

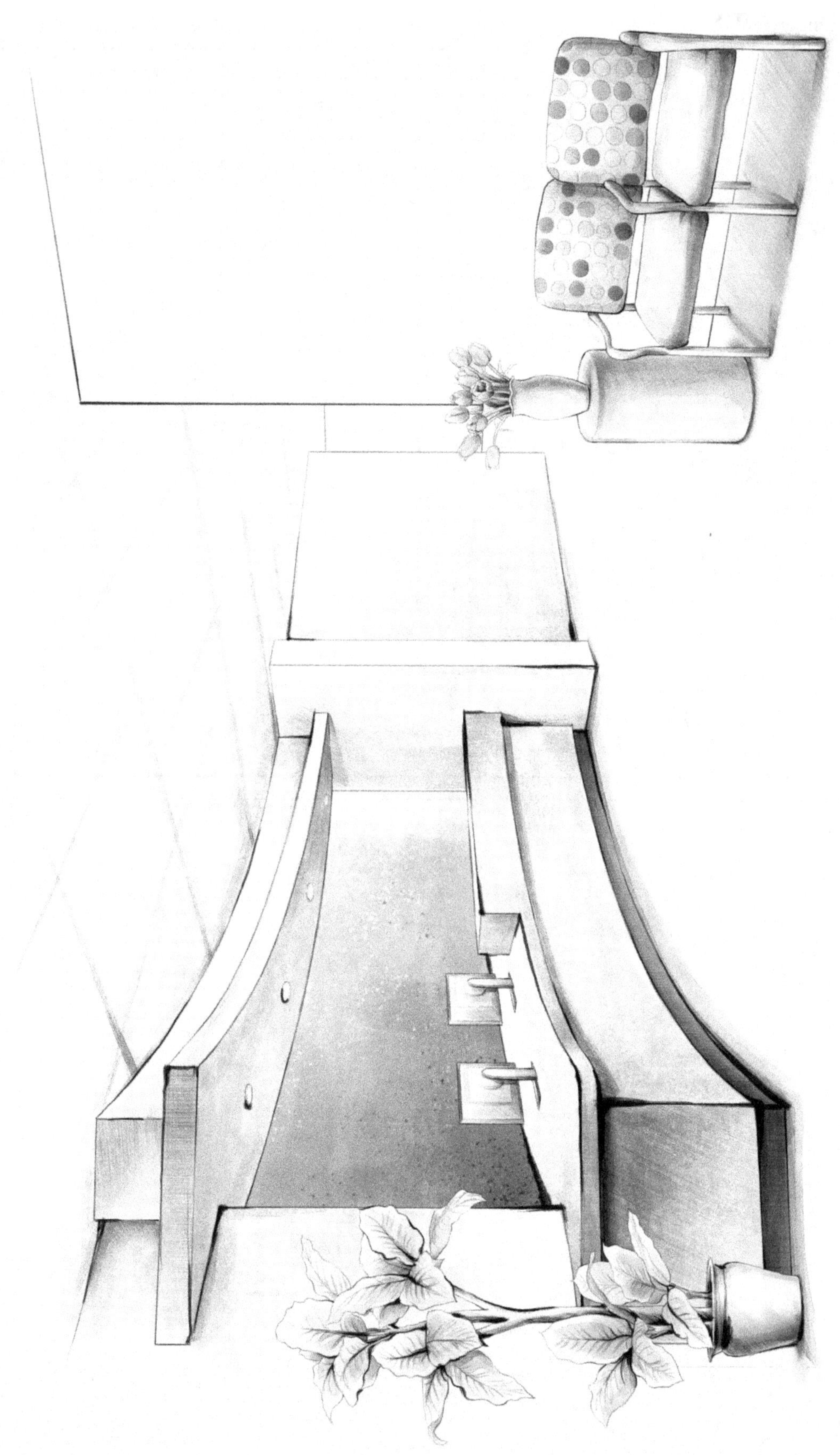

VEHICLES

INTRODUCTION

Drawing Vehicles is the perfect app for students that could use a bit of assistance learning to draw various figures. This app provides step-by-step instruction on drawing and decorating a number of vehicles. From the basics of understanding perspective and elemental proportions of vehicles, to the application of colour media to define shapes and contours, this course demonstrates everything needed to make your drawings look like the professional quality artwork being done in automotive styling studios today.

EXERCISE

Sketch a basic box shape and details such as the wheels, headlights, grill, windows and interior. Add some shading to the wheels. Erase obsolete lines. Shade the form, using uniform line work to create a smooth appearance. Add another layer of dark to the wheels and shadows, giving them more contrast against the lighter values of the vehicle. Rich dark and graduated values give this Jaguar a shiny metallic appearance. It is important to make uniform pencil lines to create the smooth, metallic look for the vehicle's surface.

Remember, the same principle of **perspective** is used in the drawing of a vehicle, which you have studied in house drawing. The portion close to us looks large and the farther portion looks smaller.

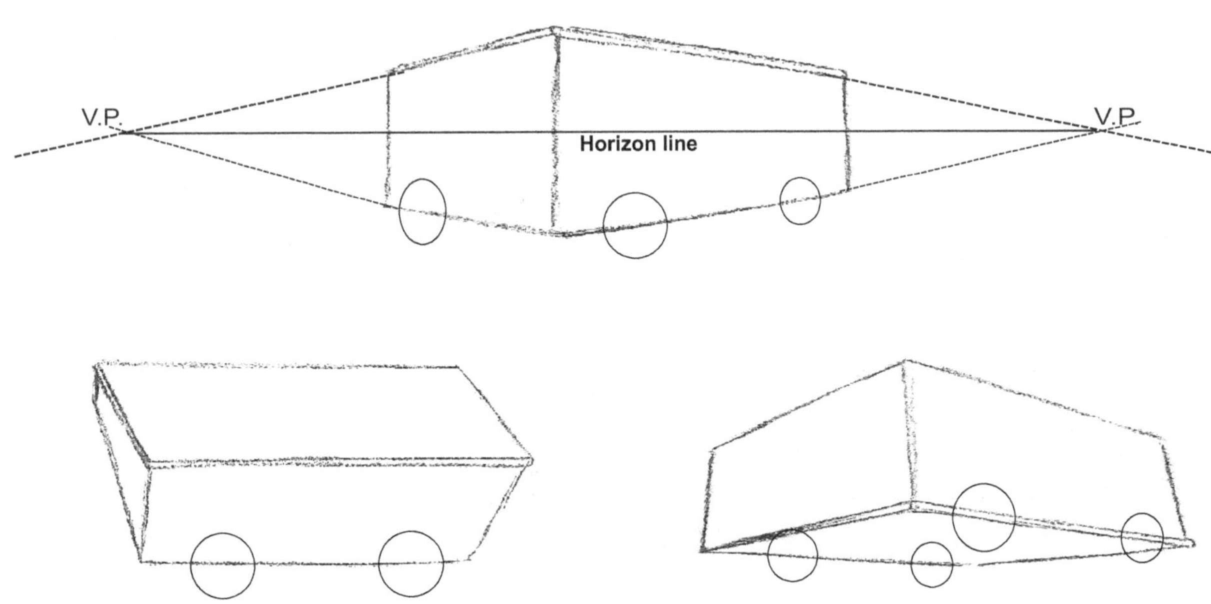

STUDY FROM DIFFERENT ANGLE (RENDERING)

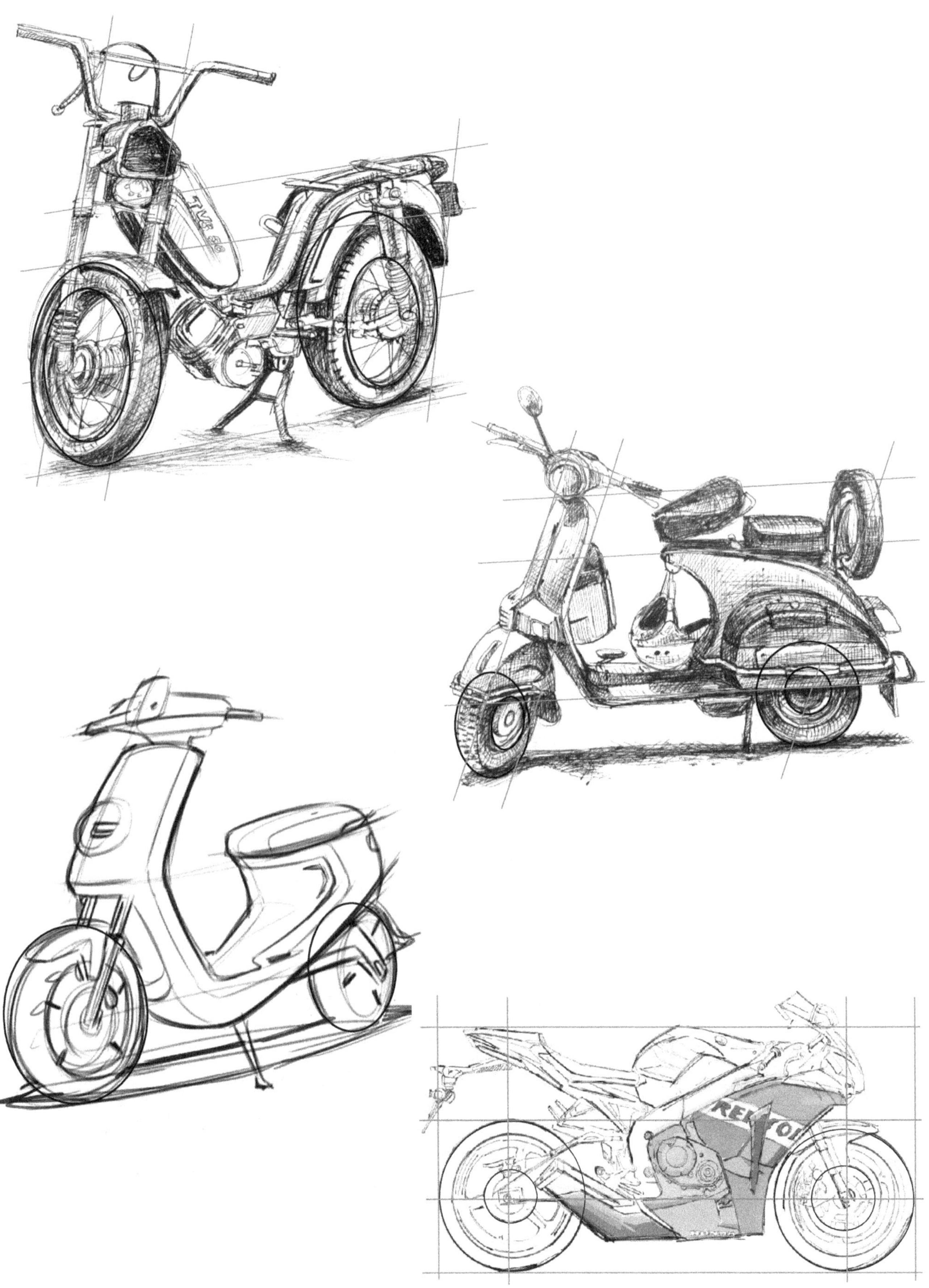

PORTRAIT

INTRODUCTION

Earlier you have studied about basic structure of human head in various angles and parts of the head- nose, ears, eyes and lips. Now we are going to study about portrait drawing. To portray include different types of subjects, character and the mood of the people like children, women, men or even self portrait.

You can draw a portrait using any of the popular **media:** pencil, charcoal, pastel, pen and ink, water colour, felt- pen, etc. Each one of them, however, will produce different effects due to the specific characteristics of the **medium** and the **technique** used.

In a portrait drawing the special attention required on **lighting, pose, eyes, facial expression, clothing, hair** and the **background.**

EXERCISE

First draw basic outlines in light hand. You can either grid or freehand your outlines. An HB pencil is perfect for outlines, not too dark and not too light. This step is very important in obtaining a likeness of your subject. If your outline doesn't resemble the person, your final product won't either. So take your time and get features and proportions correct. It's not uncommon for your outline to take a few hours. Next start working on the hair. But pay attention to which way the hair is flowing. Always work from top to bottom, left to right, just like reading. The mechanical pencil use to add the fine details and the 6B to push the darker areas, adding contrast.

Understanding planes: A head is more complex, but it can still be reduced to a few masses consisting of light, half tone, and shadow. Within each mass are various "planes," or the different side of an object. For example, a cube has six planes, of which we see only three at a time. So when shading a portrait, Change the direction of lines as per the mouldling. Study the given example below.

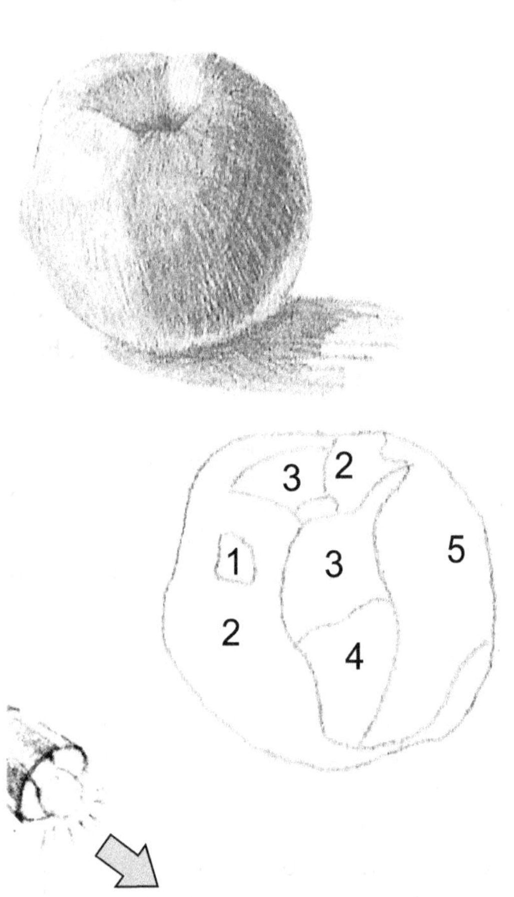

LIGHT: When drawing a portrait it is very important to consider the direction of the light falling on the model. If light falls on the face from the left corner of the page, the effect would be as shown below. Exercise using live models and photographs and try to achieve the same shaded effect on your own, by varying the pressure on the pencil.

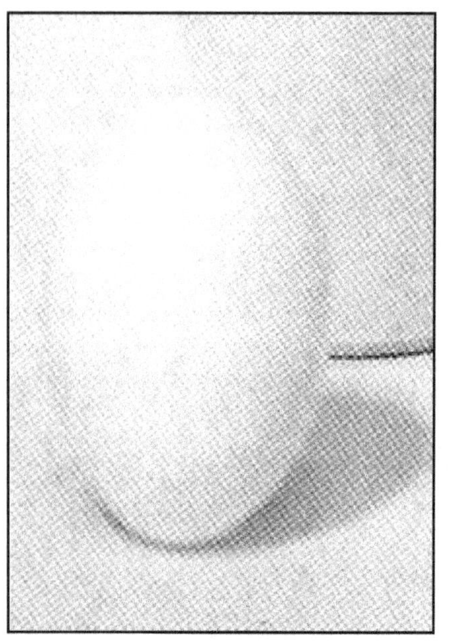

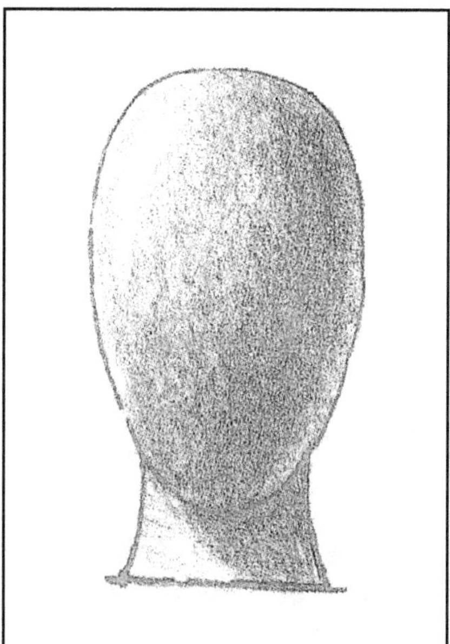

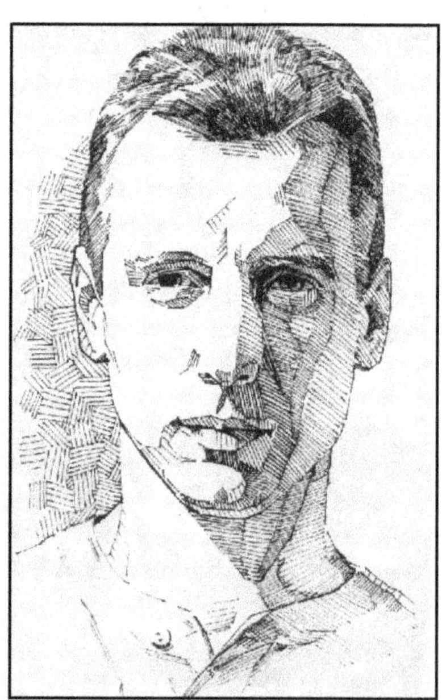

Blending Pencil Techniques:
        In portrait drawing you can use following techniques to smudge or blend marks made with charcoal, Conté crayon, pencil or other drawing media. Different values can be obtained   by Varying pressure on the pencil and using different grades of pencils.

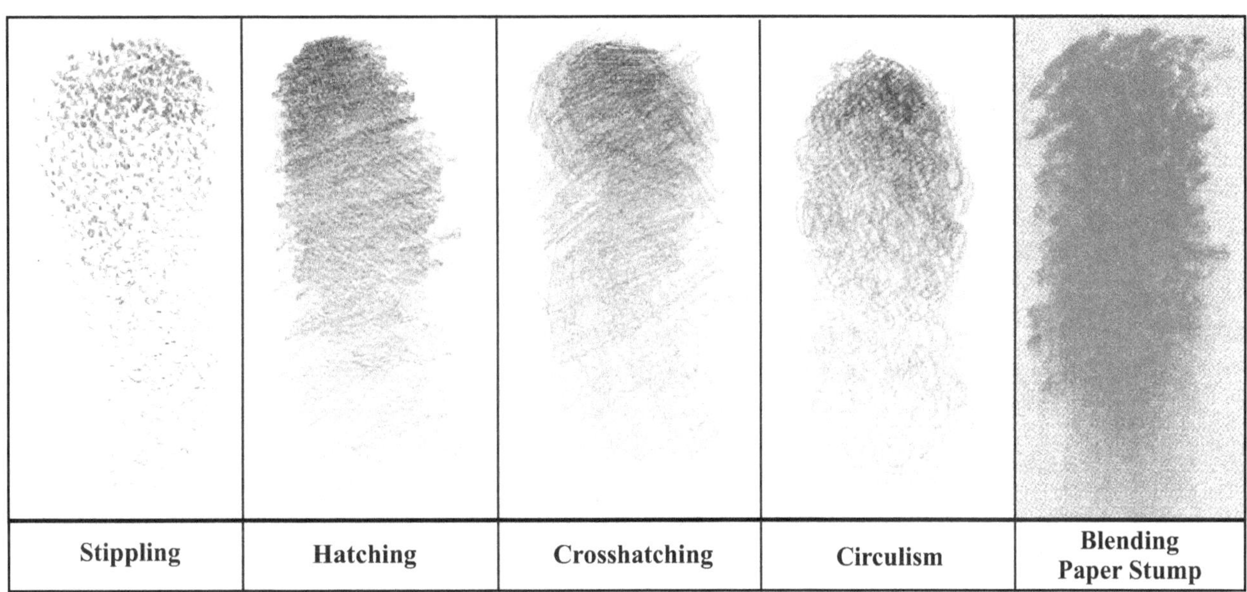

Gray scale created using pencil tones

STUDY OF TONES FOR DIFFERENT MOULDINGS

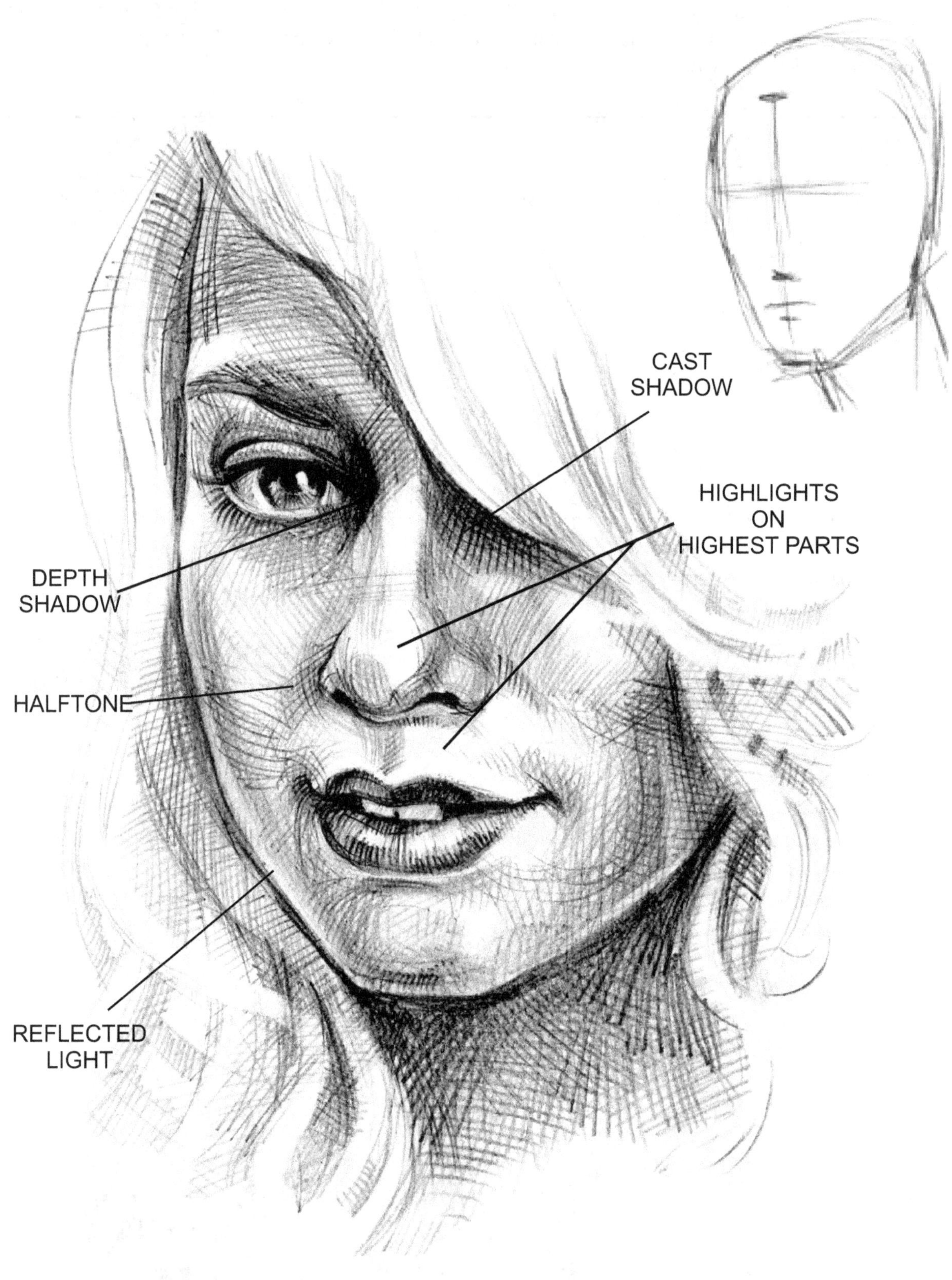

PORTRAIT COMPOSITION

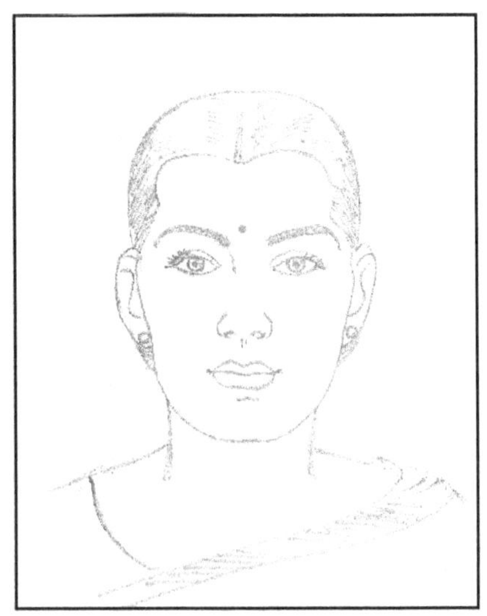

FULL FACE PORTRAIT

CLOSE UP PORTRAIT

HALF SIZE(TORSO) PORTRAIT

THREE QUARTER PORTRAIT

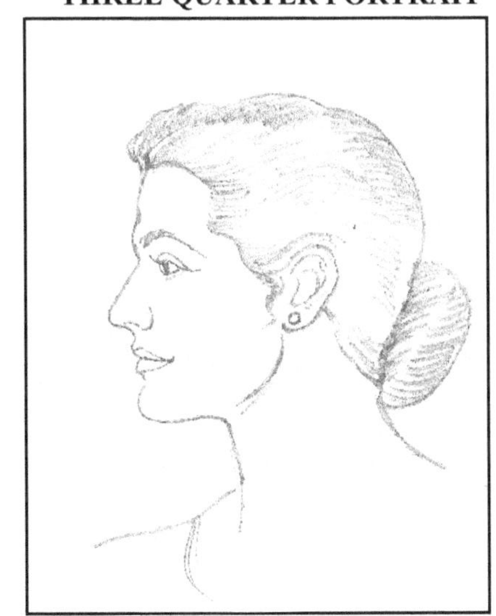

PROFILE PORTRAIT

LIFE SIZE PORTRAIT

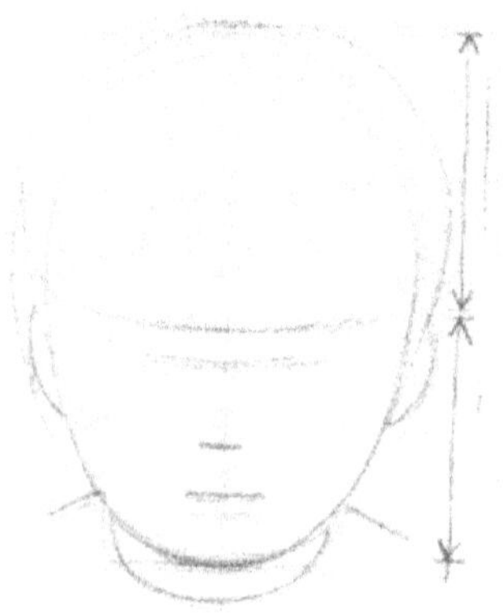

CHILD

When drawing a child, remember that children have round and bigger heads in proportion to their bodies. Big eyes, small nose and fully round cheeks are their identity.

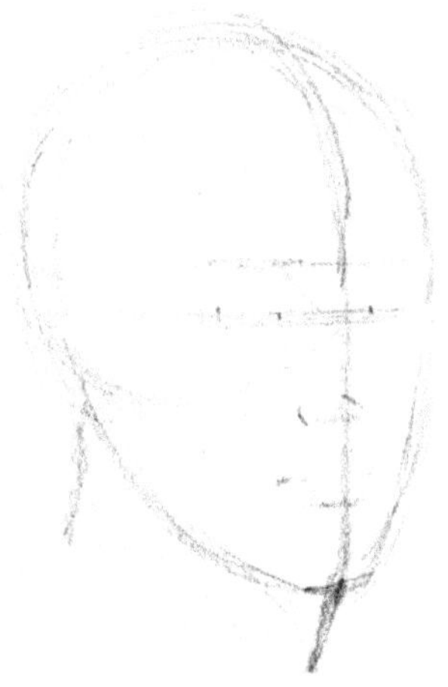

BEAUTIFUL FACE

Drawing Indian females be careful about glow in her eyes, use soft and thin strokes to define the planes of the forehead, cheeks, Draw nose and lips. You can finish it with full detail and medium tones. Use little shadow and only very necessary lines. Draw long black hairs and some loose hairs falling over the face for another identifying of portrait. Lastly draw saree-blouse,a simple necklace and small 'Bindi'.

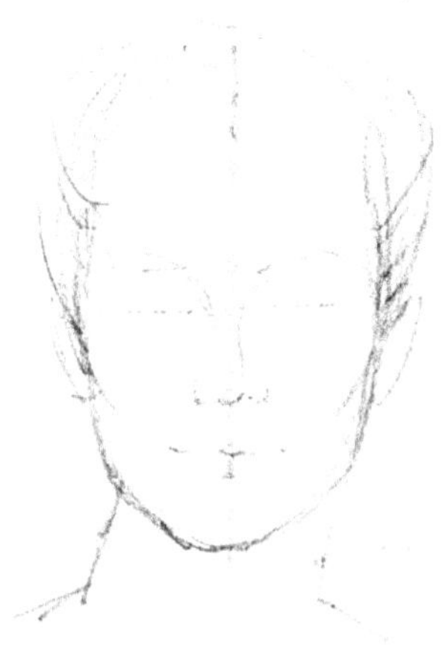

YOUTH

Some person does not need any make-up to look beautiful or handsome. Look this young chap - Hritik, have youth and energetic face. Highlight in the crystal like eyes and stylist beard is very important as these two things are capable of producing a happy and smiling face. Pointed nose and soft healthy skin had made him really attractive. Be careful not to use too many lines and details when drawing this type of person.

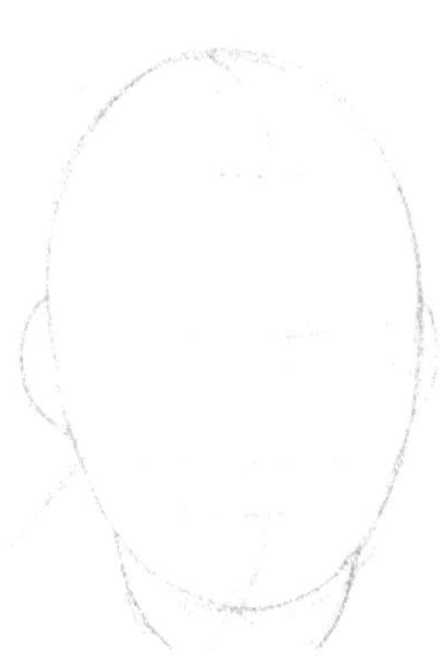

OLD

Old faces are more complicated. They have many wrinkles on the face and it is very difficult to draw than young person. Carefully observe each part of face and try to draw details. Darker tones may be apply in shadows under eyes, nose, ears and neck.

The Mona Lisa by Leonardo Da Vinci is one of the most famous paintings in the art history. The work is kept behind a bullet-proof glass safely at the Musée du Louvre gallery in Paris. Only very little information is known about the subject. It is the portrait of Lisa del Giocondo, a member of Gherardini family in Florence and wife of Francesco del Giocondo. Many researchers think her as Da Vinci's lover or mother. It is difficult to tell whether Is Mona Lisa gloomy or happy ? At the first sight, viewers feel she is happy but in next instant they sense, she is sad. The researchers found that her facial expression is 83% happy, 9% dismayed, 6% scared and 2% annoyed. The painting technique is called "Sfumato" which means pale or soft in Italian. In this method, an optical illusion is created around the mouth using shading and color.

CARTOON/COMIC

INTRODUCTION

A cartoon is a form of two-dimensional illustrated visual art. A semi-realistic sketch or drawing, usually feeling or emotion, as in a newspaper or periodical, symbolizing, satirizing, or caricaturing some action, subject, or person of popular interest. it came to refer to humorous illustrations in magazines and newspapers, and after the early 20th century, it referred to comic strips and animated films. In addition, comics is a medium used to express ideas by images, often combined with text or other visual information. Comics frequently takes the form of juxtaposed sequences of panels of images.

EXERCISE

It is first laid out in lead pencil and then inked in. When the ink dries, the pencil lines can be removed with an eraser without injury to the ink lines. Ability to handle a pen is acquired only by practice. The exercises are to be practiced until you are able to accomplish with sureness and confidence.

THE HEAD

Start from the head by making a rough circle in pencil, as shown below. Next, divide the circle, as shown. Add the eyes, ears, nose and mouth. Every cartoon head shapes has segments, i,e., it may be flat, cornered or pointed.

FACIAL EXPRESSIONS

The facial expression are most important in cartoon drawing. The following drawings shows the same expressing different emotions- surprise, sorrow, fright, scheming, smiling, laughing, and anger. Study these drawings and you will see that the expression is changed mainly, by altering the mouth, the eyes and the eyebrows. After you have studied the drawings on the chart, make a whole page of pencil circles and add the features as you conceive them, to express various emotions. Then try turning the heads, and next, try drawing them in titled positions.

CARTOON SHAPES OF EYES, NOSE, EARS AND MOUTH

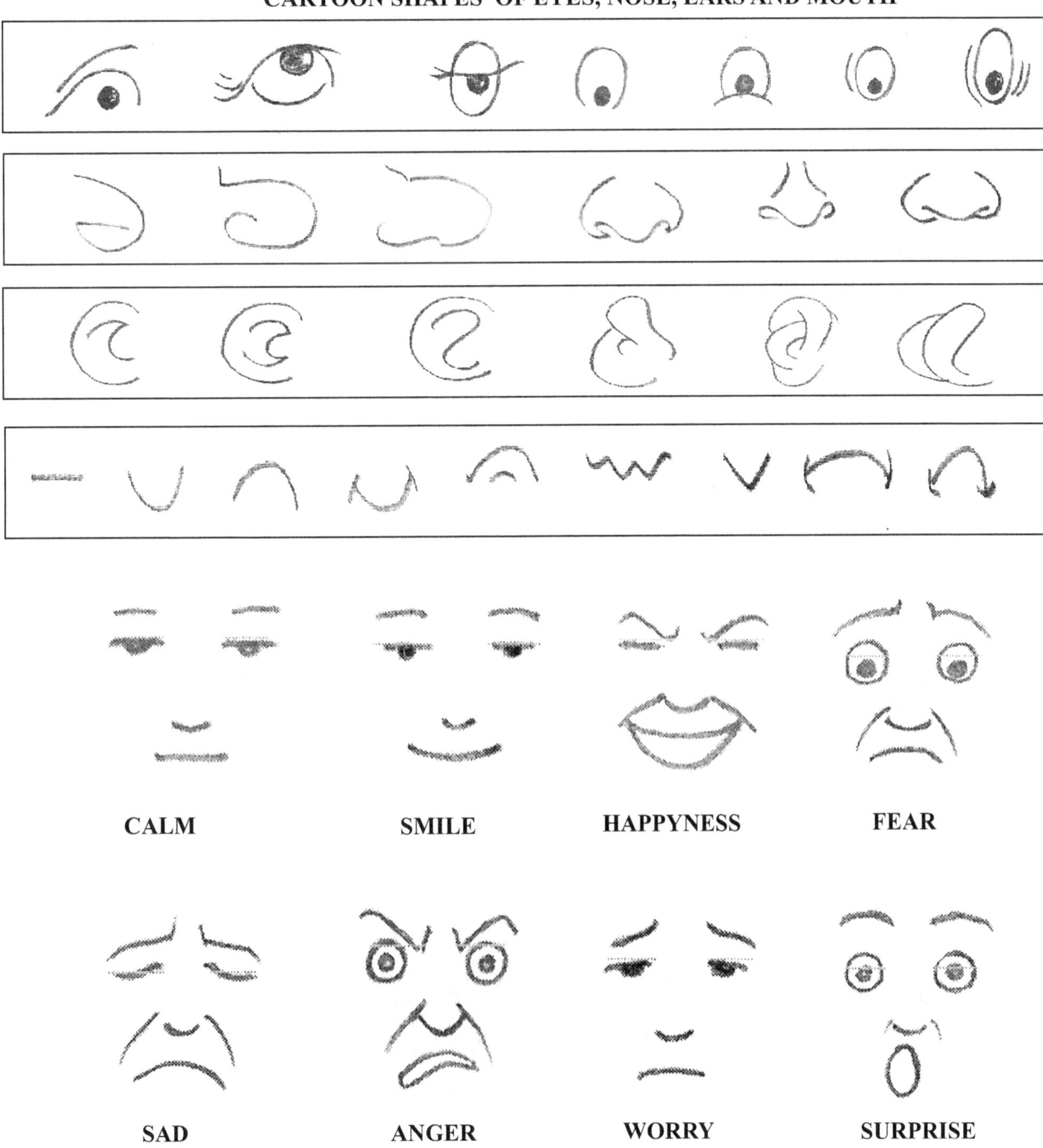

| CALM | SMILE | HAPPYNESS | FEAR |

| SAD | ANGER | WORRY | SURPRISE |

THE HANDS AND FEET

   Study the hands and feet on the plate. Bear in mind that is drawing cartoon, do not go into detail. Using the chart as a guide, practice making hand and feet until you are able to draw them in any desired position.

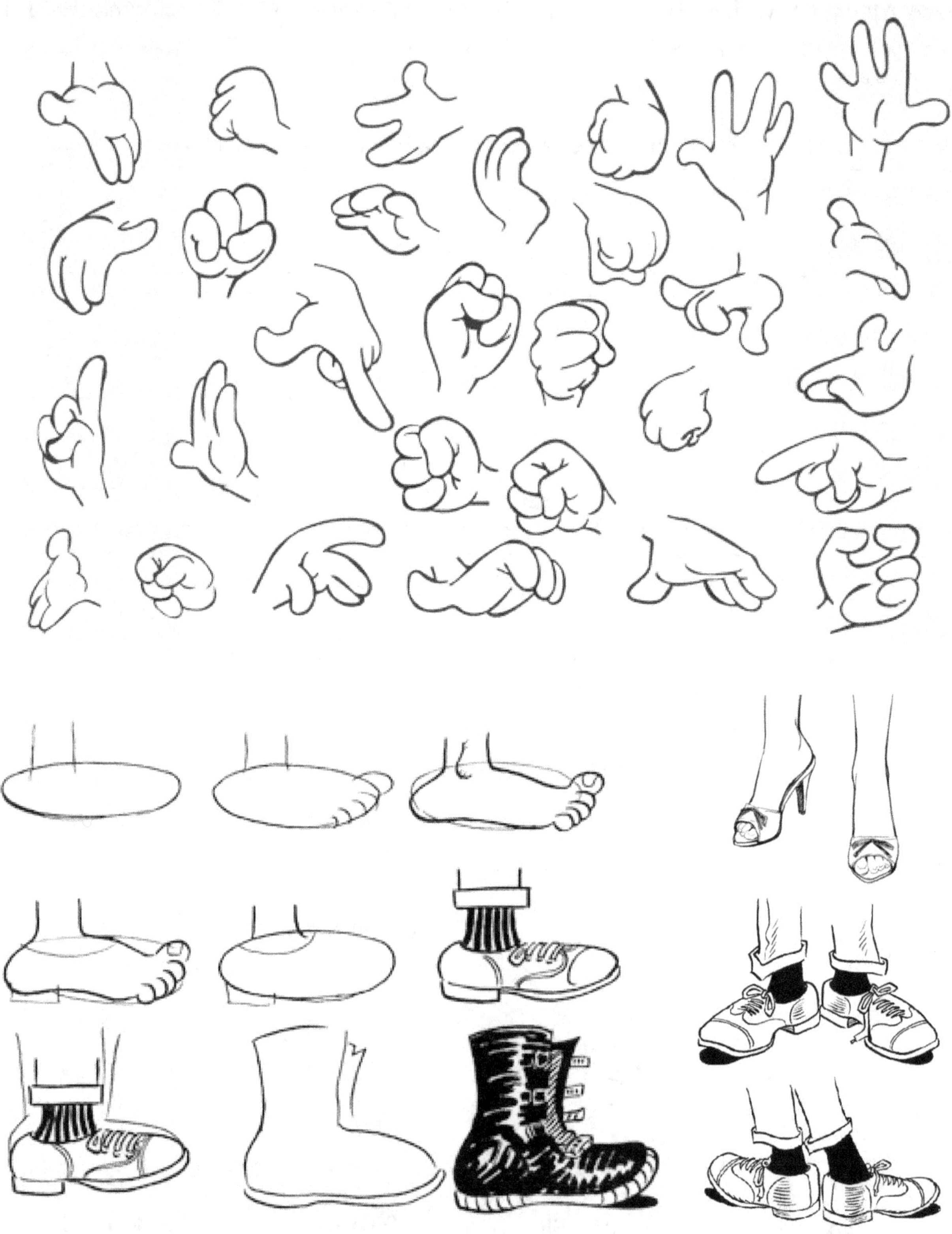

FIGURES IN ACTION

The drawings below are first roughed out, the circles are arranged to make the figures more animated. Make up a page from your own imagination.

COMIC CHARACTERS

       Up to now, all the cartoon figures have been simple and built upon the same combination of circles. Now advance to character comics. Character is achieved by varying the size of the circles. The large head and tiny body or tiny head and large body on the next character.

Study these characters, and then make several pages of your own.

ANIMALS

Comic animals are constructed with a circle understructure just as human figures are. Note how the cat, dog and horse were first roughed out and then finished. Notice the that the cat is walking like a human being. This doesn't happen in real life, but in drawing comics, you can take many liberties. Try a few pages of these animals, using the same characters are drawn here, but put them in different positions.

CARICATURE

A picture, description, or imitation of a person in which certain striking characteristics are exaggerated in order to create a comic or grotesque effect. Caricatures of politicians are commonly used in editorial cartoons. When drawing the person's character, artist can sketch-head,nose, ears, eyes, lips, etc. in any shape than the normal proportions but person should be recognise as special features of his/her character(hair style, eyes, nose, ears, mouth, costume etc.).

ABSTRACT ART

INTRODUCTION

Abstract art uses a visual language of shape, form, color and line to create a composition which may exist with a degree of independence from visual references in the world. On the other hand, The term abstract art can be applied to art that is based an ***object, figure or landscape***, where forms have been simplified to create an abstracted version of it, means that does not attempt to represent an accurate depiction of a visual reality but instead use shapes, colours, forms and gestural marks to achieve its effect.

There are many theoretical ideas behind abstract art. Art for art's sake – that art should be purely about the creation of beautiful effects, is one of the main theories. That art can or should be like music is another theory – in that just as music is patterns of sound, art's effects should be created by pure patterns of form, colour and line.

Abstract art developed from its beginnings in the early twentieth century to become a central stream in modern art. More recent artistic production is often called Contemporary art or Postmodern art.

An Abstract Painting By Pablo Picasso-Guernica

SOME GUIDELINE OR POINTS

1.Start with one simple strong shapes

2.Spend some time exploring the principles of composition. Learn about important aspects, such as direction, balance and harmony.

3.Choose an abstract artist - look on the net, Photographs - who uses simple, strong shapes - and copy a few of them. Then try to create your own design of simple shapes using those as a starting point.

4.Start with nature. Picasso said 'There is no abstract art. You must always start with something. Afterward you can remove all traces of reality'. Try looking at some realist paintings and reducing them to bare bones, simplifying the main shapes. Forget about the things being shown, just indicate the main volumes - the rough shape of a figure, the vertical shape of a tree, a horizon.

5.Look at scientific images. Space photos, electron microscope images, DNA sequences, microbes, diagrams, mathematical formulae - these things can have a curious beauty.

6.Limit your palette. Try creating a minimalist palette(colors).

7.Repetition can be very effective.

8.Create some textures and techniques- patch work, dry brush, impasto, hard edge, collage, print impression etc for get more beauty.

9.Study some folk art style but don't copy or influenced.

10.Use least number of strokes.

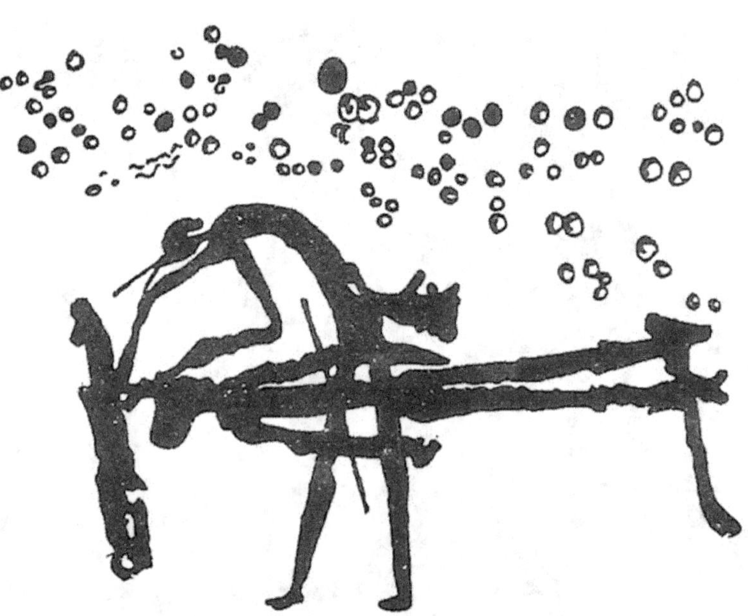

An Abstract form: A doctor attending a patient
Mesolithic rock painting, Bhimbaithka, M.P.

AN ABSTRACT LANDSCAPE
1. Simple shape
2. Geomatrcal shape
3. Collage work
4. Texture
5. Folk art style
6. Least number of strokes.
7. Hard edge
8. Repetition

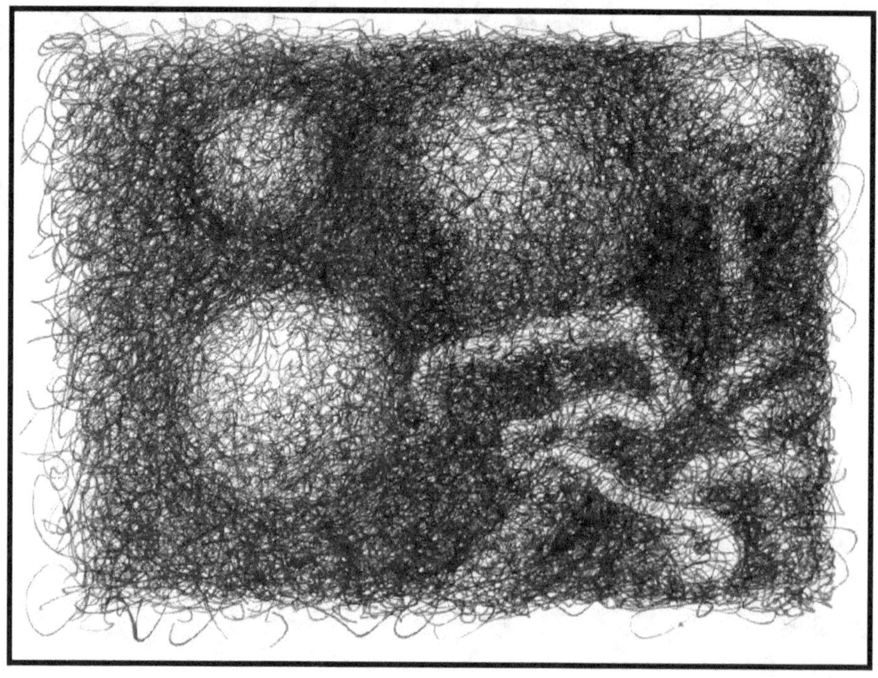

Beyond the Brush : There are many ways of applying different materials and medium to create beautiful textures in abstract painting. Here are some of the alternative to a brush.

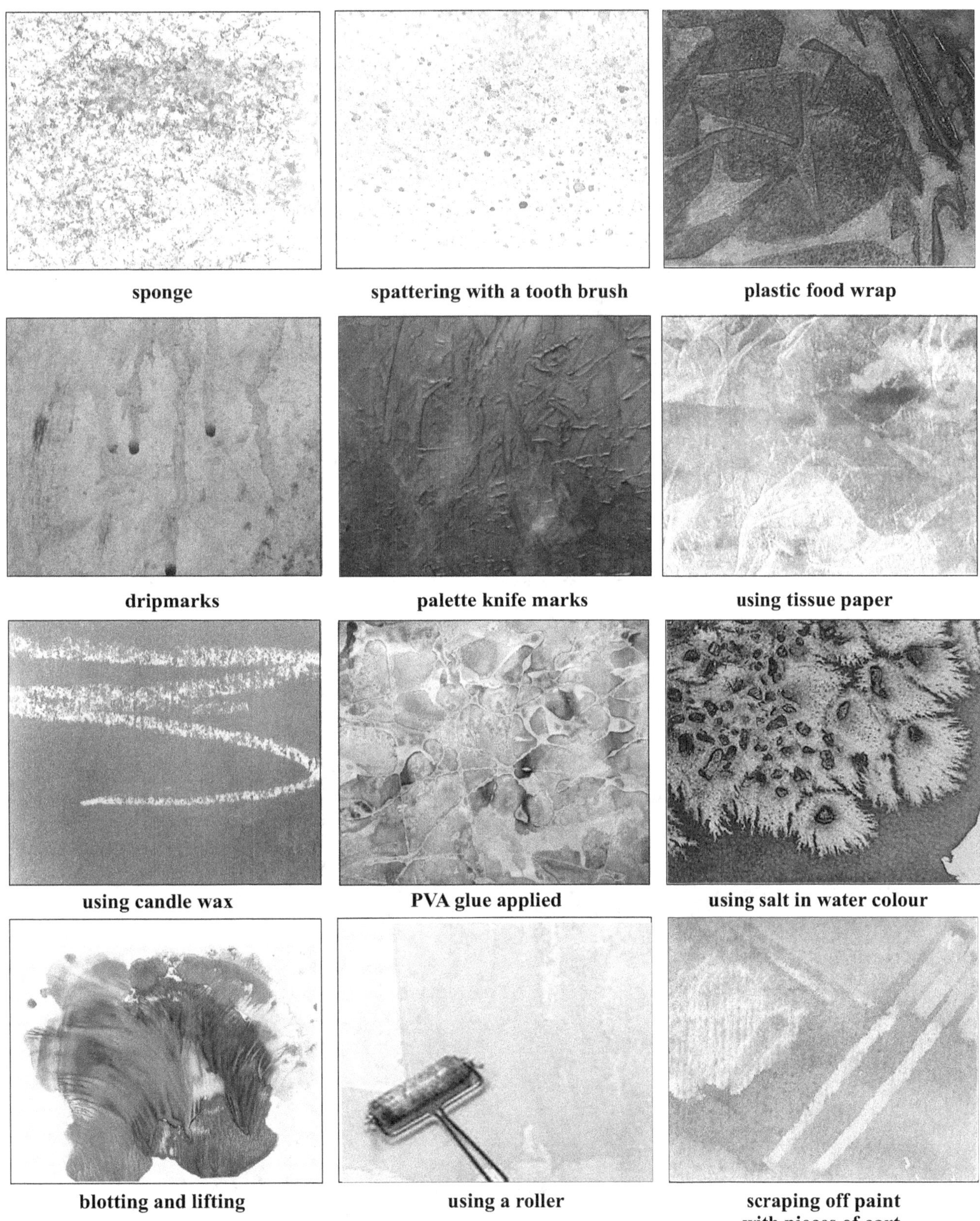

sponge	**spattering with a tooth brush**	**plastic food wrap**
dripmarks	**palette knife marks**	**using tissue paper**
using candle wax	**PVA glue applied**	**using salt in water colour**
blotting and lifting	**using a roller**	**scraping off paint with pieces of cart**

Mixed media : A work of visual art that combines various traditionally distinct visual art media-for example, a work on canvas that combines paint, ink, and collage could properly be called a "mixed media" work. Found objects can be used in conjunction with traditional artist media to attain a wide range of self-expression in abstract art .

MONOGRAM, LOGO & SYMBOL

INTRODUCTION

A logo/monogram is a graphic mark, sign or emblem commonly used by commercial enterprises, organizations, nation and even individuals to aid and promote instant public recognition. They are either purely graphic (symbols/icons) or are composed of the name of the organization or trademark or brand.

It requires a clear idea about the concept and values of the brand as well as understanding of the consumer or target group. Broad steps in the logo design process might be formulating the concept, doing an initial design, finalizing the its concept, deciding the theme colors and format involved. Sometimes motif made by overlapping or combining two or more letters or other grapheme to form one symbol.

Its design may be protected by copyright, via various intellectual property organizations worldwide which make available application procedures to register a design to give it protection at law.

EXERCISE

Some logo/monogram designs feature simple, beautiful typography whilst others more are fun and colourful. all symbol should be memorable and able to integrate with your design effortlessly. One of the best ways of getting inspiration for a logo/monogram design is by looking at what other designers have created. A great design that uses a bold font and hides a lightning bolt in the middle of the logo/monogram.

MONOGRAM

LOGO

SYMBOL: A symbol is an object that represents, stands for, or suggests an idea, visual image, belief, action, or material entity. Symbols take the form of words, sounds, gestures, or visual images and are used to convey ideas and beliefs. For example, a red ribbon may be a symbol for "AIDS". On a map, a picture of a tent might represent a campsite. Numerals are symbols for numbers. Personal names are symbols representing individuals. A red rose symbolizes love and compassion.

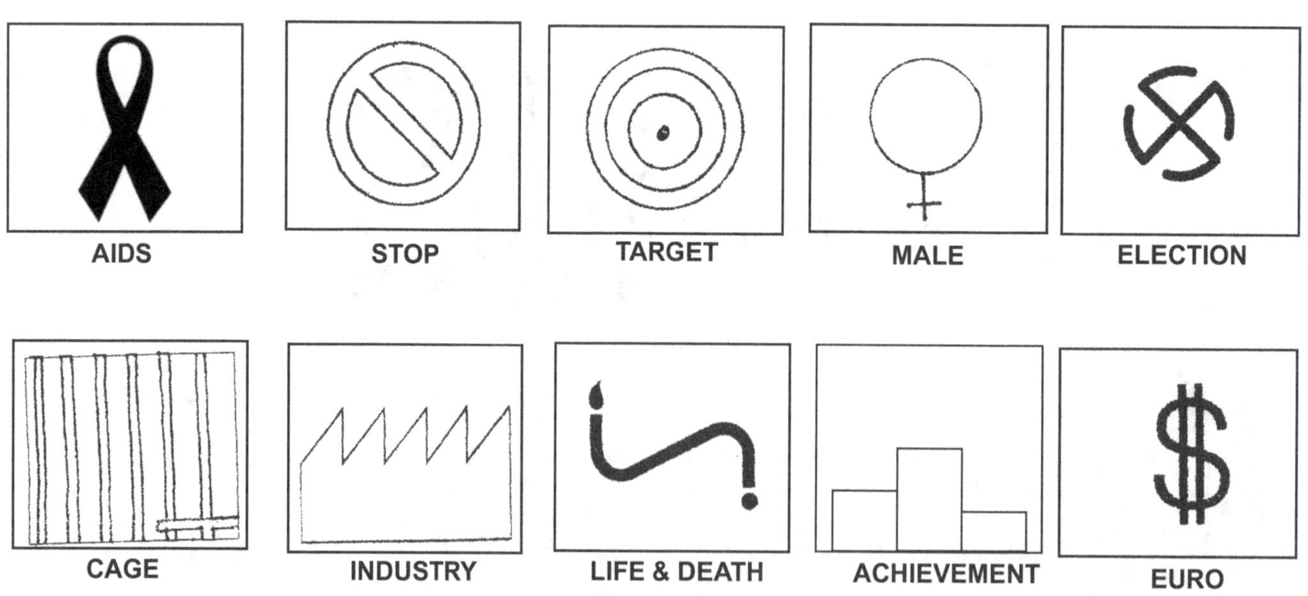

FASHION ILLUSTRATION

Fashion reflects a society's prevailing customs; it's political, economic and geographical state at any given point of time. It also reflects the wider spectrum of aesthetics, art and design trends in contemporary society. In the past, fashion emerged from the courts and the royal patronage, but today fashion is a colossal global and employing millions of people in either fashion industry or fashion business.

Fashion producers fall into three basic categories: haute couture; ready-to-wear designer labels; and the mass-produced ready-to-wear industry. The haute couture producers are the highly creative design houses that produce very expensive garments made to order for individual customers. The ready-to-wear designer labels are known for products designed by their talented designers. Their fine quality, innovative styling is made in standardized sizes and usually manufactured in factories. The mass-produced, ready-to-wear garments are manufactured off-shore, coming out of low wage countries at much lower costs. The primary objective is per piece production at a competitive price. In addition to apparel other fashion accessaries are important to contribute, in a secondary manner, to the wearer's outfit, often used to complete an outfit and chosen to specifically complement the wearer's look.

The illustrated drawing will inspire as well as fuel your fashion illustrations, with a stronger connection to the fashion design studio or classroom experience. The goal is to accelerate comprehension, application, and diversification of your drawing skills. This chapter, on basic figure drawing, have been expanded with trendier, elongated fashion forms, Model Drawing, in all new layouts, now reflects your classroom experience, with more figure analysis and new runway poses. It provides a broader platform to help you fully develop your fashion design illustrations.

Art Materials :
Paper, Tracing Paper, Graphite Pencils, Pens, Colored Pencils, Brush Pens, Markers Brushes and water based paints.

Supporting Sources: Fashion Magazines.

Model Making: Beside the drawing and painting work, student should practice model making by different materials with the help of **YOU-TUBE** for DAT-NID,CAT-NIFT, and NATA Exam.

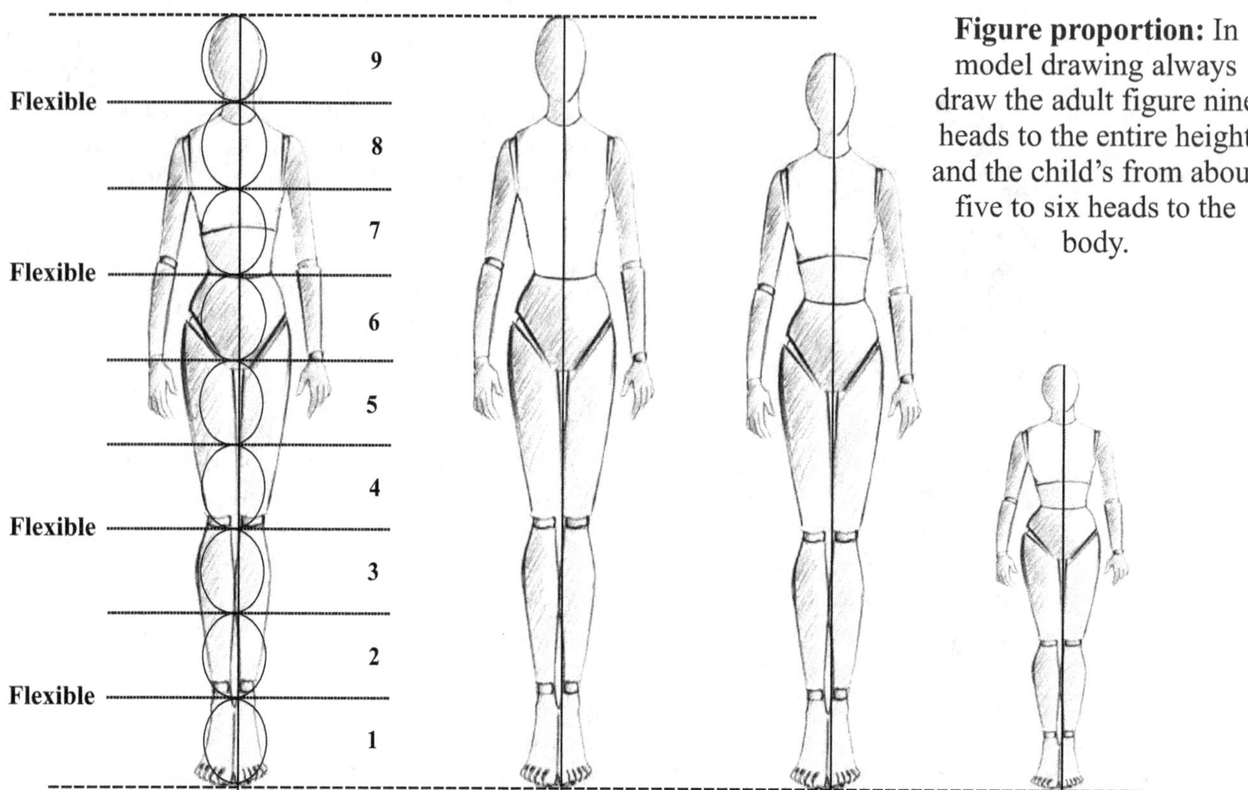

Figure proportion: In model drawing always draw the adult figure nine heads to the entire height and the child's from about five to six heads to the body.

Study from Basic Simple Form -Step By Step : First draw the balance line, this is a the first line of your sketch, and it represents your model's center of gravity. Second draw the torso, head, arms and legs.

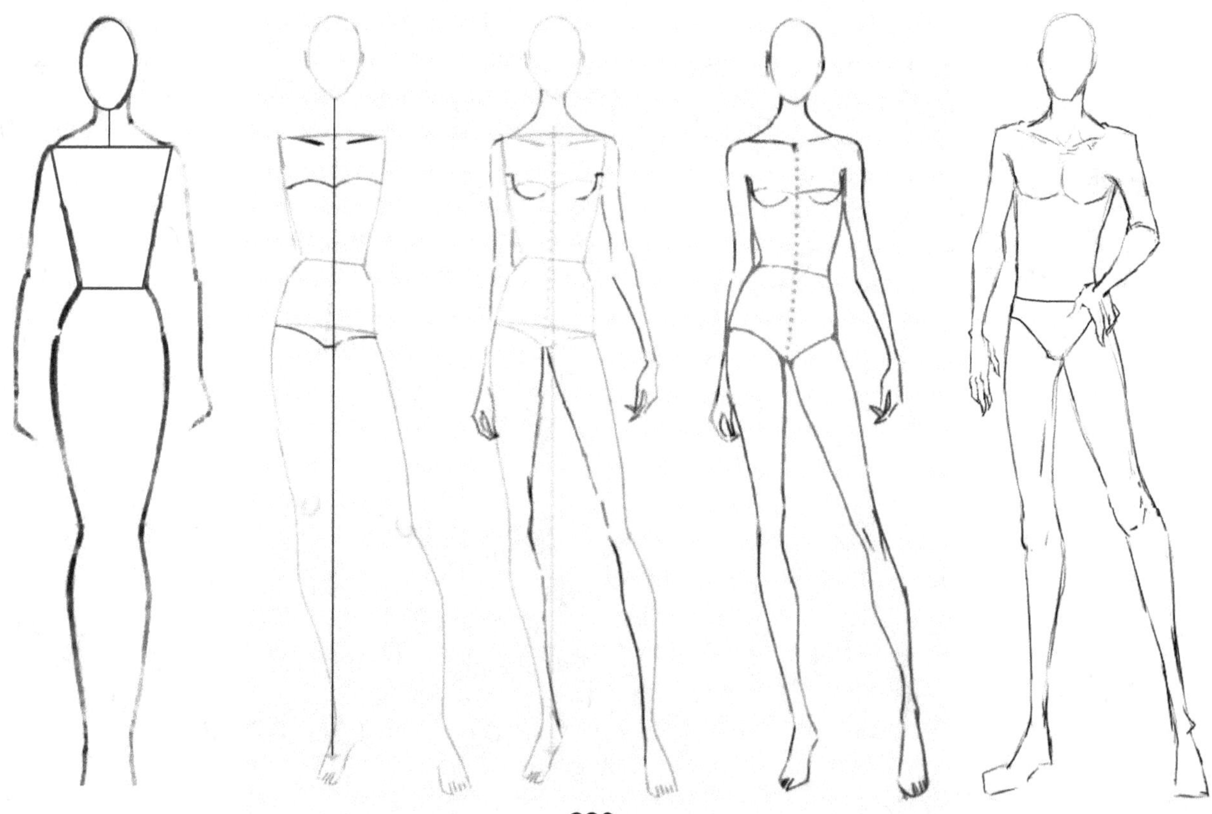

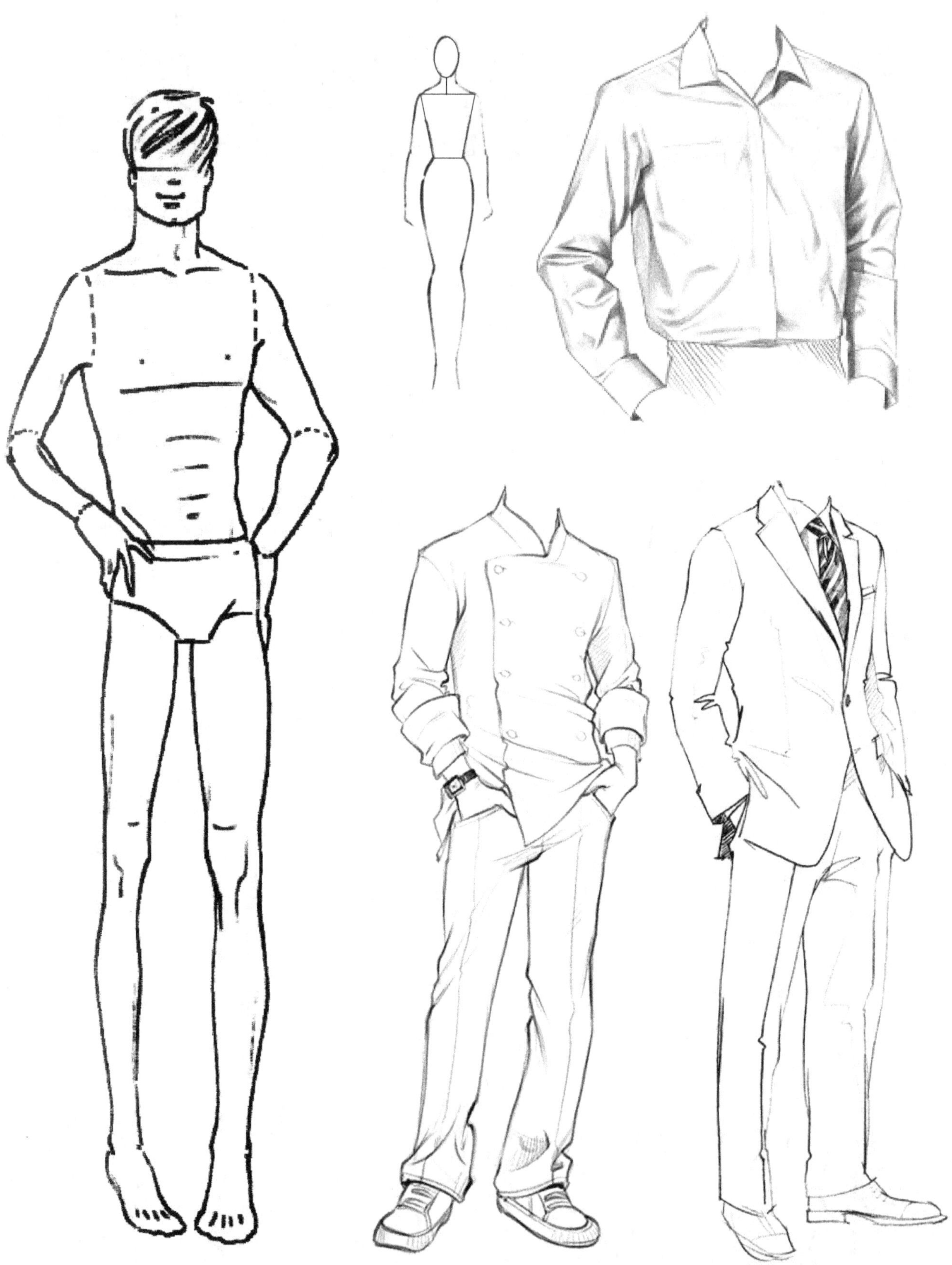

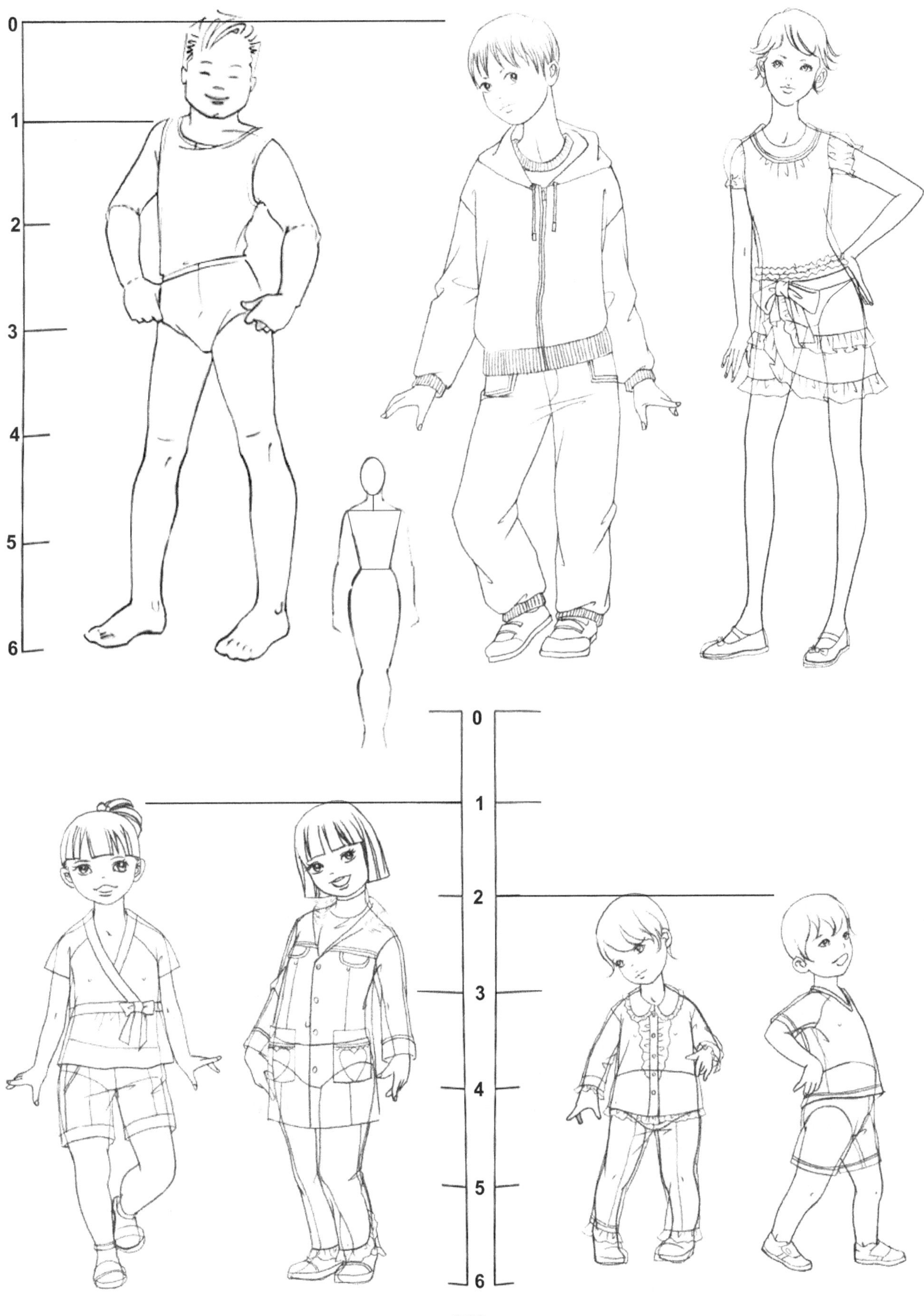

-230-

Male Garments Designs

Children Garments Designs

Different Hair Styles

Some Fashion Accessories : The drawing of fashion accessaries are varied according to occasion and shapes are inspired by many motifs.

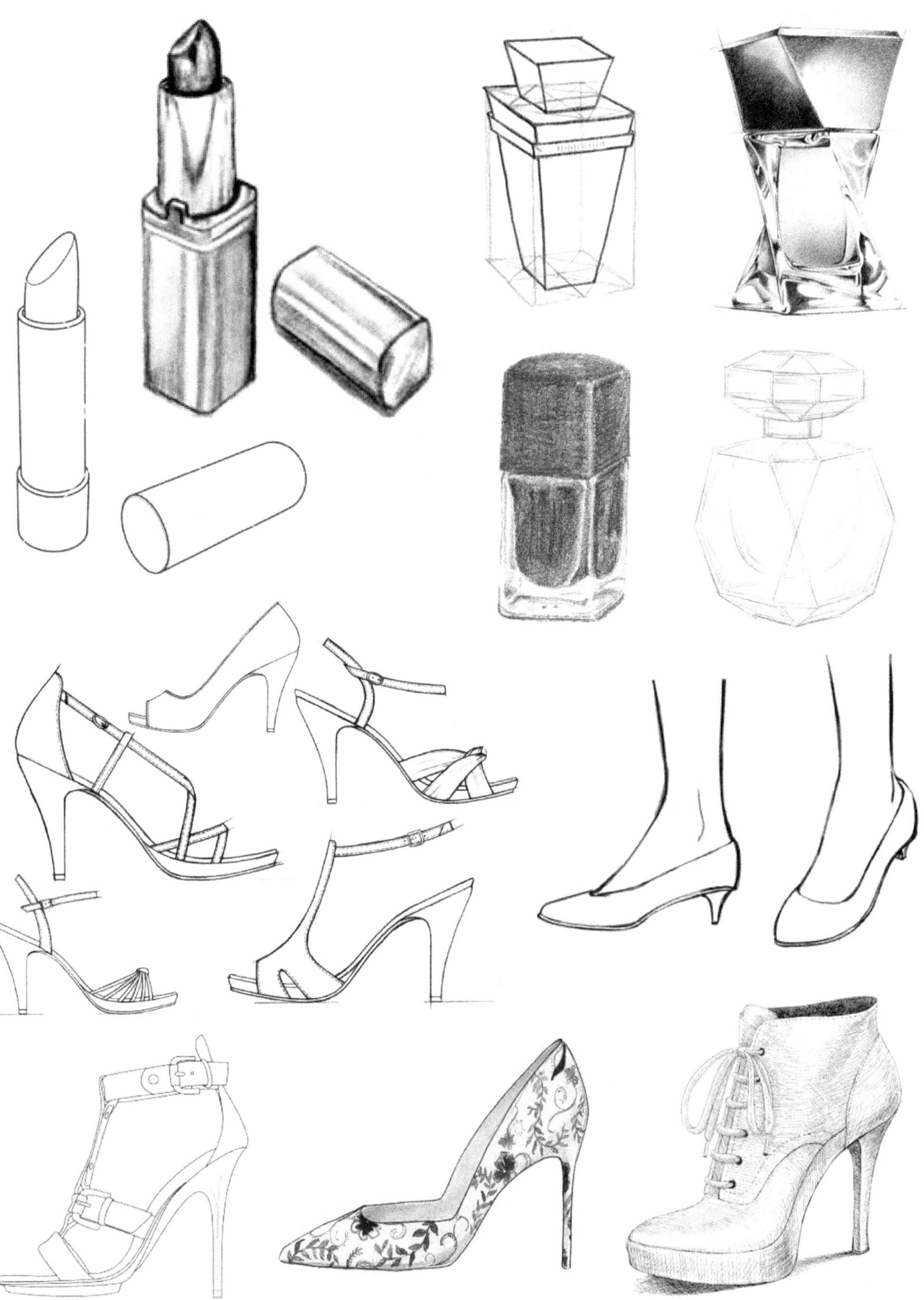

GLOSSARY

Glossary of Painting Terms:

Art Concepts: Theories and ideas about art and how it contributes to human growth, how it may be understood in terms of styles and techniques, and how it rests on philosophical and aesthetic assumptions about making art.

Aesthetics: Branch of philosophy that provides a theory of the beautiful and of the fine arts; a systematic attempt to explore human feeling, form, beauty, and style expressed in disciplines involving creative effort; dealing with questions of definition, meaning, value, and evaluation in the arts.

Applique: Textile decoration in which cut fabric shapes are stitched to a fabric ground as a design.

Baseline . A line that establishes the placement of a subject and helps you work out the proportions of a drawing.

Aesthetics: Philosophy applied to art, which attempts to formulate criteria for the understanding of the aesthetic (rather than utilitarian) qualities of art

Aerial perspective: A way of suggesting the far distance in a landscape by using paler colours (sometimes tinged with blue), less pronounced tones, and vaguer forms in those areas that are farthest from the viewer. By contrast objects in the foreground are painted in sharply outlined, brilliant, and warm colours, and background objects are shown in muted, cooler colours.

Body colour: Watercolour made opaque by mixing with white. Also: term used in painting to describe solid, definitive areas of colour which are then completed or modified with scumbles and glazes.

Body Painting: Ancient art of decorating the body.

Brush: Implement for applying paint, usually of hog or sable hair set in a wooden handle.

Brush stroke: The individual mark made by each application of paint with a BRUSH, usually retaining the mark of the separate brush hairs.

Brushwork: General term for manner or style in which paint is applied, and often considered by art historians as an identifying characteristic of a particular artist's work.

Bleed: The effect of two or more wet colours running into each other or the effect of one colour applied to a wet support.

Cast shadow: The shadow of an object that appears on a different surface or object.

Colour wheel: A diagrammatic chart showing the placement of colors in relationship to each other. For more details.

Chalk: The common name for calcium carbonate, which is found as a natural deposit all over the world, and is composed of the remains of tiny crustaceans. Traditionally used in painting and drawing.

Classicism: The quality of classic or classical art. The term is applied in particular to the type of art that was the antithesis of Romanticism during the 18th and 19th centuries, when it was held to represent the virtues of restraint and harmony, in contrast to dramatic individual expression.

City scape: Painting or drawing of city scenery.

Contour sketch (or Continuous line sketch): A sketch or drawing that is done with a single line.

Contrast: Differences between the values in a composition.

Craft knife: A small knife with a sharp, pointed, replaceable blade.

Crop: Determine the area of a scene to be included within an artwork.

Crafts: A category embracing most decorative arts.

Drawing : A finished representation of a subject.

Dry Brushing: Technique used in paintings using more pigment then water.

Decorative art: Collective name for art forms like ceramics, tapestries, enamelling, stained glass, metalwork, paper art, textiles, and others, which are deemed to be ornamental or decorative, rather than intellectual or spiritual.

Easel painting (or picture) : mall or medium-sized painting executed at an easel. These were usually intended for collectors and connoisseur, although the term may also be used generally for any portable painting, as opposed to mural painting.

Easel: An easel is used to support your canvas while painting. Can be a collapsible tripod, studio types and as a combination sketch box unit. Some sketch boxes contain lids that serve as easels.

Fixative Spray: For fixing charcoal drawing on canvas before painting. Fixative spray is available in spray cans, or for use with mouth atomizer.

Foreground: Part of a two-dimensional artwork that appears to be nearer the viewer or in the "front" of the image. Middle ground and background are the parts of the picture that appear to be farther and farthest away.

Foreshortening: the use of the laws of perspective in art to make an individual form appear three dimensional.

Focal point: The place in a work of art at which attention becomes focused because of an element emphasized in some way.

Format: The overall shape of a composition.
Figurine: small model or sculpture of the human figure, like prehistoric Venus Figurines.
Fine art: art whose value is considered to be aesthetic rather than functional, i.e. architecture, sculpture, painting and drawing, and the graphic arts. Compare applied art and decorative art.
Graphite: A soft black substance used in the core of some pencils.
Gesture Drawing: This quick drawing captures the energy and movement of the subject. It does not necessarily have to be realistic.
Gouache: (Tempera) Opaque watercolors and the technique of painting with such colors using white to make tints.
Genre: The representation of people, subjects, and scenes from everyday life.
Glass Painting: technique of decorating glass, not very clearly distinguished from glass enameling, although it may be more transparent and smoother. Early glass painting was not fired, and therefore not permanent.
Impasto: Thick mass of paint or pastel; hence impasted, or impastoed.
India Ink: In fine art, a drawing ink made from a black pigment consisting of lampblack and glue.
Iconography: recognizable emblematic motifs and symbols in works of art: Hatching: drawing technique that uses closely spaced parallel lines to indicate toned areas. When crossed by other lines in the opposite direction it is known as cross-hatching.
Harmony: The principle of design that creates unity within a work of art.
Hue: The gradation or attribute of a color that defines it's general classification as a red, blue, yellow, green, or intermediate color.
Installation art: The combining of elements into a singular artwork that is specifically located in one place; an artwork that exists only in the place in which it was/is installed, and is not able to be relocated like a painting or print.
Horizon line: The line where land or water meets the sky, in reference to linear perspective.
Intensity: This term is used to describe the brightness, or the dullness of a color.
Life drawing: drawing from a live human model.
Linear: artistic style that emphasizes lines and contours; hence linearity and linearism.
Light source. The origin of the light shining on elements in a composition.
Linseed Oil: Used as a medium. The tradional "binder" for oil colors.

Light box: A device that shines light evenly through a translucent surface. This allows the viewer to see slides, transparencies or drawings laid on its surface.
Masterpiece: originally a test piece of work done by the medieval apprentice in order to qualify as a Master of his Guild. The term is now used more freely to mean a work of obtaining importance or quality.
Medium: the means or material with which an artist expresses himself. In painting, the medium is the liquid in which pigment is mixed and thinned, e.g. linseed oil.
Motif: a repeated distinctive feature in a design.
Mixed media: An artwork in which more than one type of art material.
Miniature Painting: very small piece of work (Manuscript Illumination).The term was more specifically applied to small portraits painted on paper ,palm-leaves, ivory etc .
Monochromatic : Use of only one hue or color, that can vary in value or intensity.
Media: (1) Plural of medium referring to materials used to make works of art. (2) Classifications of artworks, such as painting, printmaking, sculpture, film, etc.).Middle ground Area of a two-dimensional work of art between the foreground (closest to the front) and background (furthest receded).
Mood : The state of mind or emotion communicated in a work of art, through color, composition, media, scale, size, etc.
Mechanical pencil: A pencil consisting of a thin stick of graphite encased by a holder similar to a pen. Mechanical pencils need no sharpening.
Medium: The art material that is used in a work of art such as clay, paint or pencil. Describing more then one art medium is referred to as media. Any substance added to color to facilitate application or to achieve a desired effect.
Motif: A repeated pattern, often creating a sense of rhythm.
Movement: The principle of design that deals with the creation of action.
Negative space: Shapes or spaces that are or represent the areas unoccupied by objects.
Neutral colors: Black, white, gray, and variations of brown. They are included in the color family called earth colors.
Nonobjective: Having no recognizable object or subject; also, nonrepresentational.
Repetition: Repetition is created when objects, shapes, space, light, direction, lines etc. are repeated in artwork.

Reflection: Personal and thoughtful consideration of an artwork, an aesthetic experience, or the creative process.

Oil Paint: : "Oils are one of the great classic media, and have dominated painting for five hundred years. They remain popular for many reasons: their great versatility, offering the possibility of transparency and opacity in the same painting; the lack of color change when the painting dries; and ease of manipulation."

One-point perspective: A way to show 3-D objects on a 2-D surface, lines appear to go away from the viewer meet at a single point on the horizon known as the vanishing point.

Organic: Refers to shapes or forms not of geometric shape, having irregular edges, surfaces, or objects similar to natural forms. Reference materials. Pictures from various sources, used to examine a subject more closely, or from different angles, or under different conditions.

Oil Cup: A container that can be clipped to your oil palette. One cup for the medium, the other cup for the brush cleaner.

Oils Oil: based pigment used with paint thinner, turpentine, or other non-water-based suspension.

Sandpaper pad: A very small pad of sandpaper sheets attached to a handle; used for sharpening pencil tips.

Pattern: A design, image, or shape repeated in a predictable combination.

Pencil extender: A device that attaches to the end of a pencil that has been shortened by use, used to extend the pencil's life.

Perspective: A technique that gives the illusion of depth to a fl at picture.

Palette: slab of wood, metal or glass used by the artist for mixing paint. Also: figuratively: the range of colours used by the artist.

Palette knife: spatula-shaped knife for mixing or applying thick, bodied paint

Proportional dividers. Dividers that have points at both ends and are used for proportionally enlarging or reducing a hand-drawn image.

Paper weight: The thickness of a sheet of paper; common weights for sketch paper are 50 lb. to 70 lb. (105gsm to 150gsm). For drawing paper common weights are 80lb to 90lb (170gsm to190gsm).

Paint Box: A piece of equipment used for storing brushes, paint, palette, and accessories when painting outdoors.

Painting Knife: Knives come in a variety of shapes and sizes. A trowel-type flexible knife.

Pigment: Pigment is the material used to create the effect of color on any surface.

Performance art : A type of art in which an event or events are planned and enacted before an audience for aesthetic reasons.

Point of view: The angle from which a viewer sees the objects or scene in an image.

Portfolio: A systematic, organized collection of artwork, usually student artwork.

Positive Shapes: Positive Shapes or spaces in an image that represent solid objects or forms.

Properties of color: The characteristics of color that are perceived: hue, value, and intensity.

Proportion: The scale relationships of one part to the whole and of one part to another. In images of figures, the appropriate balance between the size of body and its limbs.

Panorama: painting of a view or landscape; especially large-scale painting around a room, or rolled on a cylinder.

Polymorphic painting: multiform painting, produced by some modern kinetic artists. The appearance of the work changes according to the position of the observer.

Polymorphic painting: This scheme used two or more colour combinations.

Proportion: in painting, sculpture and architecture, this describes the ratio between the respective parts and the whole work, as annunciated (for instance) in the Canon of Proportion, a mathematical formula establishing ideal proportions of the various parts of the human body.

Reflection: Personal and thoughtful consideration of an artwork, an aesthetic experience, or the creative process

Sketch.: A drawing in rough, unfinished form.

Straightedge: A metal ruler or similar tool used for drawing straight lines.

Structural sketch: The primary line work that the values (lights and dark) and line work of a drawing are built upon.

Symmetrical: Balanced composition, with equal elements placed as if reflected in a mirror.

Shade: Using a mixture of black mixed with a color to make it darker. The opposite of shade is tint.

Spectrum: The colors that are the result of a beam of white light that is broken by a form of prism into its hues.

Stencil: The process in which an area is cut out of paper, or material such as cardboard to enable paint or ink to be applied to a piece of paper, or canvas through the cutout.

Study: A detailed drawing or painting made of one or more parts of a final composition, but not the whole work.

Symbol: A symbol is a picture or image that tells a story of what it is without using words.

Sketching: Typically a sketch is a rapidly executed or casual portrayal of a subject, in pencil, charcoal, pen and ink or other portable medium, often produced as a preliminary work in preparation for something more detailed.

Stencil art: An image created by applying ink or paint through a cut-out surface.

Stippling: a drawing technique which employs many small dots or flecks to construct the image, or shading.

Shape: A two-dimensional area or plane that may be open or closed, free form or geometric. It can be found in nature or created by humans.

Space: The area between, around, above, below, or contained within objects. Spaces are areas defined by the shapes and forms around them and within them, just as shapes and forms are defined by the space around and within them.

Subtractive: Artistic method accomplished by removing or taking away from the original creative material, (the opposite of additive)

Structure: The way parts are arranged or put together to form a whole.

Style: A set of characteristics of the art of a culture, a period, or school of art; the characteristic expression of individual artists or groups.

Tertiary colors: Colors that represent a mixture of secondary colors.

Tint: Tint is the opposite of shade. Tinting is combining white with a color to make it lighter.

Shaded Tint: If we mix back colour with any primary colour get the tint shade.

Tone: Color with gray added to it.

Turpentine : Used for cleaning equipment and to thin mediums.

Theme: A subject or topic of discourse or of artistic representation.

Thematic Works: A series of artworks that have a commonality, i.e., the same subject matter, style, technique, concept such as works about life and leisure, life and work.

Two-dimensional: Having height and width but not depth (2-D)

Three-dimensional : Having height, width, and depth (3-D).

Thumbnail sketch: A small, quick sketch.

Tooth: The roughness of a paper surface.

Tracing paper: Thin, translucent paper used in the process of drawing.

T-square: A straightedge with a perpendicular attachment that allows the tool to glide along the side edge of a drawing board or paper pad.

Under painting: Preliminary painting used as a base for textures or for subsequent painting or glazing.

Unity: A feeling of completeness is created by the use of elements in the artwork. Unity A principle of design that connects a variety of elements of art and principles of design into a work of art with harmony and balance.

Value: Shadows, darkness, contrasts and light are all values in artwork.

Value scale: A value scale shows the range of values from black to white and light to dark.

Vintage: A photograph printed within a few years of the negative being made. Value Lightness or darkness of a hue or neutral color. A value scale shows the range of values from black to white and light to dark.

Vanishing point: In perspective drawing, a point at which receding lines seem to converge.

Variety; A principle of art concerned with combining one or more elements of art in different ways to create interest.

virtual: An image that is of the imagination, not of the real world.

Visual : metaphor Images in which characteristics of objects are likened to one another and presented as that other. They are closely related to concepts about symbolism.

Visual Concepts: Descriptive qualities of form and structure such as straight and curved, open and closed, spiral and concentric.

Volume : Describes the space within a form, such as that of a container or building.

Value sketch: A thumbnail sketch used to plan the lights and dark of a drawing.

Vantage point: The point from which the viewer observes a scene.

Viewfinder: A device used to crop a scene.

Wash-A highly fluid application of color.

Watercolour: A translucent, water-based paint that comes in cake or tube form.

Wax Crayon: These crayons are ideal to use to loosen up your drawing style. Crayons are cost effective, and it is difficult to create really detailed drawings.

wash: A thin layer of translucent (or transparent) paint or ink, particularly in watercolor; also used occasionally in oil painting.

Glossary of Printmaking(Graphics) Terms

Block: In printmaking, a piece of flat material, such as wood, linoleum or metal, into which a design has been carved.

Dry point: Similar to etching, but the lines are simply scratched into the plate manually, without the use of acid. The hallmark of a dry point is a soft and often rather thick or bushy line somewhat like that of an ink pen on moist paper.

Etching: process in which the design is drawn on a metal plate through a wax ground; the design is cut into the plate with acid, and printed. Also: a print produced by this method.

Embossing: A process used to create a raised surface, or a raised element printed without ink. End grain Block A wood block usually boxwood, maple, cherry, or other fruitwood, cut across the grain and used for wood engraving. top

Engraving: The general term for incising lines directly into a metal plate or, in the case of wood engraving, an end grain block of hard wood, in intaglio, engraving differs from etching in that the plate is not grounded, and it is the pressure of the tool, not the use of an acid bath, that creates the lines in the metal.

Intaglio: decoration produced by cutting into a surface, used in engraving, etching, gem carving.

Line engraving: the art or process of hand-engraving in Intaglio and copper plate, using a

Lithography: printing method in which a design is drawn on stone with a greasy crayon and then inked. Landscape painting: Composition in which the scenery is the principal subject. Also: scenic areas of a painting or drawing.

Linoleum cut: A relief print, much like a woodcut, but using battleship linoleum rather than a wood block. The linoleum is somewhat easier to cut and prints more evenly because it lacks the grain.

Lino cut: print produced by carving a design into a block of linoleum.

Iris print: An type of inkjet print printed from an Iris printer.

Linoleum Cut: A relief print carved into linoleum rather than wood.

Monotype: printing process that takes an impression from a metal or glass plate, producing only one print of each design, which must then be redrawn. Mono print- A print that has the same underlying common image, but different design, color or texture.

Mass: The outside size and bulk of an object, such as a building or a sculpture; the visual weight of an object.

Metal Cut: A form of relief printing from an intaglio plate. In the 15th century, metal cuts often employed drill holes that printed as white dots. Engraved lines will print white rather than black in metal cut since the surface, rather than the marks in the plate, is inked.

Tie-dye: method of dyeing by hand in which coloured patterns are produced in the fabric by gathering together many small portions of material and tying them tightly with string before immersing the cloth in the dye bath. The dye fails to penetrate the tied sections. After drying, the fabric is untied to reveal irregular circles, dots, and stripes. Varicoloured patterns may be produced by repeated tying and dipping in additional colours. This hand method, common in India and Indonesia, has been adapted to machines.

Offset litho: lithographic technique in which ink is transferred from a plate to a rubber roller, and then onto the paper.

Repousse: Technique of metalwork art, where metal is decorated by hammering from the side not seen, so that the design stands out in relief.

Relief print : A print in which the non-image areas have not been cut away and only the surface of the block or plate is inked and printed. Included in this category are woodcuts (the most ancient form of printmaking) and linoleum cuts. top

Relief printed etching (or reverse etching): A print from an etching plate in which the surface is inked with a hard roller and any ink that penetrated the incised lines is wiped away. The opposite of intaglio printing.

Wood block: Print produced from a design on a wooden block.

Silver print: This generic term covers all prints made on paper that is coated with silver salts. Black and white photographs are usually silver prints.

Woodcut: A relief print usually carved in the plank grain of a piece of wood. After the relief image has been carved in the plank with knives or gouges it is inked with a dauber or roller. It can then be printed by hand (in which case a sheet of paper is laid down on the inked plank and rubbed from the back with a smooth surface such as the palm of the hand or a wooden spoon) or with the help of a mechanical press.

Print: any image, pattern, or lettering produced on fabric or paper by a variety of graphic processes.

Glossary of sculpture Terms

Bronze: Alloy of copper and tin, used for cast sculpture. Bronze sculpture is made from this alloy. Hence bronzist, a maker of bronze sculpture, plaques, etc.

Bust: Portrait sculpture showing the sitter's head and shoulders only.

Bas-relief: Form of sculpting characterized by only a slight projection from the surrounding surface.

Carving: an object or design carved from a hard material as an artistic work.

Chisels: a long-bladed hand tool with a beveled cutting edge and a handle which is struck with a hammer or mallet, used to cut or shape wood, stone, or metal.

Cire Perdue: (lost wax"): Casting process used in bronze sculpture.

Casting: The duplication of a model in metal or plaster by means of a mold; the model thus formed is a cast.

Direct carving: Method of stone sculpture where form is carved immediately out of the block, and not transferred from a model.

Earthenware: This type of clay needs to be glazed, it is porous and not waterproof. Earthenware is a low-fire clay.

Firing: To harden clay, you have to heat it at high temperatures which fuses the clay particles.

Freestanding: a sculpture intended to be viewed from all sides.

Greenware: When clay is hard, but not yet fired it is referred to as greenware. The clay can be made wet and turned back into a useable material.

Glaze: transparent layer of paint applied over another; light passes through and is reflected back, modifying or intensifying the under layer. Also: vitreous layer made from silica, applied to pottery as decoration or to make it water-tight.

Lost-wax casting: A casting technique in which a wax form is placed in a container that is then filled with a material that can withstand high temperatures, such as plaster. The container is heated to melt the wax and create a mould.

Mobile: a three-dimensional, moving sculpture, that hangs from the ceiling. A type of sculpture in which objects are suspended and balanced so that they are moved by currents of air.

Modeling: three-dimensional representation of objects.

Mold: A negative (hollow) form that is filled with a material such as plaster or metal and removed when the material hardens into the shape of the mold. A mold can be used to make copies of an object.

Mosaic: a picture or pattern produced by arranging together small pieces of stone, tile, glass, etc./A colourful and variegated pattern.

Oxides: Applying metal oxides to the clay, mixing with water, you can create an effect of stained wood.

Plaster: When mixed with water, this powder will harden into a chalk-like solid used to create sculptures, and other forms of artwork.

Porcelain: Porcelain is a combination of kaolin, silica and feldspar. You can work with porcelain as you would clay, but when you fire it correctly, the result will be similar to that of glass.

Pottery: A form of ceramic art, in which wet clay is shaped, dried, glazed and fired in a kiln to create a variety of vessels, and ornaments. For history and styles of Antiquity.

Repousse: Decorative relief on metal formed by hammering from the back, so that the design is pushed through in relief. The piece can be turned over and worked from the other side.

Replica: An exact copy or reproduction of an artwork, sometimes made on a smaller scale than the original.

Resin : A solid or liquid synthetic material that can be carved, cut, drilled and polished in its solid form, or used in its liquid state in moulds.

Relief sculpture: carving, etc in which forms project and depth is hollowed out; the type of relief is determined by the degree to which the design stands out; thus alto rilievo (high relief) and bas relief (low relief), in which the projection is slight.

Terra-Cotta: a type of fired clay, typically of a brownish-red colour and unglazed, used as an ornamental building material and in modelling.

Slab built: Clay slabs are cut into shape, and joined together with scoring and wet clay called slip.

Slip: A liquid form of clay. Slip is used to fill in pores, and even out the color. Slip is used to join clay.

Style: Refers to a set of characteristics of the art of a culture, period, school of art, or individual.

Stoneware: Sturdier then earthenware, stoneware is waterproof even without being glazed.

Sculpture: Three-dimensional artwork to be seen either in the round (from all sides) or as a bas relief (a low relief in which figures protrude only slightly from the background).

Glossary of Applied Art Terms

Abstract: Artwork in which the subject matter is stated in a brief, simplified manner; little or no attempt is made to represent images realistically, and objects are often simplified or distorted.

Applied art: The designing and decorating of functional objects or materials to give them aesthetic appeal, e.g. printing type, ceramics, glass, furniture, metal work and textiles. The term is frequently used to differentiate this type of work from the fine arts (painting, drawing, sculpture) whose value is primarily aesthetic.

Airbrush: Instrument for spraying paint, propelled by compressed air. it has been much used by commercial artists, whether for fine lines, large areas, or subtle gradations of colour and tone.

Animation: The rapid display of images to create an illusion of movement; still images can be created by hand or digitally.

Batik: The art of decorating cloth in this way, using wax and dye, has been practiced for centuries. To make a batik, selected areas of the cloth are blocked out by brushing or drawing hot wax over them, and the cloth is then dyed. The parts covered in wax resist the dye and remain the original colour. This process of waxing and dyeing can be repeated to create more elaborate and colourful designs. After the final dyeing the wax is removed and the cloth is ready for wearing or showing.

Ceramics: The art of making objects of clay and firing them in a kiln.

Computer Art: Visual images either computer-generated or computer-controlled using software or hardware tools. Also referred to as Digital art.

Design: Plan or blueprint for a visual work of art as well as the outcome or product of applying.

Designer: Professional artist whose major concern is the development of efficient, functional products that are satisfying aesthetically.

Digital Media: Technology driven by computer access with emphasis on web based and print output design.

Enamel: vitreous substance (usually lead/potash glass) fused to metal at high temperature (about 800 degrees Cent) and often used for decorative objects.

Figurative: A term used to describe art which is based on the figure, usually in realistic or semi-realistic terms; also loosely used to describe an artist who paints or sculpts representationally, as opposed to painting or sculpting in an abstract or non-objective manner.

Graphic design: Derived from the German word graphic. Describes the applied art of formulating/arranging image/text to communicate a message. It can be applied in any media, such as print, digital media, animation, packaging, and signs.

Imagination: The act of recalling natural and human-made objects, animals, people, places, and events from one's past experiences and rearranging them in a new or unusual order or format.

Installation Art: This typically employs mixed media(sculpture),which typically fills an entire space, such as a room or gallery. It is commonly site-specific.

Key block: A block or plate carrying the full design with which all other blocks and plates are registered during printing in more than one color.

Multimedia: Computer programs that involve users in the design and organization of text, graphics, video, and sound in one presentation.

Narrative Drawing: A way of telling stories visually; a narrative drawing can consist of a single image or a sequence of images.

Patchwork: A group of smaller brush strokes applied together to create a larger unit .(art work).

Poster: Either advertising lithographic designs, propaganda posters or reproductions of famous paintings.

Panorama: painting of a view or landscape; especially large-scale painting around a room, or rolled on a cylinder.

Overpainting: The final layer of paint that is applied over the under painting or under layer after it has dried. The idea behind layers of painting is that the under painting is used to define the basic shapes and design so that the overpainting can be used to fill in the details of the piece.

Tapestry: wall hanging of silk or wool with a nonrepeating pattern or narrative design woven in by hand, during manufacture.

Tribal Art: Also called Primitive Native Art, it embraces the traditional art of tribal societies in the Americas, Africa, India, the South Pacific, and Australasia.

Technique: Specific method or approach to art making, including the use of tools and equipment, the application of media, manipulation and control of materials, etc.; any way of working with art materials to create an art object.

Portfolio: A collection of documents and art works representative of a person's completed works and/or works in progress.

SAMPLE QUESTIONS

1)Draw the group of objects placed before you in the rectangle, large enough to suit the size of the paper you may use any medium for painting or shading.

2) Draw a 16 cm square. In this square draw a design with the help of following units and colour it with a suitable colour scheme.

a) Decorative different size of fishes.

b) Two forms of flowers and leaves.

c) Mixed unequal geometrical shapes.

d) Two or three rhythmic lines.

3) Draw design for a lampshade. Use any geometrical natural, decorative or abstract forms use suitable colour scheme.

4) Draw design for a shopping bag. Use decorative forms of leaves, flowers, birds, fishes, butterfly and any other form with suitable colour scheme.

5) prepare design for vase, umbrella, hand fan hexagon circle with the help of mixed shapes in beautiful colour scheme.

6)Arrange two or three objects before you shade with pencil.

7) Make a composition in pencil and colour with any medium.

a) Children playing football on the ground.

b) Farmer family working in the field.

c) Balloon seller and children.

d) A women is cooking in kitchen and her two children are playing nearby.

e) Family enjoying a picnic.

f) Marriage ceremony.

g) Any Indian festival.

h) Family watching television at home.

8) Make a poster design on any of the following subjects in any medium of your choice.

a) Global warming.

b) National Integration

c) Terrorism

d) Common wealth game (New Delhi)

e) Pollution Problem

f) World peace

g) Population

f) Art education